Chicken Soup
for the Soul.

Reboot
Your Life

To Sarojani
with l[...]
Gran[...]

D0959412

Chicken Soup for the Soul: Reboot Your Life
101 Stories about Finding a New Path to Happiness
Amy Newmark, Claire Cook
Published by Chicken Soup for the Soul Publishing, LLC www.chickensoup.com

The publisher gratefully acknowledges the many publishers and individuals who
granted Chicken Soup for the Soul permission to reprint the cited material.

Front cover photo courtesy of iStockPhoto.com/createsima (© createsima).
Back cover photo courtesy of iStockPhoto.com/alvarez (© alvarez).
Interior photo courtesy of iStockPhoto.com/digitalskillet (© digitalskillet).
Photo of Amy Newmark courtesy of Susan Morrow at SwickPix

Cover and Interior Design & Layout by Brian Taylor, Pneuma Books, LLC

Distributed to the booktrade by Simon & Schuster. SAN: 200-2442

Publisher's Cataloging-in-Publication Data
(Prepared by The Donohue Group)

Chicken soup for the soul : reboot your life : 101 stories about finding
 a new path to happiness / [compiled by] Amy Newmark [and] Claire Cook.

  pages ; cm

 ISBN: 978-1-61159-940-4

 1. Happiness--Literary collections. 2. Happiness--Anecdotes. 3. Self-actualization
(Psychology)--Literary collections. 4. Self-actualization (Psychology)--Anecdotes. 5.
Anecdotes. I. Newmark, Amy. II. Cook, Claire, 1955- III. Title: Reboot your life

BF575.H27 C45 2014
158.1   2014943303

PRINTED IN THE UNITED STATES OF AMERICA
on acid∞free paper

24 23 22 21 20 19 18 17 16 15 14   02 03 04 05 06 07 08 09 10 11

Chicken Soup for the Soul®

Reboot Your Life

101 Stories about
Finding a New Path
to Happiness

Amy Newmark
Claire Cook

Chicken Soup for the Soul Publishing, LLC
Cos Cob, CT

Chicken Soup for the Soul

Changing your world one story at a time®
www.chickensoup.com

Contents

Introduction, *Claire Cook* xi

❶
~Do It Now~

1. Must Love Midlife, *Claire Cook* 1
2. Conquering the Giant of Provence, *Dawn A. Marcus* 6
3. Life Launch, *Kristi Paxton* 10
4. Following My Nephew's Dream, *David Cranmer* 14
5. A Risky Jump, *Sioux Roslawski* 18
6. Winters of Solace, *Heather Zuber-Harshman* 21
7. Just in Time, *P. Avice Carr* 25
8. The Dry Truth, *Kathy Whirity* 28
9. A Family Reunion, *Peter W. Wood* 31

❷
~Follow Your Heart~

10. Run for Your Life, *Dean Karnazes* 39
11. Finding "Perfect Love", *Shari Hall* 44
12. Mobilized by Fear, *Andrew E. Kaufman* 49
13. Time of Possession, *James C. Magruder* 53
14. Happiness Is a Big Loud Garbage Truck, *Roz Warren* 57
15. Movie Critic, MD, *Tanya Feke* 60
16. Becoming Real, *Amy L. Stout* 64
17. A New Operating System, *Sabrina Zackery* 67
18. Self-Discovery, *Val Jones* 70
19. There Are Writers in There, *Shawnelle Eliasen* 73

❸

~Take a Chance~

20. A Real Stretch, *Rebecca Olker* 81
21. From Corporate to Carrots, *Kamia Taylor* 85
22. 365 Envelopes, *Karen Martin* 88
23. Jumping Fences, *Arlene Ledbetter* 92
24. Laying Myself Off, *Sharron Carrns* 96
25. The Life of the Party, *Giulietta Nardone* 99
26. Safely Stuck in a Rut, *Tanya Rusheon* 103
27. The Tuesday Night Ladies League, *Pat Wahler* 106
28. Moments of Clarity, *Erin Latimer* 109
29. Moving to Hong Kong, *MaryLou Driedger* 112
30. Running Away to Join the Circus, *Denise Reich* 115

❹

~Find Your Purpose~

31. What's Your Story? *Amy Newmark* 121
32. Making a Difference, *Lisa Morris* 124
33. Finding My Happiness, *Brenda Lazzaro Yoder* 128
34. A Happiness Throttle, *Alli Page* 130
35. Lost and Found, *Marijo Herndon* 133
36. Restaurant Epiphany, *Robert J. Brake* 136
37. Family of Rejects, *Sylvia Ney* 139
38. The Confidence to Change, *Angela Ogburn* 143
39. Unexpected Changes, *Jane Lonnqvist* 147
40. Express Yourself, *Jan Bono* 151

❺

~Start Over~

41. A New Model, *Jennifer Sky* 157
42. A Long Walk, *Christopher Clark* 161
43. I Should Thank Him, *Heather Ray* 165

44. The Adventure of Starting Over, *Patricia Lorenz*...............168
45. Rewriting My Story, *Deborah K. Wood*.............................172
46. Finding Me at Fifty, *Liz Maxwell Forbes*..........................175
47. The Power of Positive Pigheadedness, *Lynn Kinnaman*.......178
48. Doors Wide Open, *Jennifer Chauhan*...............................181
49. Never Too Old, *Kay Thomann*...185
50. Laid Off and Living the Dream, *Sean Marshall* 188
51. Meeting Mom, *Katherine Higgs-Coulthard*.......................190

❻

~Mind Your Health~

52. Who Would Have Thought? *Esther Clark*...........................197
53. Back in the Saddle Again, *Jennie Ivey* 200
54. No Smoking, *Elizabeth Smayda*.......................................204
55. A Kick in the Keister, *B.J. Taylor*.....................................208
56. Made to Order? *Marsha Porter* 212
57. Running for My Life, *Melissa Face*...................................216
58. My Big Wake-Up Call, *Lori Lara* 219
59. The Comeback, *Brian Teason* 221
60. How I Became a Muddy Girl, *Maggi Normile*.....................225

❼

~Overcome Adversity~

61. From Homeless to Happy, *Kamia Taylor* 231
62. Jersey Shore Promises, *Theresa Sanders* 235
63. The Café de l'Espérance, *Cherie Magnus*...........................239
64. Finding Hope after Despair, *Debra Wallace Forman*............243
65. The Joy I Choose to See, *Janet Perez Eckles*........................246
66. Mirror, Mirror, *Sara Etgen-Baker* 250
67. Life Reignited, *Jessie Wagoner*...253
68. A Long Hard Fight, *Jeanette Rubin*...................................256
69. Two Sisters, *Ann Michener Winter*....................................259

8

~Listen to Your Friends~

70. The Year of Exploration, *Nicole K. Ross* 267
71. How Running Helped Me Heal, *Kristin Julie Viola* 271
72. A Journey of a Lifetime, *Stacy Ross*................................274
73. What Would You Do? *Jaime Schreiner* 278
74. Starting All Over, *Jay H. Berman* 280
75. Gratitude, Schmatitude, *Susan A. Karas* 283
76. I Think I Can, *Tyler Stocks* 287
77. Dear Daddy, *Paul Bowling II* 290
78. Nose to the Wall, *Garrett Bauman* 293

9

~Take Time for You~

79. Doing Nothing Perfectly, *Ferida Wolff*.............................301
80. Annual Reboot, *Connie Rosser Riddle* 303
81. Awakened by the Creator Within, *Christine Burke* 306
82. My Writing Roller Coaster, *Lisa McManus Lange* 309
83. Clean Start, *Pam Bailes*..312
84. One Year of Celibacy, *Shannon Kaiser* 315
85. Back to School, *Angela Joseph*.....................................317
86. A Happy Heart, *Terri Elders* 320
87. Second Chance, *J.C. Andrew* 324
88. Dancing with a Cane on My Head, *Sue Mannering*............328

10

~Adjust Your Attitude~

89. Eight Thousand Miles, *Carol Strazer*................................335
90. Forgiveness and Freedom, *Nancy Julien Kopp*....................338
91. Steady the Course, *Eloise Elaine Ernst Schneider*.................341
92. The Bedtime Ritual that Changed My Life,
    Dallas Woodburn 344

93. Best Day Ever, *Dorann Weber* 348

94. Picture This, *Carol Ayer* 351

95. All Things New, *Kathleen Kohler* 355

96. The Relationship Dance, *Chris Jahrman* 359

97. Just Drive Warrior, *Diana Lynn* 362

98. Pickles, *Fallon Kane* 364

99. My Perfect Imperfect Life, *Marilyn Boone* 366

100. The Stay-at-Home Mom, *L.A. Strucke* 368

101. Thriving, *Lynn Dove* 372

Afterword, *Amy Newmark* 375

Meet Our Contributors 377

Meet Our Authors 394

Thank You 396

About Chicken Soup for the Soul 397

Introduction

'm thrilled to be a part of *Chicken Soup for the Soul: Reboot Your Life*. I loved immersing myself in all 101 of the fabulous stories you're about to read, and it was a joy and an honor to be asked to write a story myself.

I was so inspired by these brave and thoughtful men and women—who all feel like new friends now—and I know you'll be inspired by them, too. What struck me most in their stories is that we can bury our dreams for years, even decades, but they still linger beneath the surface and never really go away. I knew this from my own personal experience, but to see it multiplied by one hundred is incredibly powerful.

So, bravo to every one of these contributors, who took long, hard looks at their existing lives, realized they were stuck, and had the courage and the tenacity to change them into the lives they'd dreamed about.

You'll hear about M. Sean Marshall's awesome wife, who helped him celebrate his layoff and turn it into an amazing adventure.

You'll cheer on Kamia Taylor as she fights her way back from homelessness.

Fallon Kane will share the lessons she learned working in a pickle shop.

You'll walk along with Heather Clausen as she gets herself back in shape.

You'll be glad it was Rebecca Olker, and not you, who found herself at a writing retreat where the participants were naked.

You'll go belly dancing with Sue Mannering.

You'll learn how to change your negative thoughts to their opposite along with Carol Strazer.

You'll go to Paris with Cherie Magnus, Hong Kong with MaryLou Driedger, and South Africa with Christopher Clark.

And you'll read my story about finally writing my first novel in my minivan when I was forty-five and, at fifty, walking the red carpet at the Hollywood premiere of the adaptation of my second novel, *Must Love Dogs*, starring Diane Lane and John Cusack.

If you're feeling stuck in your own life, if you find yourself whining about the cards you've been dealt and pointing fingers at everyone but yourself, this is the book for you. Not only will you feel less alone as you hear from people who were once standing right where you are now, but you'll find the motivation you need to take the plunge and create a better life, and you'll learn some practical strategies for getting there.

What are you waiting for? Enjoy!

~Claire Cook,
bestselling author of *Must Love Dogs* and *Never Too Late*

Reboot Your Life

Do It Now

Must Love Midlife

It's never too late to be what you might have been.
~George Eliot

The Hollywood premiere of the *Must Love Dogs* movie was held at the mammoth Cinerama Dome on Sunset Boulevard. I was the author of the novel it was based on. I was thrilled that, because my name was on the movie poster, I was entitled to four tickets to the premiere, which meant my husband and two kids and I could all go. We were even given a suite at the Hollywood Roosevelt.

I had no expectations, other than thinking it would be fun and we'd probably get free popcorn. I remember wandering Hollywood Boulevard early that afternoon with my daughter, poking around in all the tourist shops. I bought a knock-off Gucci bag shaped like a dog and a pink feather boa collar to clip around its neck, and decided it would be only fitting to carry a copy of the book to the premiere in it. Clearly I was thinking like a tourist rather than an author whose movie adaptation was about to premiere in a few hours, since I also bought a refrigerator magnet with a picture of the Hollywood sign on it.

By that point I'd heard premiere stories from other authors. The one that stuck in my head was from an author whose name must not have been on the movie poster because he only got two tickets to the premiere. He brought his mother. The day came and they pulled up to the red carpet. The limo driver rolled down the window and gave his passenger's name and said he was the author.

As the driver got out to open the doors for the author and his mother, the event publicist leaned into her microphone. She announced his name and told the long line of media people standing behind the ropes on the edge of the red carpet that he was the author.

"Nah, we don't want him," a television reporter standing with his cameraman said loudly. Everybody else in the long line concurred with a headshake or a brush of their hand, or just ignored the announcement entirely. The author and his mother slunk along the length of the red carpet as quickly as they could and disappeared into the theater.

I'd warned my family what to expect and I wasn't really worried about it. I mostly wanted to watch the movie. Gary David Goldberg, the movie's producer/director, had shared every draft of the script, as well as a few short promo clips, but he hadn't wanted me to watch the whole thing until tonight.

It was early on a hot summer night and the sun was still relentless. Our stretch limo pulled up. The driver lowered his window, gave my name and said I was the author. He opened our doors and the event person announced me. I got ready to be ignored.

Well, it turned out that not only had the actors not arrived yet, but unbeknownst to me, one of the Boston affiliates had asked *Access Hollywood*, which aired on the same network, to get some footage of me for them to show on the local news that night.

"We want her!" the crew from *Access Hollywood* yelled.

And because *Access Hollywood* wanted me, *Entertainment Tonight* yelled, "We want her!"

And then *Xtra* wanted me. And then everybody in the whole media line wanted me. The event publicist started escorting me toward the line. "How do you feel about director Gary David Goldberg changing Mother Teresa, the St. Bernard in the book, to a Newfoundland in the movie?" a reporter yelled.

"I would have been fine with a possum," I yelled back.

And so I walked along the red carpet, which was actually a dog-themed green faux-grass carpet dotted with fire hydrants, taking questions from the media line. After I finished chatting with the big outlets, the event person pulled me aside and whispered that I'd done the important ones, so I could stop now if I wanted to.

"Are you kidding me?" I said. I talked to every single one of them, including the guy from a radio station in, I think, Singapore at the very end of the line. I did thirty-five interviews on that green carpet. The paparazzi were even yelling "Claire, Claire" and taking my picture when I looked. At one point I remember asking a group of them if they were really the paparazzi because they seemed so much nicer in person than I'd heard they were.

And the next morning I awoke to find out there was a picture of me, holding up my knock-off dog purse with a copy of *Must Love Dogs* peeking out, on the front page of *The Hollywood Reporter*. And in an AP piece that was picked up by hundreds and hundreds of publications, Michael Cidoni wrote that in his twenty-five years of covering Hollywood premieres, he had never seen an author have as much fun at a premiere as Claire Cook. And of course, "*Must Love Dogs* author Claire Cook says she would have been fine with a possum!" was just about everywhere.

This was the year I turned fifty, which in Hollywood years I'm pretty sure is at least eighty-two. My green carpet media blitz was a total long shot, and I was not in any way prepared for it or expecting it to happen. A minute or two later one of the actors—Diane Lane, John Cusack, Christopher Plummer, Elizabeth Perkins, Stockard Channing—could have arrived and the media would have dropped me in a Hollywood minute. But in this tiny window was a colossal opportunity to get the word out about my books, and when that happens, you've just got to go for it.

Eventually my long-suffering family and I made it inside the theater. And I was right—not only did we get free popcorn but also free soda, both delivered to us by handsome tuxedo-clad waiters. We were even seated in the front row of the first balcony, with the actors surrounding us.

Way down below, in front of the movie screen, Gary stood up to speak.

"None of us would be here tonight," he began, "without Claire

Cook and her wonderful novel. I started out as a fan of her work, and we quickly became personal friends, and I now consider her one of the few people in the world I can always count on for the truth presented in the kindest way possible."

Behind me, some of the actors hooted. Dermot Mulroney caught my eye and gave me a thumbs-up. I was stunned. I was overwhelmed. It was one of the most beautiful moments of my life.

Just over five years before that, I'd been sitting with a group of swim moms (and a few good dads) at 5:30 A.M. My daughter was swimming back and forth and back and forth on the other side of a huge glass window during the first of two daily practices that bracketed her school day and my workday as a teacher.

The parental conversation in the wee hours of that morning, as we sat bleary-eyed, cradling our Styrofoam cups of coffee and watching our kids, was all about training and form and speed, who was coming on at the perfect time, who was in danger of peaking before championships, even who just might have a shot at Olympic trial times.

In my mind, I stepped back and listened. *Whoa*, I thought, *we really need to get a life.*

And right at that moment it hit me with the force of a poolside tidal wave that I was the one who needed to get a life. A new one, the one I'd meant to have all along. I was not getting any younger, and I was in serious danger of living out my days without ever once going for it. Without even *trying* to achieve my lifelong dream of writing a novel. Suddenly, *not* writing a book became more painful than pushing past all that fear and procrastination and actually writing it.

So, for the next six months, through one long cold New England winter and into the spring, I wrote a draft of my first novel, sitting in my minivan outside my daughter's swim practice. It sold to the first publisher who asked to read it. Lots of terrific books by talented authors take a long time to sell, so maybe I got lucky. I've also considered that perhaps if you procrastinate as long as I did, you get to skip some of the awful stages on the path to wherever it is you're going and just cut to the chase.

But another way to look at it is that there were only three things standing in my way all those years: me, myself and I.

My first novel was published when I was forty-five. Not only did I walk the red carpet at the Hollywood premiere of the movie adaptation of *Must Love Dogs* at fifty, but I'm now an actual bestselling author of eleven novels, as well as my first nonfiction book about reinvention, *Never Too Late*. Not many days go by that I don't take a deep breath and remind myself that this is the career I almost didn't have.

Anything can happen. It is never, ever too late.

~Claire Cook

Conquering the Giant of Provence

The road leading to a goal does not separate you from the destination;
it is essentially a part of it.
~Charles de Lint

"I do." Those simple words, spoken amid smiles and tears on a warm June afternoon changed my life. No, this was not my wedding. My husband and I had already been happily married for twenty-eight years and had settled into a comfortable empty nester life with our two Terriers. We enjoyed hikes in the woods and had just started a new hobby identifying wildflowers. We'd also grown comfortable with the twenty-five extra pounds we'd put on, which didn't interfere with photographing flowers.

The wedding couple was in their twenties. We knew their families, but no one else at the reception. We selected a table with two other couples and introduced ourselves. The husbands were fraternity brothers who got together yearly to keep their friendship alive.

During the entrée and dessert, they shared plans for a bicycling trip through Provence, in southern France, starting Labor Day. The trip accommodated different levels of cyclists, although the big event would be a climb up Mont Ventoux, known as the "Giant of Provence," which is a highlight of the Tour de France. There'd be lunches at vineyards, overnights in old castles, and great food. The more they talked, the more enthusiastic we became. Several glasses of wine later, my husband and I were hooked.

When I spoke with a travel agent the next morning, it became quite clear that this trip was for avid bikers. She asked, "What size bike do you ride? What level rider are you?"

After a long pause, I said, "I'm not really sure," which translated into "We haven't touched a bike in twenty years." The travel agent got us signed up and I happily told my husband the trip was a go.

Then we began investigating the biking planned for each day. Basically, it was breakfast, a brisk climb to a vineyard for lunch and wine tasting, then another ride with good climbs to the hotel for dinner. I should have thought hills, knowing Provence sits at the bottom of the Alps, but was horrified to see how long and how steep each day would be.

The trip itinerary said, "We begin with a short descent and then the consistent climb to Ménerbes."

After several nights of nightmares about the Ménerbes climb, we dusted off our boys' old mountain bikes and hit the park. Our local park has a popular five-mile flat loop circling a lake and many roads climbing big hills. As we rounded the lake, the "flat" loop didn't seem quite so flat and had a long, gentle hill I'd forgotten about. In my lowest gear, sweat dripping down my face, I huffed and puffed to get up the gentle rise.

I thought I was doing pretty well until I started getting passed by walkers. My husband joked that people *with* walkers could pass me as my front tire veered left and right to keep me from falling over. I took frequent stops to catch my breath and drink from my water bottle. I was in big trouble. The last time I'd biked, I'd only ridden on the flat trails made from converted railway beds. And as I recalled, I'd gotten tired after about twenty miles or so of flat. Here I was, at least twenty-five pounds heavier, nearly two decades older, and planning to ride thirty to fifty miles a day with big hills.

What was I thinking?

I have two strong traits — I'm stubborn and I'm cheap. I'd set my mind to this challenge and the trip was already paid for. So my husband

and I decided we could transform ourselves from flab to fit in three months. My husband spent hours poring over maps, measuring the distance, elevation, and steepness of each climb, while I rid the pantry of sweets, treats, and high-fat snacks. The minimum biker level we could sign up for on the trip was at least thirty miles a day with total climbs of 3,600 feet. My husband plotted out a ten-mile, 1,200-foot climb loop for us to work up to doing three times a day.

We also began to look at other bikers in the park. We noticed three things — they wore spandex, they had tiny butts, and they had thin and shapely legs with well-defined calf muscles. The first part was easy. We dug out the old spandex shorts our sons had worn on their high school rowing team. Our transformation was underway. Wearing spandex in public when you've got rolls and bumps you've been hiding under jeans is great motivation to lose weight.

Then we traded in the old mountain bikes that wouldn't shift gears for new road bikes, and learned gear shifts are done by pushing the same lever as the brake, pedals are purchased separately from bikes, and "clipless" means you clip your shoes into pedals with cleats. And when they said to expect to fall over a few times getting used to the cleats, they were right.

Our summer was totally scheduled around biking. At the first hint of morning sun, we'd begin a ride before work. After work, it was back to the park for more miles. As the weeks wore on, I needed fewer rest breaks. My previously wide butt was becoming narrower, and one day I was watching my husband's legs as he biked in front of me and exclaimed, "You've got calf muscles!" We were slowly transforming ourselves into real bikers. As the months passed, fewer bikers passed me, and I took great pleasure on those rare occasions I managed to zip past a young biker. I imagining him thinking, "Was I really just passed by an old lady?"

After two months, our conversations revolved around elevations and hill grades. We'd become masters at changing flats, dressing for rain or cold weather, and eating protein snacks as we rode. We increased the hills in our daily routine. When my butt muscles would burn in protest, I'd just think, "One climb closer to Mont Ventoux."

As August ended, we had become more confident and Mont Ventoux was looking like a real possibility.

First day jitters on the trip soon ended when we left Ménerbes in the dust. In four days, we smiled at the top of Mont Ventoux, holding bikes overhead for our celebratory photo. Some people thought we'd never bike again after our trip. For those naysayers, I have news: We just finished our first century ride this weekend, completing eighty hilly miles our first day and 100 miles the next.

The trip to Mont Ventoux transformed more than our muscles. My husband and I renewed our vows to each other. We developed a special bond formed by overcoming a challenge, stopped thinking of ourselves as soon-to-be seniors, and started looking forward to new, exciting adventures together.

That June wedding helped us say "I do" to a world of possibilities we'd never imagined.

~Dawn A. Marcus

Life Launch

*Twenty years from now you will be more disappointed by
the things that you didn't do than by the ones you did do.*
~Mark Twain

The kids grew up, moved away and left us in peace. Most evenings found us lying on separate couches in our living room. Television reflected crime scenes onto our skin, contrasting with our predictable home life. I'd fall asleep during the commercials and eventually stumble to bed with a book—where I'd fall asleep again.

We were snoozing ourselves into oblivion, and I feared this would continue. Our headstone might read, "Here lie the Paxtons—bored to death in the 21st Century."

How do you fix a dull life? We'd talked about driving Route 66, backpacking the wilderness, navigating coastal waters. All just talk. Secretly I wondered if we'd ever do anything exciting again.

Then, within a couple of months, life as we knew it changed. Denny's dad passed away, and our beloved fox terrier died of a mysterious ailment. Our daughter's young friend lost his life, and several of our peers had bouts with cancer. We turned sixty as our marriage turned forty. Alarmed, we noticed photos of people our age moving into the obits, and we launched a series of conversations about life's brevity.

As time slithered away, we revisited an old pipe dream and decided to buy a used boat. Experts recommended thirty-six to forty-two feet—a stretch for us kayakers—but comfortable for long trips or living aboard.

In case a thirty-foot increase in boat length and twin diesel engines were not enough challenge, we acquired a puppy that needed to learn the art of polite peeing on a live-aboard boat.

Now, erase the picture in your mind of a trim sixty-year-old couple wearing captain caps, perched at the upper helm on an aqua sea. They maneuver neatly into a tropical port where dockworkers rush to gather the lines.

No, it looked more like this: "What if she refuses to pee on the boat?" asks the captain.

"I don't know," the first mate answers, not feeling seaworthy. "Heaven forbid she does her jobs everywhere, and it gets all stinky and such."

First things first, we began pee pad training at home before acquiring a trawler. Puppy Smalls refused to pee on the pad. A determined sailor, I fenced in the pad and offered it at desperate moments. Success!

So began our thrilling future. Captain Paxton scoured the web for used trawlers. I scribbled numbers on tablets, wondering how long our pensions, semi-retirement jobs and pieces of our children's inheritance could fund our dream. I had calculated one to ten years, just as my captain presented a list of twenty-five trawlers. We planned a Florida boat-hunt road trip.

Only our imaginations, our checkbook, and questionable sanity limited us. We departed the couches for west central Florida. We toured boats hugging the Gulf of Mexico, crossed the skinny state, and then boarded a string of trawlers in rivers along the Atlantic.

Stories flowed from vagabonds who had lived their sea dreams, elderly sailors now selling their dream vessels to new dreamers. "We lived aboard ten years," said one aging captain. "They were the best-lived years of our marriage. My wife is ill now." A tear glistened in his eye as we dabbed at ours.

We discovered our own love-boat with a brokerage in Fort Pierce and made an offer.

What next? Will we still work? How will we operate this thing? We would make it up as we went.

Back on our Iowa couches, excitement lit our faces. "This was the best trip I've ever had!" I said. "I don't even care if we buy the boat."

A month later, we e-mailed an offer and counter offers, arrived at a price and headed back to Florida, where a professional boat surveyor would inspect our vessel. Then we'd hand over the money, fix small issues and sail away.

After survey day and a glorious cruise on a turquoise river, I lay coiled in fetal position on our El Cheap-o Motel bed. "I'm so sorry I killed our dream!" I wailed between sobs. I felt I'd just inspected a different boat — or the same boat through different eyes. Whichever it was, our love boat no longer looked like a place I'd love to live for nine months while navigating the intracoastal waterways. The surveyor detected my angst and counseled us.

"You don't have to buy this boat. If you see deficiencies you missed before, either counter offer and have the items fixed, or withdraw your offer," said the surveyor, my new hero.

We countered. The seller declined. End of pipe dream or nightmare. End of story.

Or so we thought. After a week of whining, we resumed our quest, navigating from couch to deck so we could enjoy the sunset. Each evening, we shifted puppy and books from lap to lap as we sailed through basic boating courses. Within another week, Captain Paxton presented a new list of old trawlers and a fresh road trip itinerary.

This time we started in Baltimore and drove down the East Coast, hoping past experience would help us find a sounder vessel at a better price, and it did.

Terrapin is a classy 1984 with solid mechanics, teak interior, and expansive deck. Our dream boat bobs happily in a slip at New Bern, North Carolina. This unplanned location suits us. We will stay six months or a year to enjoy the Crystal Coast and to sharpen our seamanship skills.

Back in Iowa for Christmas, our grown kids surprised us with a pirate-themed treasure hunt. At one point we were blindfolded, our hands tied together, using our feet to pull a line with a clue up a flight of stairs. Minutes later we lay on our frozen deck, fashioning a hook from a paper clip; we tied it to sewing thread and pulled a clue basket up from the snowdrift below. In the barn we uncovered a wooden chest of boating supplies. Our captors made us down a shot of rum and sing a sea shanty.

Today, from the windows of our floating home, we have new perspective in a watery world. Our brains exercise as we explore new plumbing, new knots, and new docking maneuvers. We conquer cooking challenges in a tiny galley. Our boating community regales us with stories collected from smooth and stormy voyages. We soak it all up as we form new friendships over glasses of wine.

Adventures beckon: a trip to the pump-out station, a dinner cruise to a neighboring town, a trip to the Outer Banks. The Great Loop. The Bahamas.

As I type, Smalls slumbers on a couch in the salon. She's exhausted from a romp with Hank, her doggy pal from Dock C. Soon she will awaken and make the rounds on her floating doghouse, stern to bow. Smalls embraces her new-and-uncertain life with a vengeance. We hope to follow her lead.

~Kristi Paxton

Following My Nephew's Dream

Commitment leads to action. Action brings your dream closer.
~Marcia Wieder

'm not sure why I took the selfie, but I did. Sitting on my back porch in upstate New York in the late-winter thaw, I raised my iPhone and snapped a picture of a very glum individual. But why was I unhappy? I'd always been adept at figuring out internal discord, so I mentally started taking note of all the good things in my life. I was in love with my adoring wife, and we were raising our beautiful baby girl. In a down economy, I had a good-paying job that allowed my family to travel, which we enjoyed.

I eyed the forty-two-year-old man in the picture. Bottom line, I was dissatisfied with that successful job and didn't want to leave the following morning for South Carolina where I would be overseeing a construction project. Another tedious undertaking of walking behind carpenters, electricians, and drywall installers, telling them what to do, and, like the man without the eyes in *Cool Hand Luke*, snapping the whip when it was time to push them faster.

What I really wanted as my dream job was what I was already doing on the side: writing and publishing fiction with my wife. We had started a little online magazine in 2008 devoted to short stories of any genre. It was a labor of love in the beginning, but a couple of years later during the eBook boom, we decided to try making some money from the publishing. It became a joke at my day job when I would say, "This assignment is my last." Five years later, our bags were packed for our trip to The Palmetto State. It seemed like I would never have a last assignment.

I was leaving my home in the care of my nephew Kyle, who would watch over it while taking classes at the local community college. Like me, Kyle wanted to be a writer, and I had published his first poetry collection the previous year. He and I had been great buddies. I was the zany uncle, a close confidant. When I went away to the military, we lost touch, and when I came back, he was going through typical teenage strife with the added troubles of drugs and alcohol. Our relationship had changed. We struggled to find our lost common ground. We eventually found it in books and movies, though our relationship remained strained. I could see, despite his continued tribulations, that he was still an intelligent, loyal young man who was trying. When he said he would care for my house, I knew he'd do his best. And I would continue to help publish his work when I had time.

Charleston turned out to be a rewarding city with a rich history and beautiful parks and beaches, but the job itself was taking a toll on me. Unexpected delays cropped up at every turn. What was supposed to be a six-week assignment was going to take months. I didn't want to stay that long. I had a writing and publishing venture calling me.

Back in New York, Kyle's troubles were mounting once again as well. He was having a relapse from sobriety. On June 18, 2013, while I was getting ready for another stressful day of work, my wife burst into the bathroom to tell me my niece had called. Our house was on fire and they couldn't find Kyle. I reeled from the shock.

I went into work as usual, anxiously awaiting news from home. Two hours later, the call came from my sister with the heart-wrenching words… they found Kyle's remains by the back door; he didn't make it out.

I left work, unable to focus or control the tears.

I took my little family back to New York for the service and spoke at the funeral. I stumbled around in shock. When I returned to work in Charleston, it was even harder than before as I tried to balance a job

I already disliked with the loss of my nephew. I cried hard every day for the following month and searched for meaning wherever I could find it. Nothing seemed to help ease the pain. While our family had banded together and found strength, I needed something more. I strived relentlessly to get Kyle's second poetry collection in print. I delved deep into his words. Still, no solace. And then one day, it happened.

After the assignment ended, and we returned to New York—again—I had the opportunity to read through Kyle's dream journals that had been found in his parents' house. Among the usual assortment of flights of fantasy and distorted meanderings of daily events, this chestnut popped up: "David had ended his career to write short stories and wear sweatpants and grow a beard ([Allen] Ginsberg) and write and I was ardent with admiration."

That dream reassured me that my nephew cared for my happiness and me. The date in the journal entry showed he had dreamed this at a time when we were still somewhat at odds, long before I had published his first poetry. I cried again but with tears of joy.

I leafed further through his journals and found an entry about abstract time travel, an adventure where he went into the past to save me from a work-related danger. At the end, he wrote, "The dream was also about how proud and reverent I am of my uncle, or how much I look up to him."

Kyle's words gave me strength for my next step. I knew it was time to use all of my vacation (two months' worth) to just write… a thought that no doubt goes through the mind of every wannabe author with a day job. My wife and I had talked it over before, and we had been saving for several years, waiting for the right time to take the chance on writing and publishing. It hadn't happened because there's never a right time to throw caution to the wind and strike out across the desolate plain where there's no certain income, no insurance, no security.

While the vacation days dwindled away, the passages from Kyle's journals preoccupied me. My thoughts lingered on the poet, who had so much to offer, running out of time. The nephew who imagined his uncle a writer. His words, "I was ardent with admiration," came back to me. I needed more time, and I was delaying the inevitable.

I wrote my boss and told him I wanted to go on intermittent status indefinitely. If they wanted to let me go, fine. I needed to follow not just my dream, but Kyle's too.

And here I am, working from home. Mostly seven days a week. Watching what I spend. Some months enough comes in to pay the bills and other months I'm scrambling. But you know what? Now I'm smiling in all my pictures because I know Kyle is out there, proud of me. Just as I am of him.

~David Cranmer

A Risky Jump

When once you have tasted flight, you will forever walk the earth
with your eyes turned skyward, for there you have been,
and there you will always long to return.
~Leonardo da Vinci

I was in a blah phase of my life. I was carrying extra weight, my hair looked awful, and my favorite clothes were baggy jeans or sweatpants. My shoes were rubbery ugly-looking flats, perfect for the way I was plodding through life.

A teacher during the day, I spent my leisure time knitting and reading. My children were grown and had lives of their own, so that challenge was over. My life had become uneventful.

I needed to take a leap. I needed to do something risky.

There was something that attracted and terrified me at the same time. My former father-in-law had spent his middle-aged years participating on a competitive skydiving team. Looking at photos or hearing him tell stories about his competitions, I would always say to myself, "Someday."

Sadly, it took a colleague's death to spur me into action. A fellow teacher—still in her thirties—died after waging a nasty battle with breast cancer. With what should have been a full life ahead of her, she left behind a husband and young children. I kept thinking that someday I would summon enough courage to go skydiving, but what if I ran out of somedays before I got the chance to do it?

Before I could change my mind, I called and scheduled my jump for the next Saturday. I could hardly refrain from squealing, the result of equal parts excitement and terror.

Driving the hour to the skydiving center, I felt like I might be driving to my death. Certainly, thousands and thousands of people safely skydived, but there were enough deaths that this was considered a dangerous sport. Before they even started the training, the skydiving staff had me fill out a six-page form; each place I initialed seemed to say, "If your parachute doesn't open, it's not our fault. If you break a leg when you land, it's not our fault. If you die, it's not our fault." I stopped reading the form and blindly initialed the places that were highlighted. I didn't want any more reminders about how risky this was.

After I watched a video about what the jump was going to be like, I worked one-on-one with Brian, my instructor. My first jump would be a tandem jump, which meant I would have my instructor strapped to me.

With his help, I learned that once I leaped out of the plane, I'd have to arch my back and put my arms out. Brian showed me a couple of different landing options, but assured me that he would make that decision when we were a few feet away from the ground. He explained that there would be a mix of veteran jumpers and beginners like me in the plane, but the experienced divers would go first.

"Each time a jumper goes, we'll scoot closer to the back end of the bench. I won't hook us together until right before it's our turn." Brian helped me into a flight suit. Everyone was loaded into the plane, and we headed toward the clouds.

It only took a matter of minutes to reach the needed elevation, but my panic level rose faster than that plane. The inside of the airplane got hot—at least it felt that way to me. It was as if I was in an oven and the oven had wings. My heart beat so fast it felt like it was going to thump its way out of my chest. My screams hadn't escaped from my throat yet, but it was only a matter of time.

As the veteran jumpers started stepping off the bench and leaping out into the sky, I had to wait my turn. But I didn't want to. I didn't want to wait. I wanted to jump out. Right then. Immediately. And I didn't care if my instructor was hooked onto me or not.

I bit down to keep from screaming. I managed to keep my seat planted firmly on the bench until it was our time to jump. Brian, behind me, hooked my harness to his and we got up.

My diving teacher walked to the gaping opening on confident legs. My legs, however, felt like they were made of rubber. A minute earlier, I was ready to leap out on my own. Now I was not so sure this was a smart thing to do.

The moment before we leaped out into the blue sky, the exhilaration that coursed through my veins was worth it. Above me was sky. Below me was sky. It was the oddest—and most exciting—experience of my life.

When the two of us leaped out, it felt like we were totally free.

I won't lie. When Brian indicated it was time to pull the cord, I was relieved when the chute opened. With the nylon canopy above us, I figured I might end up with a broken leg but at least I didn't have to worry about plummeting to the ground and getting squashed like an egg.

We finally returned to the ground and gathered the armfuls of parachute. My adrenaline was still pumping through my veins. And I knew. I knew. My life would never be the same. Even as we walked back to the skydiving center, I still felt thousands of miles high.

I no longer plod through life, all because I made that one leap.

~Sioux Roslawski

Winters of Solace

You cannot be lonely if you like the person you're alone with.
~Wayne Dyer

"I haven't skied much," my friend Nyna said. "So I'm not up for spending a weekend in the mountains, especially when it takes five hours to get there."

"But you can't improve without practice," I said.

"I wish I wanted to go, but I don't. I'd rather stay home, go hiking."

"Hiking?"

I pictured the rush of sliding down the slopes and weaving between pine trees at Mammoth Mountain, my favorite resort. Hiking couldn't compare to my winter playground.

"Let's conquer a new trail," Nyna said.

"Thanks, but I'm sticking with snowboarding. I just need to find someone to tag along."

I hung up and walked into the garage to survey my gear. My one-year-old snowboard with perfectly white bindings rested against the wall. The helmet I'd purchased after smacking my head on the ice during a magnificent crash leaned against the base of the board as though napping. The gear hadn't been used since I'd gone boarding with my last boyfriend the year before. He'd convinced me to try the sport and helped me learn to turn on the snow.

Now, a season later, I did a mental scan of friends for possible companions. Two people were avid skiers but had moved to Colorado.

Another friend wanted to snowboard if she could ever afford it. The rest weren't interested in winter sports.

I was starting to feel lonely even though I had been feeling content about being single again. I needed to do something, figure out how to get on the mountain without my friends, otherwise I'd backslide to a dark place.

I opened my computer. A search revealed a local ski club. Great! That would be easy. Then I looked at the price per trip. Too much.

What about an informal group who carpooled and hung out on the mountain? I found one of those, too, but the members seemed a lot older and were married.

My research options exhausted, I walked to the kitchen to make hot cocoa. As I reached for a mug, the answer to my dilemma slapped me in the face like a brisk breeze on a winter day.

I should go by myself.

By myself? But I could barely snowboard and didn't know the mountain well.

Despite my counterarguments, the idea took shape with each marshmallow I dropped in the cocoa. Leave early in the morning. Plop. Stay at a hostel. Plop. Board on groomed trails. Plop.

By nightfall my car was loaded. Two days later I started my first solo snowboarding adventure. By eleven that day I sat next to a couple on a ski lift.

"Are you from Mammoth?" she asked.

"Anaheim," I said.

"Do you and your friends come here often?" he asked.

"I came by myself," I said.

"Alone?" Her eyes grew wide, like I said I had twelve fingers.

"Alone."

"Good for you," he said. "Better to come on your own than not at all."

I nodded. A grin appeared under my ski mask. Maybe I could do this.

Each lift ride resulted in more affirmation of my solo journey.

Most people admired my adventurous spirit and wished they were up for doing the same.

The five-hour drive home whizzed by as I contemplated future snowboarding trips. I schemed which weekends I'd go, the time I'd leave, which parts of the mountain I'd investigate, where I'd stay. When I pulled into my garage, my calendar for the season was filled with plans and excitement.

Come May, I returned my snowboard to the garage and said farewell until the following season. With each year I got better at snowboarding and planning my trips. I even learned to enjoy the drive.

Eight years after my first solo trip I walked into a Mammoth lodge for a lunch break. The place was packed, so I shared a table with an older man.

"Need room for your friends?" he asked.

"I'm by myself," I said.

"Really? You should join my group." He gestured to the empty chairs on his end of the table. "They're not here yet, but they're a great bunch." He extended a hand. "I'm George."

"Heather. Thanks, but I'm going to head out soon."

By the time my helmet was in place and my coat was zipped up, his friends still hadn't arrived.

"Have fun," he said. "See you out there."

I smiled at his kindness, but knew I'd never see him again. The mountain was too large to run into the same person twice.

The next day I went to a restaurant after my last run. As I sat by the fireplace and enjoyed the mountain view George walked by.

"Hey there," he said.

"Hi," I said, shocked he'd been right about seeing each other again.

"Ever been to the hot springs?"

"No."

"Want to join us tonight?"

I weighed the pros and cons of agreeing to hang out with a stranger and his alleged friends who I had yet to meet. He did seem sincere, though, and the springs were a public place. If I drove on my own and made sure others were there it should be safe.

"Sure," I said.

"Great. See you there at five."

The sunset view from the hot springs was breathtaking. As the last glint of light disappeared, I climbed out of the rock-lined water, ready to take my pruned skin back to my hotel room.

"Want to ski with us tomorrow?" George asked.

"We'll be doing some runs from the top before it gets too warm," one of his friends said.

George had been right again. His friends were a great bunch, so I agreed to board with them. Their skill level far exceeded mine, but they were encouraging, not cocky. They helped me trust my skills and try slopes I'd avoided by myself. It made for a phenomenal day, so we decided to meet at Mammoth again two weeks later.

At the end of our next weekend on the slopes George and I sat in a lodge waiting for the others. He cocked his head to the side and smiled.

"You need to meet my friend Dale," he said. "You'd like him."

"Sure," I said, figuring he'd never set us up, like the dozens of other people who'd said the same thing before.

"Excellent. I'll make it happen."

Six weeks later Dale and I went on our first date. Six months later we were engaged. Six months after that we were married. As I look back now I'm thankful to Nyna for not wanting to go snowboarding because it made me learn to be okay with doing things by myself, and led me down the slope to my husband.

~Heather Zuber-Harshman

Just in Time

By changing nothing, nothing changes.
~Tony Robbins

"Y ou are one of those 'Just in Case' kind of people."

"What the heck does that mean?" I asked her, and she said it meant the opposite of a 'Just in Time' kind of person. "Which are you?" I wondered out loud and immediately wished I hadn't.

"Oh, I'm a 'Just in Time' kind of gal," she said with that smirk on her face. Why did I even try to be friends with her? She always made me feel like a fool. Why did I meet her every Friday after work for coffee just so I could feel bad?

"How do you know what kind of person I am? I might be a closet 'Just in Time' kind of person and you don't know it." I tried to lighten things up a bit.

"Oh, I'll bet you have an umbrella in the bottom of that huge purse you carry all the time." She eyed my purse with disgust.

"So what if I do? What if it rains? You'll be the first one to get under my umbrella because there is no way you have one in that little change purse you carry." I was not going to let her win this one.

"You carry that umbrella 'Just in Case', and I only carry one if it is raining. See the difference? It's the way you are. You carry way too much baggage. It might even be the reason you have a weight problem."

That did it. How could anyone be so mean? I left. I could hardly wait to get home, home where I would not have to think about what kind of person I was.

I stared at the door of my apartment when I got home. The note I left for the mailman was still stuck on the mailbox. "I am expecting a parcel. If it arrives, please put it in the plastic bag, inside the box, in case it rains." I opened the door, reached over, grabbed the note off the box and slammed the door. Could she be right? Was I a boring "Just in Case" kind of person?

When I opened the refrigerator to get a drink, I noticed the rows of pickles and mustards and three kinds of "Just in Case" juices. I sat at the kitchen table and glared at my cupboards full of dishes, pots, pans, and at least fifty cookbooks that I had "just in case." Just in case what?" In case he came back to me? In case I met someone new? In case I ever found someone to love and cook for again?

I reached for a hanger to hang up my coat. What for? In case someone drops by? In case someone might think I was a less than perfect housekeeper? I was more pathetic then I thought.

Wandering through the apartment, I realized I was a "Just in Case" kind of person. The bed. Oh the bed. I had a king sized bed. Me, alone, in a king sized bed, for what? "Just in Case," that's why.

My closet was full of three sizes of clothes. One size fit me, then there was one size smaller, and one size larger. That's when I lost it. I grabbed an extra large plastic bag. Of course there were small, medium, and large to choose from. I chose the extra large plastic bag and started to throw out the small and large sized clothes. I kept holding dresses, shirts and skirts up to me. They were already out of style and they never really looked that good. They were all safe clothes; the colours went with everything, and the styles were as plain as unbuttered toast. One jacket could go with any skirt, and any shirt could go with all the pants. When did this happen to me?

I sat on the floor of my bedroom sorting shoes. I had had some for ten years and never wore them. Why? Because I might need them "just in case."

It was after midnight when I finished loading the car. The Goodwill was the first stop early in the morning, then the second stop was the park for a run. The rain couldn't stop me. Shopping works in all kinds of weather too. I bought clothes in my favourite colors and got my hair cut in the style I'd always wanted but was too afraid to try. It was late and I was hungry, so I stopped at the neighbourhood bar for something to eat just in time for the evening hockey game. The place was packed so I looked around for a place to sit. Arriving anywhere without a reservation was not my style. When a man offered to share his booth with me I hesitated: I couldn't just sit down with a total stranger. Could I? I did.

He was new in town but the movers wouldn't arrive until tomorrow. He just thought he'd drive around his new neighbourhood and see how it looked at night. We talked until the game was over and noticed the bar was clearing out.

I smiled when I arrived home and threw the parcels on the bed. I decided I'd keep my king sized bed. Just in case.

~P. Avice Carr

The Dry Truth

Desire is the starting point of all achievement, not a hope, not a wish,
but a keen pulsating desire which transcends everything.
~Napoleon Hill

At twenty years old I married my husband, Bill. We were young and as compatible as rum and Coke, which was my drink of choice, one I began abusing on a regular basis. I began to notice that, while other friends would have a few drinks on the weekend, we were imbibing on an almost nightly basis.

One night I remember walking through our apartment complex, noticing how other apartments were decorated so comfy and cozy. Through opened blinds I could see walls adorned with family photos and knickknacks on shelves that gave a warm, homey feel.

This was in sharp contrast to our meagerly decorated apartment where a lone poster of Rocky Balboa hung on the front room wall. This was the late 1970s.

Between the drinking and the hangovers I'd try to convince myself that someday I too would have a beautiful home and a family—which is really all I ever wanted. Then one night in the shadow of my buzzed behavior a small voice whispered: "Nothing changes if nothing changes."

Although I wasn't fully heeding the message I knew that for things to change it would have to start with me.

Nothing changes if nothing changes. That concept literally changed my life.

I was twenty-three years old and into the third day of my sobriety when I woke up in the wee hours of that September morning. I hadn't slept well and woke up feeling an anxiety attack about to strike.

Walking over to the kitchen sink I looked out the window as the sun began to rise above the darkened sky. I stood there taking in the quiet and tranquil sight, and with the serenity came the self-assurance that I was going to be all right.

Another amazing outcome was that my husband also quit drinking completely—cold turkey like me. The only thing that stayed the same was the love we felt for each other.

Recently Bill and I celebrated thirty-seven years of marriage—thirty-four of those years happily sober. We are the proud grandparents of four grandchildren, with our fifth due on Bill's birthday.

As I write this I am sitting in the new home Bill and I built ten years ago. The walls are covered with framed photos that tell the history of our family.

In my home office the lettered sentiment above the doorway reads our truth: "Love Is All That Matters."

In the dining room hangs a framed collage of wedding photos from both our daughters' weddings. The sentiment: "Family Is A Gift That Lasts Forever" is etched above the happy smiles and it speaks to the thoughts of my heart, the meaning more precious than gold to me.

Our beautiful home and all its inspiration is a far cry from that lifetime ago when we lived in that apartment with a Rocky poster on the wall.

As a woman of faith I strongly believe that it was God's nudging that put me on a different road. Me listening was the key to my success. I doubt if I would have reached the destination on my own. Only when I quit drowning my feelings did I allow my inner light to shine—just as God intended.

Thirty-four years ago I gave up an addiction to alcohol and have never looked back.

For more than twenty years now I have been blessed to share my writings in a public way. Writing from the heart is what fuels my soul, it is the reason I put pen to paper every day. I'm writing about what

I know, focusing on the joys of family life, a life that I once thought was out of reach for me.

And that is the story of my dawn of new beginnings.

"Nothing changes if nothing changes." Those five words are a powerful truth. I know. I've put them into action.

~Kathy Whirity

A Family Reunion

To know when to go away and when to come closer
is the key to any lasting relationship.
~Doménico Cieri Estrada

My daughter and I unpack our luggage in our Florida motel room and slip into more comfortable clothing—cotton shorts, T-shirts and sandals. We have flown down from New York to visit my eighty-eight-year-old mother who recently broke her hip. My older brother, David, who has been undergoing dialysis three days a week for over ten years, has moved in with her.

"It's a family reunion," I tell my daughter, Zoe.

But, truthfully, it isn't much of a reunion because there was never much of a union to begin with. That's because there wasn't much of a family to begin with. When I was six and my brother was eleven, our parents divorced and my mother married a man who was saddled with four needy kids of his own. My mother later admitted, "After six months of marriage, I knew it was a big mistake." But she compounded her error by staying married for twenty miserable years. That was our family.

My sixteen-year-old daughter and I park our rental car in my mother's concrete driveway and step out into the Florida heat. My mother's pink-stucco, two-bedroom home nestles within a modest community built around a small golf course and features a plush green lawn, well-manicured shrubs, and tastefully arranged palm trees.

As I open my mother's front door, my daughter sees an invalid sitting in a hydraulic-lift chair. This woman is watching television and the remote control is resting on her lap. Her hair, normally dyed and coiffured, is gray and hangs loosely down.

This invalid is my mother. But my perspective is different from my daughter's. I see a young, beautiful fashion model, a successful New York City clothes designer who still is able to move around with the help of her walker.

"Hi, Mom," I say. I pretend to hope for nothing more than some pleasant conversation and a hug or two. More importantly, I hope my daughter might finally get to know her remarkable grandmother. Maybe she'll even get to know her mysterious uncle David.

"Hi, honey!" beams my mother, reaching out. "And look at you, Zoe! You've grown so tall!"

I bend down and kiss the top of my mother's head.

Sitting on the couch beside her is my brother. I know very little about David. Perhaps that's because he has always wanted it that way. By the age of fourteen, he discovered a coping mechanism to deal with our mother's toxic second marriage: heroin. My heroin was boxing. Instead of sedating my sadness and anger, I punched it out. But all of that belongs in the past. David has moved on, and so have I. He is sixty-five years old and has graduated from Columbia University with a degree in social work. Me? I'm sixty and teach high school English.

"Good to see you, brother," David says, embracing me. We've never been close, but I feel his warm hug and I notice the serenity in his face. It feels good.

"Good to see you, too," I say. Our relationship has never grown much beyond "Good to see you, brother." Our brotherly bond has always been fragile and, as the younger brother, I never was able to develop a sense of trust around him. Consequently, we keep our topics easy and non-threatening. Today, we speak about his recent retirement and the inept Florida Marlins.

While talking, I sense we both are attempting to establish a semblance of brotherly affection. But I am certain he wouldn't want me to dig too deep and start asking delicate questions about his health or his personal relationships. So I remain silent.

Superficial and comfortable is best. We offer only the outlines of our lives, at least the version that we like best.

We are both smart enough to have left our guns at the door. It won't be necessary for us to wear our protective armor this afternoon. All of our arguments, yelling and putdowns are in the past.

After an hour of easy conversation I feel more relaxed and trusting. Perhaps, at this late date, it's best we aim for comfortable friendship rather than stressful brotherhood.

"You know what I like to do?" he says, looking out the window at the back yard. His voice is soft, tender and humble, and that surprises me. "Every week, I drive to the grocery store, buy a big bag of peanuts and bring it home. Then I scatter the nuts on the grass under the tree in the back yard. Every day I just sit here and look out the window and watch the squirrels, birds and the cat enjoying the nuts." David's voice, I notice, exudes a new sense of calm and equanimity, something I've never heard before.

My mother smiles with undisguised love and pride at David's emotional tranquility and his recognition, and appreciation, of small pleasures.

My initial expectation for this family reunion had been small because our individual histories have been vast, bewildering and convoluted. My mother's fashion career offered her a luxurious and expansive lifestyle, touring the world in grandeur. By comparison, David's life anchored him to the streets of New York, where he cared for the city's downtrodden. Me? As an English teacher, I have explored the world, and people's minds, from the safety of my classroom and the printed page.

I look at David's worn face and I feel the bite of mortality. My mother, brother and I are growing older and I fear that in profound ways we still don't know each other very well. We have made ourselves unknowable behind our blind teenage rage, our middle-aged selfishness and now, perhaps, with our mature etiquette and polite superficiality.

There is no hint of anger or revenge. Complaints and accusations are nonexistent. Disagreements are left unsaid and past hurts are submerged, like icebergs, and will remain submerged. Maybe this is as good as it gets.

"Let's watch *Judge Judy*," smiles my mother, as she points the remote control at the television.

Throughout the day, I've noticed Zoe sneak quick glances from her iPhone at me, my brother, and my mother. Does she understand what has happened today? Does she understand that we were once enemies locked in combat? Is she aware that she is witnessing her family members finally at peace with each other?

Does she realize that her grandmother, her uncle and her father have emerged from our various personal journeys scarred, wiser and triumphant?

"Will we see you for breakfast tomorrow?" asks my mother.

"Bright and early," I say, kissing the top of her head.

I look down at my mother sitting comfortably in her hydraulic-lift chair and realize her once expansive life will now become more and more limited. But that is life. "Mom, you're still the prettiest woman in the room," I say.

She laughs and her bright eyes twinkle. Her long, gray, un-coiffured hair and wrinkles don't make her look old, they make her look eternal.

I look over at my beautiful daughter as we walk out to our car. I am so proud of her. At sixteen, she has already distinguished herself. She has maintained a high-honor roll status and has been selected captain of her tennis team. She makes friends easily and seems to be confident and have a healthy self-esteem.

"Zoe, I want the dysfunction to end with me." I don't actually say this to her, but it is exactly what I am thinking as we slowly drive home.

~Peter W. Wood

Chapter 2

Reboot Your Life

Follow Your Heart

Run for Your Life

A sister is a gift to the heart, a friend to the spirit, a golden thread to the meaning of life.
~Isadora James

I used to babysit an angel. Her name was Pary and she was my younger sister. She was the youngest and my brother Kraig was sandwiched between us. Being the oldest, I was often called upon to watch over Pary when my parents ventured out, as they frequently did.

Times were different back then, safer. Our household was a free-spirited place and we were always encouraged to wander openly. Boundaries were few, and a skateboard and five-dollar bill could carry you far.

Still, when it came time to babysit, we were not to leave the house. Three rambunctious housebound kids became a recipe for mischief, and poor Pary bore the brunt of our practical jokes, like the time we mixed cayenne pepper in her milk or the time we put a goldfish in her sock. Yet, no matter how cruel our pranks became, she never got upset with us. She never cried, and she never told on us. She seemed to accept our antics as nothing more that boyhood immaturity, which they truthfully were. She would just laugh along with us. "That was a good one, you guys," she'd say, trespasses forgiven.

Eventually, I lost all desire to play tricks on her. It didn't seem right. I'd developed a certain respect and admiration for the way Pary responded to our unkindness, and I couldn't bring myself to inflict pain upon such a compassionate soul. She taught me a valuable lesson in life, one that even as a young boy I could somehow appreciate.

As we grew older, Pary and I developed a close friendship. Even though she was younger, Pary possessed a wisdom and understanding well beyond her years. She was open-minded, amazingly kindhearted, emotionally intelligent yet pleasantly whimsical. She never passed judgment or criticized others, no matter how poorly they behaved or how much their position deviated from her own viewpoint. But she wasn't a pushover, either, and always stood firmly for her beliefs and values. Above all, Pary remained true to herself no matter the circumstance or the setting.

Sometimes I would confide in her that I didn't like certain things in my life, like playing in the school band. "If you don't enjoy it, don't do it," she would tell me. "Do what you love, Dean," she said. "You'll be happier that way."

We lived in Southern California, where the weather seemed perpetually clear and sunny. I'd taken up running and used to run along the seashore, often stashing my shoes in the bushes and running barefoot along the soft sand. Sometimes Pary would walk down and we'd watch the sunset together from the bluffs overlooking the sparkling Pacific.

"You really love to run, don't you?" she would say to me. "I can see how happy it makes you."

She was right. I did love to run, and it had become my solace and freedom. Though she wasn't a runner herself, she could sense this.

As the sun dropped below the horizon, setting the evening sky ablaze, she'd say, "That was a good one. Best one ever..."

She would say this every time we watched the sunset. Sometimes I would tease her: "Pary, that's what you said last time."

"Well, it was," she'd respond, "Tonight was the best one ever."

In high school, Pary was stunning, with beautiful brown eyes, olive skin, and golden flowing hair. Still, she didn't think much of her physical beauty. There was no vanity or pretention in the way she acted or how she treated others. Pary was just Pary.

I was a senior when she was a freshman, and as I watched a cadre of boys swoon over her, I was concerned. But she was surprisingly adept at seeing through their showmanship and attempts at attracting her attention. Even as a freshman, she had things pretty well figured out and didn't require much counsel on my behalf.

Pary was far and away the smartest member of the family and her marks in school were always the highest. In fact, she occasionally helped me with certain subjects, though she downplayed the amount of assistance she provided (which, in actuality, was quite substantial).

I managed to scrape my way through high school and head off to the craziness of college. I stopped running and started partying. Pary and I remained close. Whenever I returned home, we had a great time together, picking up right where we'd left off. Throughout high school Pary never lost her way, as I sometimes had. She graduated with honors and was looking forward to a long summer at the beach before starting college.

August rolled around. It was Pary's eighteenth birthday. Although I was away attending summer school, we had talked earlier in the day. I told her I missed her and wished her a happy birthday. She had said that her girlfriends were taking her out for dinner. She was looking forward to it.

Early the next morning there was a knock on my apartment door. When I opened the door, a priest stood before me.

"I have some sad news for you," he said. "Your sister has passed away."

I went numb. "What?" I finally said. "You must have the wrong address."

He said that Pary had been killed in a car accident. "That can't be," I insisted, "It was her eighteenth birthday."

"I know," he said mournfully. "I am sorry."

And just like that, my best friend in the world was taken from me.

Bereavement is a disjointing process. At first, I refused to believe this had actually happened, despite carrying my sister's body as a pallbearer at the funeral.

Then came the anger. It wasn't fair. How could this be? I was mad at everybody, mad at the world. And it showed in my behavior.

Reckless nights of drinking and raucousness followed. I was out of control and didn't care.

Somehow I managed to make it through college and land a decent job. One thing led to another and I found myself in San Francisco in a corporate position. Over time I repressed the anger and the hurt, replacing them with the material trappings of prestige and fortune. The partying didn't stop, though it moved to trendy nightclubs and upscale bars.

On the night of my thirtieth birthday I found myself in one such bar, doing what one traditionally does on one's thirtieth birthday (i.e., drinking myself into oblivion with my buddies). But something fractured that night, something powerful and transformational.

My buddies were perplexed when I announced that I was leaving at 11 P.M. "What?" they said. "The night is young—let's have another round of Tequila shots!"

I informed them that I was going to run thirty miles to celebrate my thirtieth birthday.

They laughed at me. "You're not a runner," they said. "You're drunk."

This was true, but I was still going to do it. I walked out of the bar and stumbled off into the night.

People think that change takes time. This isn't always so. The desire to change may be simmering quietly under the surface for years, but once that flame reaches a flashpoint, ignition can take place instantaneously.

I didn't like my life, didn't enjoy the corporate world. It wasn't who I was. The fancy cars, the opulent hotels, the lucrative bonus program—these things weren't perks, but corporate handcuffs that only served to imprison me.

I longed for the freedom and grand sense of adventure that I'd felt as a boy when I was running. Those were the moments when I felt most complete. I wanted to experience those feelings again. So that night I took back my life.

It had been more than a decade since I'd last gone running, but even in my drunken state, it was amazingly transformative. Something just felt right, like I'd finally found my place in the universe. I thought about Pary a lot as I ran, about the way she always told me that if you do what you love, you'll find your happiness. I began to believe again that she was right. I could feel her shining down upon me from the stars above.

So much of what Pary had told me was true. Every sunset was indeed the best one ever. Every footstep was indeed better than the last. Every moment of life was indeed worth savoring. As I ran along that moonlit highway, the anger and the denial and hopelessness I'd felt over losing her dissipated. It was replaced by a commitment to live every moment of my life to its fullest in celebration of my kid sister.

The sun was peeking over the eastern skyline when I arrived at my destination, thirty-miles from my starting point. Running straight through the night forever changed the course of my life.

I quit my corporate job shortly thereafter and decided I would make a living running. How, I had no idea, but Pary always encouraged me to follow my heart, so I did. Now, some two decades later, I've realized more happiness and greater fulfillment than I ever dreamed imaginable. I've used my sister's wisdom to find my true calling in life, and she has been guiding me forward every step of the way. Whenever I lose my sense of direction, I turn to her for insight and perspective, and she always steers me back on course. Instead of being angry and resentful that she is no longer in my life, I am filled with gratitude and joy that she is.

You see, I used to babysit an angel, and now that angel babysits me.

~Dean Karnazes

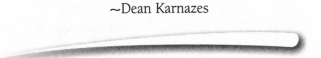

Finding "Perfect Love"

If you want to make your dreams come true,
the first thing you have to do is wake up.
~J.M. Power

I grew up on the west side of Buffalo, New York in a low-income, interracial, musical household. Although my early years were filled with the turmoil often found in a broken home, I remember hearing the soothing sounds of my father's jazz guitar at night. It was his way of unwinding after a hard day patrolling the housing projects. Those memories are few however, since I was raised primarily by my mother, a Barbizon graduate beautician, an aspiring school-teacher, and a woman with whom I had much conflict as a child. Still, it was my absentee father who instilled in me the knowledge that the Universe is a grand and awesome place, and I should be thankful for the time I am given in it.

Like all children, I had dreams... of stardom, wealth, a loving family with children, and everlasting love. I also had a burning desire to do good and be influential in a positive way in the lives of all those with whom I would come in contact. Many children do not have the opportunity to fulfill their dreams. Many grow into adults who feel their lives lack passion and purpose, or have not lived up to their expectations. I didn't want to be one of those children.

As an adolescent, I struggled to accept a stepfather in my life. Learning the new rules of the house was difficult for me, and school and music became a refuge from my teenage angst. The piano provided solace and the lyrics became a vehicle for me to share my innermost feelings of sadness and confusion with anyone who would listen. It was the one thing that reliably brought me joy and happiness, and kept me close to my distant father. The drama of the musical theater stage became a way for me to escape into a life other than my own.

But the past has a way of shaping one's choices for the future, and despite knowing deep within my heart that music was my passion, I chose to excel in academics and start on the journey to medical school. Being a doctor meant a life of security, financial stability, and social status, out of the projects and into the Ivy-covered walls.

At Columbia University College of Physicians and Surgeons, despite an inner knowledge that I'd betrayed my musical soul, I persevered and became an anesthesiologist. During my fellowship year studying to specialize in cardiothoracic anesthesia, and working with surgical greats like Drs. Mehmet Oz and Craig Smith, once again, I reached towards music to help see me through this emotionally trying time. With the encouragement of a group of fledgling songwriters at a small New York City bar called Downtime, and the assistance of a young producer named Julian Harris, I wrote and recorded a six-song demo CD. This was my first experience in a professional recording studio, and it was exhilarating! It was also my first encounter with a keyboard player by the name of Paul Gordon. As a favor to Julian, Paul played piano on a few of my songs, and that was the last time I saw or heard from him for years to come. I accepted a job offer in Florida against Julian's advice, who believed my creativity would be stifled by the Florida heat and my short-lived career in music would end. He was right.

I excelled at being a doctor and had a natural gift for connecting with and caring for my patients, but I felt empty inside and left my private practice job after only two years. I felt as if I were suffocating and needed to escape. Fleeing to Australia, I met and married my husband of the next ten years. We had two beautiful children, but we were not happy, and I was increasingly discontented with being a doctor. We travelled from Australia to the U.S., went from job to job, state to state, one unhappy year after another. For some reason, enduring this challenging marriage, simultaneously working and childrearing, and having multiple different full-time jobs depleted me of all my creativity. The fatigue and stress, the lack of "me" time, the depression and lack of love saw me deeply entrenched into a song-less decade.

Yet, there's nothing like heartbreak and death to bring on the emotion that creates the inspiration for a good song. That was certainly the case with me. In the same year my husband and I inevitably divorced, my mother unexpectedly passed away. It was the one-two punch that sent me into a downward spiral for several months. Every time I put oxygen on a patient, visions of my mother slowly suffocating in the intensive care unit entered my mind. Any time during a crisis, I would snap curtly at the OR nurses, something not at all in my character. So, with the encouragement of my colleagues, I took a three-month medical leave of absence, never to return.

I moved back across the Pacific Ocean, became a single mother of two little girls, and searched for a new job on my own. It was one of the worst years of my life but it began for me one of the most prolific times in songwriting that I've ever known. Over the next five years I wrote the songs of my life, of grief and pain, new relationships, and love lost and found. The floodgates were opened and I was once again creating beautiful music.

In August 2012, I reached out to a contact of mine who is a professional musician and asked him if he would listen to some of my songs. Finally, after all those years of stifling my passion, I wanted to be a songwriter. I thought that perhaps if he liked them that maybe somebody like Mariah Carey or Mary J. Blige would like them too! Stanley agreed and after listening to my GarageBand demos, he sent me a Facebook message saying, "Shari, I was pleasantly surprised by what I heard! I wasn't expecting this. I don't think that you should shop your songs as a songwriter. In fact, I think you're good enough to consider being the 'artist' yourself! You should record these songs."

It was the vote of confidence I needed and something I had never considered. Certainly a woman who was approaching her fiftieth year of life could not possibly embark on a new career in the music industry. Well, coincidentally, as if He knew it was my time, just a week later, Paul Gordon, the keyboard player from New York, reappeared in my life. Over the past twenty years he had worked with artists like Prince, Bon Jovi, The Goo Goo Dolls, Lisa Marie Presley, Natasha Beddingfield, and most recently the B-52s.

Once again, thanks to the wonders of Facebook, Paul reached out to me and gave me two VIP tickets to see him and the B-52s in Washington, D.C. The show was an amazing experience and afterward Paul and I caught up on the last two decades. He was married with two little boys, living in Nashville and working as the keyboardist and guitarist for the B-52s. I was living and working in D.C. at the military hospital part-time and raising my two children alone. Paul asked if I'd written any music lately. With some cajoling, I decided to share with him a few demos I had on my iPhone, and watched him intently as he scrolled through song after song detailing the events of my life over the past five years. He listened, occasionally nodding and saying "oh yes" or "that sounds like so-and-so" and looking at me, at the song titles, and at me again. Thirty minutes later, he looked up at me with a bright smile and said, "Shari, you're ready for an album." I burst out laughing in disbelief.

"I'm serious. I loved your music then and I love it now. You have a unique style, your lyrics are heartfelt, and I hear the story in each and every song. If you're willing to come to Nashville, I have the month of October off and would love to work with you!"

The Universe has a funny way of calling your attention to things left undone. And miracles happen when you least expect them too. But through a confluence of forces, Paul and I were brought together again to create *Perfect Love*, my first full length CD. Despite seeing an increasing number of wounded warriors in the operating room, my sympathetic musician Chairman created a flexible work schedule that allowed my frequent trips back and forth to the Nashville studio. Despite the monetary constraints of being a single mother supporting two teenage children, paying down a mortgage on a house, and only working part-time, I somehow managed to find a way to fund the project.

On June 25, 2013, my forty-ninth birthday, *Perfect Love* was officially released to the world, and is now available on iTunes, Amazon, and CD Baby. And suddenly, as if it were always meant to be, my life feels complete, and I know I have done what I was meant to do. I have learned that true everlasting love comes not from others, but from the love we have for ourselves, from deep within, in that place that no one else can reach, except for our Creator of course, and I definitely have that... I love me. I share this message with you so you too can believe that it is indeed possible, no matter what your life circumstances, your age, your heartaches, or past traumas in life, to make your dream come true, and to live a happy, loving, spiritual, and passionate life.

~Dr. Shari Hall

12

Mobilized by Fear

You block your dream when you allow your fear
to grow bigger than your faith.
~Mary Manin Morrissey

I remember sitting in the doctor's office. I remember hearing the word *malignant*. I remember discussing treatment options—but all I could think was, *Is this really it?*

The ground beneath my feet had already been shaky before walking into the doctor's office. Now the floor had been pulled out from under me. My mother had recently been diagnosed with cancer as well—hers was stage four and it was inoperable. Suddenly, we were both fighting for our lives.

To make matters worse, I'd been struggling with my direction after leaving a successful ten-year career as an Emmy-nominated television news writer and producer. Suddenly, my priorities had taken a sharp and sobering turn. The question was no longer a matter of what I'd do with the rest of my life—it was how long the rest of my life would actually be.

In the weeks that followed, I did what I'd always done when things got rough: I wrote. I kept writing, and I didn't stop. I wrote from my hospital bed after they removed part of my kidney, and I wrote in the weeks that followed.

I just kept writing.

I didn't realize it then, but I was writing my way through recovery. Those words would later become my first published work in *Chicken*

Soup for the Soul: The Cancer Book, and I knew they were the most important I'd ever write—not only because they gave me hope, but because they might give others hope as well.

Then I got an idea.

I had always wanted to write a book, but it seemed that time and circumstances would never allow it. Uncertain where my future might lead me—or whether there would even be one—I had nothing left to lose. It was time to take the leap, to follow my passion.

In the months that followed my surgery, I continued working on my novel, titled *While the Savage Sleeps*, and page by page, I felt my love for the written word take hold of me with more power than ever. Inspired, I found a reason to fight. A reason to live.

I was fully aware that my first novel could very well be my last, but I didn't let that stop me. In fact, now my resolve to become published was stronger than ever. If this awful disease got the best of me, I'd at least leave this world without any regrets over letting my dream slip away.

And I had plenty of encouragement. My mother was the one who had inspired me to become a writer, and there was nobody who wanted to see my novel get published more than she. As her disease advanced—through the chemo treatments, the discouraging test results, the nights she was too sick to sleep—never once did her enthusiasm and delight over my progress falter, and she'd always ask the same question: "How's the book coming?" She was so excited and couldn't wait to read it.

I remember her answer when I finally finished my first draft and asked if she wanted to have a look.

"Oh no," she said, shaking her head, with a smile that reached into her eyes. "I want to wait until it's done. I want to enjoy every word."

So I got back to work.

But I'd soon find that my battle had only just begun, that the road ahead was paved with pitfalls. After finishing my novel, I spent a year facing one rejection after another from just about every agent in New York and beyond. I can't say how many there actually were, because I stopped counting at a hundred. Many never even bothered reading the pages I'd sent, and the ones who did seemed to feel my book would never sell. It was heartbreaking, and it was discouraging, but I refused to give up. I couldn't. I'd already struggled through so much to write this novel.

But by June of 2010, it seemed pretty clear that I was spinning my wheels and getting nowhere. Out of desperation, and as a last-ditch effort, I took the only option that seemed available and uploaded my book to Amazon's Kindle Direct Publishing Platform. I figured there was nothing left to lose. I'd let the people who really mattered — the readers — decide whether my work was worthy, and whatever that decision was, I'd live with it. At least I'd know that I had given myself a fair shot.

Then I got my answer. Four months later, *While the Savage Sleeps* began moving up the bestseller list. My book, the one that nobody wanted to publish, the one that no agent even wanted to represent, eventually passed two of Stephen King's current releases on its way to number one. My perseverance had paid off.

Unfortunately, my mother never got to see our dream come true. She passed away before I could finish the book. But I still remember the day I hit the bestseller list. With a tearful smile, I said, "Look, Mom. We did it."

Three surgeries later, after my health finally began to improve, I found my stride and kept writing. In December of 2011, I released my second novel, *The Lion, the Lamb, the Hunted: A Psychological Thriller*, and the results were even better. That book moved into the upper tier of Amazon's Top 100, becoming their seventh highest selling novel out of more than a million titles available nationwide, and I was soon named one of the top-grossing independent authors in the country.

Within three months, my sales had pushed well into the six-figure mark, and before long, movie studios, literary agents, and publishers began contacting me. It was quite a change, going from being ignored to suddenly in demand, but it felt wonderful, and I wasn't bitter at all; in fact, I was thrilled. This wasn't about saying, "I showed you." It was about finally being able to say, "I showed *me*."

But it seemed this would just be the beginning of my real-life reboot. I eventually signed with one of the biggest literary agencies in the country, and soon after that, was offered an international, dual-publishing deal.

After releasing my third bestseller, *Darkness & Shadows*, and with a new book soon on the way, my novels have also topped lists in several countries, further confirming what this journey has taught me: when life throws challenges onto my path, I can let fear mobilize or paralyze me, but choosing the former is the only way out.

It's been five years since that day the doctor told me my future looked questionable. Five years of good health and unquantifiable happiness, of living my dreams instead of longing for them.

Of learning that life is all about the lesson.

~Andrew E. Kaufman

13

Time of Possession

When I approach a child, he inspires in me two sentiments:
tenderness for what he is, and respect for what he may become.
~Louis Pasteur

I loved my job in corporate America. I worked for a Fortune 500 company, the market leader in our industry. As a creative writer and incentive travel planner in the marketing division of the firm, I was traveling the world, having fun and doing what I loved most — writing. Well, at least, part of the time.

Like every job, there was also a mix of stuff I dreaded or downright loathed. After fourteen years, that got me thinking. In a perfect world, wouldn't it be nice to design a job around what you enjoy most, where your greatest strengths lie, and where you possess optimal potential? The theory being that you should spend your career doing what you love most in life.

Was this possible or was it a pipe dream? I started to research the feasibility of becoming a full-time freelance advertising copywriter and executive speechwriter. Much of my educational background, professional training, and work experience were in these disciplines.

I began talking to freelance copywriters and speechwriters. I read books by the most successful among them. I got on the phone with them to discuss how to directly apply their ideas to my situation in my marketplace.

I looked into self-employment insurance, income taxes for sole proprietorships, and personal property taxes. At first, freelancing full-time with a family of four on one income seemed like a leap of faith. In time, more information meant less fear and freelancing became a viable career option.

Since my wife, Karen, was a stay-at-home mom with our two young sons, there was no margin for error. I had to succeed. I set a launch date a year out. My preparation included setting up a sole proprietorship, creating a company name, finding an accountant, designing and printing business cards and letterhead, purchasing state-of-the-art computer equipment, software, a printer and office supplies.

Next was the hard part—testing my talent by writing for a broad clientbase. I started to write for local design firms and advertising agencies to prove to myself that I could write successfully on virtually any product, service, or subject. The criterion for success was simple—obtain repeat business.

As I built a reputation for myself, I expanded my portfolio and earned repeat business with every client. I continued my day job and freelanced at night. My days were long.

Launch day finally arrived. I had practiced my resignation speech a hundred times. Still, I felt the full weight of my decision. I set up a meeting with my boss and gave him notice. He was not surprised. He knew I had a dream to chase. He congratulated me, and we set my departure date.

I was never so excited. At thirty-seven, I was building a business around my strengths and the one thing I was most passionate about. Soon, I'd gained a few large clients and won several advertising awards.

I cherished the best fringe benefit of the freelance life—extended time with my wife and kids. My sons, six-year-old David and four-year-old Mark, watched me write from home for almost a decade. We played touch football in the back yard and baseball in an adjacent yard. We took short ice cream runs and long nature hikes, complete with walking sticks. I made up my time away from my business by working late after the boys were asleep.

It was a time of building family traditions. Football became our trademark. We teamed up with the neighborhood kids. I was the steady quarterback on both teams so I could play offense with each of my sons. I knew their skills so I could pit them against each other and still keep the score even until David would make a leaping catch in the corner of the end zone near the fence and evergreen tree. Or Mark would run for daylight and dive head first into the opposite end zone near the rotted willow tree stump.

At bedtime, as I tucked David in, he asked, "Dad, do you think I will ever be good enough to play in the NFL?"

"It depends on how hard you're willing to work."

"Do you think I will ever be as good as Joe Montana?"

I wondered how I would answer. Joe Montana, the San Francisco 49er quarterback, won four Super Bowls and was a legend in his own time. He was destined to become a NFL Hall of Fame quarterback. Yet, I wanted to keep the dream of my then nine-year-old alive.

"If you keep practicing, there is no telling how far your talent will take you," I said as I pulled the covers up to his chin.

Ten years after that conversation, David called me from his college dorm room late one night. We talked about his freshman classes, his desire to study journalism, and his hope to someday become a writer. And we talked about football.

"Pops, do you remember when we used to play football in the back yard?" he asked out of the blue.

"I sure do."

"Do you remember how badly I wanted to be like Joe Montana?" he said with a laugh.

"I remember."

"Do you remember how important it was for me to play football in the NFL?"

"Yeah. How could I forget?"

Then there was a long pause and I wondered where the conversation would go. The next words out his mouth were magical.

"Dad, if I could choose only one or the other, I would rather have played football in the back yard with you all those years than to play in the NFL."

This conversation is permanently etched in my heart.

In football there is a statistic called time of possession. The team that possesses the ball the longest has the best chance to win. Looking back, I realize by choosing to freelance, I won something in this game called life; time of possession with my sons.

~James C. Magruder

14

Happiness Is a Big Loud Garbage Truck

Children make you want to start life over.
~Muhammad Ali

Given a choice between spending time with a kid or a grown-up, I'll take the child every time. Children are more interesting than adults. They'll tell you exactly what they're thinking. The world still fascinates them, and it's still full of magic. And children are full of surprises. You never know what a three-year-old will say next.

I'm particularly mad about babies. If I hold a baby for ten minutes, I'm high for the rest of the day. I'm the rare person on the airplane who hopes the exhausted single mom struggling down the aisle with the fretful infant in her arms is going to sit next to me.

When my own son was born, twenty-four years ago, I left the practice of law to stay home with him. Although trading legal briefs for bath toys wouldn't work for every thirty-four-year-old professional, I was exactly where I wanted to be, on the floor, singing "The Itsy Bitsy Spider" to my kid.

"You may not be getting quality time," I often told him as I hunkered down beside him in the sandbox, "but God knows you're getting quantity time."

The sad truth about motherhood, though, is that if you do your job well, and raise a happy, secure and confident individual—you put yourself out of a job.

At fifteen, Tom no longer needed active mothering. Now he needed space and independence. I had to let go. And I did. But it hurt!

I was proud of my accomplished, confident teenager. But I missed the little boy who had wanted nothing more than to read books, paint pictures, make his stuffed animals come to life and explore the neighborhood with me.

I could have returned to the practice of law. But I'm really good with kids. And I realized that I needed them in my life. So I did something unusual for a fifty-year-old woman with a law degree.

I started babysitting.

I took at part-time job at my local library and put up a notice: "Wise, fun, mature library worker, great with kids, seeks occasional babysitting in your home."

I was a little nervous on my first job. I hadn't taken care of a toddler in over a decade. But I needn't have worried. Moments after meeting happy, bright-eyed Olivia, we were building towers with her blocks, acting out goofy stories with her stuffed bears and reading board books.

I was back where I belonged. On the floor, with a child.

In the decade since, I've cared for dozens of neighborhood kids. I only have two rules. I won't drive. And I don't watch TV.

I'll often find a new charge in front of the screen, expecting that I'll spend the next few hours watching along.

"It's beautiful outside," I'll suggest. "Let's go for a walk and explore."

That's usually all it takes. But if not, I don't give up.

"Want to read a story?" I'll ask. "Play hide and seek?"

The Disney Channel can be very compelling. But I persist.

"Let's walk the dog. You haven't got a dog? Let's borrow a neighbor's dog and take him for a walk."

There isn't a kid who wouldn't rather play than watch television. Cable is great, but I'm from a generation that went out to play, roaming the neighborhood until it was too dark to see.

I take care of twenty-first century kids as if it's still the fifties.

Milo, formerly addicted to Elmo, now adores the playground. Zoey makes up songs on the piano for her sister (and their hamster) to dance to. Sam writes picture books to sell to his parents when they get home.

One of the best times I've ever had was a morning I spent with two-year-old Suzi, a little girl who is fascinated by heavy machinery, following a compellingly noisy garbage truck around the neighborhood. She was totally blissed out.

I, too, was perfectly contented.

"It doesn't get better than this," I said to her.

Babysitting is so cool that I often wonder why more empty nesters don't try it.

I've taken care of five-year-old Hanina every week since he was a baby. I'm such an integral part of his life that, for a while, he insisted I was actually a member of his family. (A pretty neat trick, given that he's an Orthodox Jew and I'm an atheist.)

"You love Roz," his folks told him. "And she loves you too. But she's not family."

"Yes she is," he insisted.

So he asked me. "We're family, aren't we?"

"You can't choose your family," I told him. "But you can choose your friends."

"I choose you!" he said.

None of my legal clients ever felt like that about me.

I look forward to caring for Hanina as he grows, to attending his Bar Mitzvah, and to dancing at his wedding as joyfully as I recently danced at my own son's wedding.

When Hanina is too old to need a babysitter, letting go will be hard. But by then there could be grandchildren.

~Roz Warren

15

Movie Critic, MD

Chase down your passion like it's the last bus of the night.
~Terri Guillemets

"I quit." Those were words I never expected to hear coming from my mouth. I had been raised to persevere in even the direst of situations, but those two little words led me to a new job in a new city with a new home and new patients. I am a family physician, and I had developed the courage to leave a medical practice I felt had stifled my growth as a clinician. I had started over but soon learned I hadn't started over far enough away.

Sitting in my new office during a lunch break, I sighed at the mountain of paper charts sitting on my desk. I had a tendency to skip lunch to tackle all that chart documentation, but something told me to grab a ham sandwich and give my brain a break with a lighthearted Internet search. What I soon discovered made me giddy as a schoolgirl. After a few phone calls, I scampered into the front office and found several pairs of receptionist eyes looking up at me.

"I need to take some time off next week," I said. "Can someone help me adjust my patient schedule?"

Loraine, a receptionist and dear friend, answered, "Sure thing, doc. Anything going on you want to share?" It may have been my happy feet dance that gave me away.

"I am going to go to the movies."

A small giggle escaped the lips of the other staff. "You are going to take time off from work to go to the movies?"

"More than that, I am going to go to a film set in Wisconsin to meet Johnny Depp."

That certainly drew some attention as questions swirled around the room. How did I know about a film shoot? Did I know if the actor would actually be there? How could I know it was not an Internet hoax? Of course, I had answers for all of them. I had confirmed the film shoot with the local Visitor Center in Columbus.

Then came the speculative looks that told me I lost my mind to fly across the country to do such a thing. After all, I was a professional and professionals are serious people; they do proper things and do not pursue obscure adventures. That was what I had always told myself but something shifted in me that day. I had quit a position that made me unhappy, had made all these life adjustments by moving and changing jobs, but I still had not found a way to find that life balance. The stack of papers on my desk told me so.

For me, movies had always been essential escapism. The silver screen could erase every worry and transport me into other worlds for hours at a time. I had dreamed of being a film critic, a female Roger Ebert, since high school and the opportunity to see that magic in action was far too tempting.

But Loraine understood. She smiled a toothy grin and gave me a pat on the back. It seemed she understood that life need not come burdened with conventional trappings.

I completed my chart documentation that day with verve.

A week later, I found myself on a plane to Chicago followed by a three-hour drive in a rental car to Wisconsin. My first stop was the Visitor Center.

"I can't believe you came!" Visitor Center director Kim Bates and I had conversed on the phone several times over the past week. We hugged as if we were long lost friends.

"I wouldn't miss it."

"You must be a big fan then."

I had been a fan of the actor since my high school days, but it was difficult to explain that this trip meant far more than that. I had always done what others expected of me. It was time to step out of that box into what made me happy. Now that I had the means to explore those options it seemed a shame to let it go.

Sadly, the film shoot with Johnny Depp was canceled at the last minute but I did get to watch Christian Bale shoot a scene with Billy Crudup for Michael Mann's *Public Enemies* at the Capitol building in Madison. I also got to tour the downtown Columbus sets and visit a home that had been transformed into a 1930's brothel. My wildest dreams of becoming one with the silver screen had come true.

I went home with an exciting story though I was missing the icing on my fantasy cake. I topped it off a week later when my new Wisconsin friends notified me that Johnny Depp had arrived in town to complete his part of the film shoot. Some would say I was a stalker to hop back on that plane, and I still get picked on to this day, but in my mind what I did was round out the experience.

Columbus was just as I left it, a movie wonderland. As I waited in a crowd that night near the Universal Studios set, a woman whispered, "Did you hear a woman was coming all the way from Connecticut?"

A little embarrassed that I had become a quirky topic of discussion, I answered, "That's me."

A teacher, a hospice nurse, a high school student, they all took me in that night with open arms, and I felt accepted by people who simply yearned for adventure just as I did. No professional roles or social expectations could stymy our enthusiasm. And at four o'clock that morning, Midwestern charm was reciprocated by the bohemian swagger of a famous actor. My heart palpitated when Johnny Depp put his arms around me in a big bear hug. The moment lasted minutes but would be a source of major change in my life.

"Thanks, Johnny."

Back home, central Connecticut regaled my tale through gossip that spreads as it always does through small towns. The patients loved it! In fact, the story had such impact that the town newspaper printed a story on my travels and offered me a position as a film critic that soon expanded to my writing for six local newspapers. I could not believe my good fortune.

A year later, that fortune expanded to the red carpet. Though there were naysayers who told me that my review column was too small or that I had not made enough of a name for myself, my Columbus adventures taught me to always expect more, to keep dreaming. I applied for press credentials to the Los Angeles Film Festival, eager to see the Hollywood premiere of *Public Enemies*. I dashed out of my medical office panting with excitement that I had made it to the big time. "LA just called. I am in!"

A whoop went up through the medical staff and Loraine nodded her approval. Unlike some who stifled others with societal expectations, she knew that you can be whatever you want to be. With her support, my childhood dreams had come to fruition and I could give myself the not so official title of movie doctor.

I completed my chart documentation that day in nirvana.

And yes, the red carpet was amazing.

I learned back then that quitting isn't always quitting. Sometimes it is starting over. By listening to my inner voice, quitting led me to my biggest win, a balanced life doing all the things I loved.

~Tanya Feke, MD

Becoming Real

Dream as if you'll live forever, live as if you'll die today.
~James Dean

I met Jill in her last month of pregnancy. The incredible irony of meeting her was not lost on me. I was a woman who had tried desperately for years to carry offspring of my own and whose arms were still agonizingly empty.

Jill had recently become single and this would be her third child. She was in need of friendship and support, and would need it even more when this new little one would enter the world.

I rejoiced in the birth of Jill's baby girl and walked through life beside her. A couple of years went by, and our friendship blossomed. We were kindred spirits. Jill and her children spent Thanksgiving with my husband and me. Her little family participated in fundraisers to help us inch closer to our dream of adopting an infant.

When our baby finally arrived, Jill gave us the book *The Velveteen Rabbit* and later attended our daughter's first birthday party.

Less than a month later, Jill was dead. Three children lost their mother. I lost a friend.

Nobody saw it coming. Jill experienced a massive seizure while driving. It was a miracle that her vehicle did not hit anyone and that no one else was injured. As her young children kept vigil at her bedside, Jill was kept alive by machines. We soon learned that she would never wake up.

After a few days, the social workers took plaster forms of Jill's hands, preserving her fingerprints. They took photos, too, preparing the children for the inevitable time when they would need to say goodbye to their mama.

Removing life support from a loved one is horrific for an adult, unimaginable for a child. As a friend helplessly watching from the sidelines, it was unbearable.

And yet this extreme and heart-wrenching time jolted me into a new perspective on my own life. I had always lived for "someday" or for "when we have kids." I had not been truly living in the present. Through the painful lens of what I had just experienced, I realized that what I have right now is all I am going to get. I will only live this moment one time. I don't get to do it over again. Life is fragile and fleeting; I am not guaranteed another day.

I also realized that I had lived the majority of my life for other people and according to their expectations. I was operating out of fear. Fear of failing, of letting people down, of disappointing them.

I was participating in activities and serving on committees that I didn't even enjoy being a part of, because I felt intense pressure to be the person others wanted me to be.

The film of my life was playing in front of my own eyes and I didn't even recognize the woman in those scenes! Who was I?

I began making changes—difficult but positive changes that enabled me to pursue the things I wanted to do, that allowed me to serve causes that I truly felt were utilizing my strengths as well as challenging my weaknesses.

Now, when individuals extend an invitation, I ask myself a few questions...

1. Is this something I want to do? Is this a way I want to spend my time?
2. Would it be appropriate for me/my family to attend? Does the activity line up with our family goals and mission? Does it reflect the values we wish to own—not just portray? Is this something we are passionate about? Is it the best use of our time?

3. Do I feel I can make a difference? Is there a service opportunity?

It took some deep inner reflection to figure out exactly who I was, what I wanted in life, and how I felt I could best serve. I had to nail down my various roles in life (wife, mom, coordinator, employee, writer) and prioritize those accordingly. I then reflected on my legacy—how I wanted to be remembered in each of those chosen roles. I then decided on what I wanted to personally invest in—which relationships, roles, and responsibilities.

Once I had this all mapped out, it was so much easier to know where to focus my time and energy. It is a wonderful thing to truly experience freedom. Knowing who I am and what I stand for is a powerful tool.

I now agree with the wisdom of the nursery toys in *The Velveteen Rabbit*: "Real doesn't happen all at once. You become. It takes a long time; but once you are Real you can't become unreal again. It lasts for always."

~Amy L. Stout

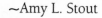

A New Operating System

A desire to be in charge of our own lives, a need for control, is born in each of us. It is essential to our mental health, and our success, that we take control.
~Robert F. Bennett

"Meeting at nine," Joel said without looking up. As I walked to my desk at my secure major software company job, the office was buzzing. I meandered over to my best buddy Joel's desk to quiz him. Was he being sarcastic this morning?

The moment I met Joel, I liked him. He was smart and funny and he was taller than I was. I had to look up to him no matter what, and when I did I always got a big smile. My task was to train him for the position I'd vacated a year earlier. Now I hid in a division that no one cared about. I knew Joel was not long for the job, though he was smart. His ideas were outside the box. He took great pride in challenging management and he was confident. My kind of guy.

"Now what?" I said as I walked into the room of glum faces. "Somebody forget to turn out the lights again?" I knocked back a large swig of coffee. Since the takeover of my division by a contract employment agency, these weekly meetings were routine. The big shots micromanaged while I did my best to sidestep their soirées. I showed up, did my work and left. I missed my old boss. I missed my autonomy. The joy had vanished from my job. What did they want now?

"Offshored." The words resonated in every cell of my body. The exit plan was in place. "You have a job to do," they said. "Your performance is important in making the transition seamless."

"To make whose transition seamless?" I grumbled to myself as I took another swig of coffee. Their pretense insulted me. Not only were we losing our jobs, we had to train our replacements with a smile. And if we cooperated, we would get a nice bonus at the end. Tears filled the room. I could see the questions in my co-workers' eyes. What next? Who would want to hire them? What would life be like without a comfortable corporate job? No one wanted to leave.

Except for me. I wanted out as soon as possible.

"Let's create our own exit plan," Joel whispered. "Do you want to find another job or do you want to have a life?"

The idea of jumping into another corporate position did not give me a warm and fuzzy feeling. To use a software term, I needed a new operating system for my life.

As Joel and I exited the boardroom amongst the tears and angst, we looked at each other and smiled. "Six months. That should be enough time for our exit plan," he said.

I matched his stride as we returned to our desks. "Exactly. Let's do it. Let's get on with the business of living. Our job here is done."

Once a week for the next six months, Joel and I commandeered the boardroom under the guise of a one-on-one meeting and formulated our exit plan. We didn't just chat about our dreams, we breathed life into them. We hashed out our ideas in an open forum. We gave criticism without judgment. Our bottom line was how to incorporate what we loved and make it a viable business. We weighed our strengths and weaknesses. We gave each other assignments with deadlines. We held each other accountable for the next step in our game plan.

Joel was both my competition and my mentor. His suggestions helped spark an idea I mentioned on our way home one day. I wanted to take my passions for horses and writing and weave them together. Joel's encouragement was inspirational. I counted the days until it was time to leave.

The day I walked out of that office for the last time, I formed my own production company. Those six months with Joel had trained me to set goals and complete them. Each day, I performed one task that pertained to my new business and my new life. I had no idea what I was doing and I had no budget whatsoever.

Each completed assignment gave me the kind of satisfaction I'd never felt while working in the corporate world. My objective was to create an instructional DVD about horse training using my own livestock. To make the DVD more marketable, I wrote an instructional manual. My company was a multi-media organization, producing instructional programming and fulfilling my dream as a writer. Each day was different. Some days, I was frustrated. On those days, Joel was just an e-mail away, and his input was a comfort. His eyes could see solutions that mine could not. One year later, the DVD was complete and the book was ready.

Five years have come and gone. Two published books, several awards, and many film festivals later, I am blessed, not just by those achievements, but also with the most important aspect of life: peace of mind. Most of all, I am happy that I made the choice to change my life using a new operating system.

~Sabrina Zackery

18

Self-Discovery

I was always looking outside myself for strength and confidence but it comes from within.
~Anonymous

was sitting poolside at my birthday party, dangling my feet in the water, when I suddenly felt old. All that seemed to be missing to complete my spinster persona was a houseful of cats. This was not what I had pictured for myself at thirty. In the midst of all my friends' wedding ceremonies and baby making, I felt lost—sad, single and hopeless.

With all my fruitless soul mate searching, an entire decade of personal opportunity had passed me by. Sitting there, scouring my memory bank, I couldn't think of a single unique or significant moment from my twenties. Aside from the typical college graduation and start of my career, I had done nothing that I considered important.

How did I allow myself to end up there? I didn't have photos of exotic locales, tales of adventure, or anything that would indicate I was doing more than breathing and occupying space. That moment served as my epiphany, and I recognized that my decade-long pity party must come to a screeching halt. Right there, in the midst of my "celebration," I made a decision to accept my life as it was and start living it from that point forward.

I realized I should have spent far more time building my experience catalog and far less time scouring Austin, Texas for Mr. Right. Only to be sorely disappointed, I might add, when he didn't materialize.

Waiting around for what I thought would make me happy only made me miserable, and if my twenties could evaporate so quickly, I reasoned it wouldn't be long until I was a blue-haired old lady sitting on my sofa lamenting about that whole bunch of nothing I did in my youth.

When I finally quit searching for the man of my dreams, I took my first step toward self-discovery. I purchased a guitar and learned to play it. It wasn't long until I'd written some songs, and before I knew it, I'd stepped further out of my comfort zone and bought that first home I'd convinced myself had to be a joint purchase.

With these two notches in my belt, I went on to audition for *Nashville Star*. I traveled by railroad. I walked sixty miles for breast cancer, stood atop the Empire State Building, mastered roller coasters, witnessed a whale breaching in the bay, landed in a helicopter on a glacier, deep-sea fished, grew my own vegetables, ran a half marathon, dog mushed, delivered a speech in my community, and played sand volleyball on a league. I met my childhood hero, Dolly Parton. I zip-lined in a rain forest. I donated my hair to cancer patients.

When I let go of what I thought I was supposed to become—a wife and mother—and embraced what I actually was—a strong single woman—I discovered my value. With every activity I attempted, my confidence soared until I had a firm grip on who I was and what I could do. Today, I'm a highly driven, creative and adventurous person, because I made a conscious decision to scare myself as much as possible.

And, sure, I had my doubts from time to time. I wasn't positive I could actually play volleyball, for example, but when game day finally arrived, I forced myself to attend. It was awkward since I hadn't even seen the courts since junior high, but there I was in the midst of total strangers, playing my heart out. It turned out that I wasn't half bad. A mouthful of sand here and there, but some solid passes and serves, too.

It was horrifying to climb a forty-foot pole before jumping off a platform and sailing 200 feet above a canyon. But I soldiered through the nausea, and afterwards, I felt as though I could master any challenge. At last I was strong, single, and hopeful!

Those victories of my thirties built the resilient woman of my forties. My newfound confidence came in handy when I was diagnosed with breast cancer. I refused to let my diagnosis boss me around. Two years later, I'm still breathing and occupying space, but now, unlike that first forgotten decade, it's with a purpose. In fact, I think it's safe to say that had I continued on the former stagnant path of my twenties, I would not have possessed the confidence or determination to face that breast cancer challenge.

Today, as a middle school English teacher, I share the lessons I've learned with my classes in hopes of inspiring them to be more. While it's obviously my educational responsibility to teach them how to be better readers and writers, it's also my personal responsibility to lead them toward their own paths of self-discovery. As recently as last week, I suggested that they invest in a small journal, not to write diary entries, but to record the special events and activities of their lives. I wish I'd started seeking growth opportunities earlier, but I remind myself that it's better to have lost ten years than twenty or thirty.

And by the way, while I was out living life, Mr. Right found his way to me.

~Val Jones

19

There Are Writers in There

We keep moving forward, opening new doors, and doing new things,
because we're curious and curiosity keeps leading us down new paths.
~Author Unknown

I sat in my minivan and watched the rain roll down the wind-shield. It was a soggy April day. And I was in a church parking lot. My church parking lot. I'd walked in those doors a thousand times.

But this day was different. This day, our church was hosting a Christian writer's conference. And I wasn't a writer. Well, I wanted to be. But that desire was a tiny dream, pressed into the folds of my heart, buried under the million real things that created my real life.

"Okay, Shawnelle," I said to myself. "You can do this." But truth was, I wasn't sold. Sure, I'd tried to dress like a writer. I'd bought a notebook and a pack of ink pens. I'd even twisted my long, red hair into a sophisticated knot. But I felt like I was a little girl playing dress up. I was a mama of five. An eight-year homeschool mama. A mama whose breast pump was on the seat next to me, peeking out from the top of my business-like new bag.

I glanced at the floorboards. There was a stack of mail strewn about. On the top, face up, was a coupon from a local department store. A good one, too. Maybe I should run away and shop for the day? But no. The registration fee, the one my husband had paid, was steep. And my encouraging girlfriend had taken my boys for the day. No. Shopping was out. I had to go in.

But there were writers in there.

And the thought scared the high-heeled writer boots right off me.

I sat and watched headlights stream into the parking lot. I watched doors open. Umbrellas bloom. People walk through those doors with confidence and grace.

"Here's your chance," I said out loud. "It's now or never."

It was true that I was scared. But it was also true that there were always words, waves and waves of words that washed through my thoughts and heart and days. Words that wrapped into and wandered through my life. Words that I had to set free.

I grabbed my bag and book and package of black pens. Then I opened the door, stepped over a puddle, and walked toward a new chapter of my life.

It wasn't that I regretted the life choices I'd made up until then. Not at all. I was the bustling, proud mother of five sons. And mothering was grand. Rich. Rewarding. I loved my days, from the moment the sun rose and I burped and bathed my baby, until the evening hours when I stayed up late to chat with my teen. But there were times when I wanted to share the ins and outs of my days. Times I wanted to reach out to people outside my home, to encourage and inspire and help others.

The one allowance I'd made for myself, writing-wise, was to pen a yearly Christmas letter. It was an attempt to record and share the small moments of life—what the kids had done, where we were as a family. The responses I received after I mailed my letters were always generous and kind. People were uplifted. Something in me felt good—fulfilled—when a friend gave me a post-Christmas-letter call or took a moment to write back. It felt like my desire to care for others had been stretched a little further.

And the stretching felt good.

But now this new stretch of being out of my element, in soggy boots, lost and confused in the very foyer I buttoned my kids' coats in every Sunday? Not so good.

"Um, excuse me," I said to the elegant lady beside me. "I'm new. Can you tell my where to go?"

"Sure." She smiled. "If you've registered, you can pick up your conference packet over there."

She pointed to a table that had been erected outside the nursery I knew so well. I thanked her, put one foot in front of the other, and went to get the goods.

A few moments later, the sanctuary buzzed with excitement. It was almost time for the keynote speaker. I chatted with my pew neighbors. Most of them were writing novels or had publishing credentials. I reconsidered that coupon on the van floor. I felt self conscious, like the words "Christmas Letter" were stamped across my forehead.

But when the keynote speaker took the podium, when this accomplished veteran author began to speak about writing and the blessing of written words, something in my spirit broke free. A streak of passion, more bold and wide than my fear, began to pulse in my chest. And later in the day, when we had the opportunity to spend fifteen minutes with one of the presenters, I knew I had to speak with Cecil.

I sat in my own church gym, in a chair like the dozens I helped to unfold each Sunday, and felt my heartbeat hammer in my neck. I looped my scarf a little tighter.

"What have you been writing? Did you bring anything with you?" Cecil asked.

"Christmas letters," I said. "I send one. Each December."

I pulled a copy from my bag. The snowmen on the stationery border suddenly looked silly. I handed it to Cecil and hoped he hadn't seen my hands shake. And then he read my letter. Quickly. Quietly. When finished, he looked up at me.

"I'll bet your friends love this," he said.

I nodded.

"The writing is a mess. But I can teach you to write. You have talent, and that's something you either have or you don't. You have a gift."

Cecil and I talked for a few more minutes. I tried to hold the tears inside. He gave me a reading list and said that he'd come back to the area to teach a workshop soon. He also put me in contact with a beautiful writer named Julie. I left the conference that evening armed with books, encouragement, goals, and hope that shone brightly on that cold, wet day.

After that, things happened pretty fast. I read all I could about writing. I won a contest and a trip to New York to learn from the editors of an inspirational magazine. I sold a manuscript. Cecil came back and held a class in my home. I had stories published regularly. I started to blog about motherhood and marriage and family.

And my life, my wonderful life, got even better.

I often think about that conference, that April, now five years ago. I was so afraid to reach for my dream. I was scared to stretch into the unknown. Goodness, I was terrified to even walk through my own church doors.

After all, there were writers in there.

It turns out I was one of them.

~Shawnelle Eliasen

Chapter 3

Reboot Your Life

Take a Chance

20

A Real Stretch

Coming out of your comfort zone is tough in the beginning,
chaotic in the middle, and awesome in the end... because in the end,
it shows you a whole new world!
~Manoj Arora

"Do you have a bathing suit I can borrow?"

Mom looked at me incredulously. "A bathing suit? Sure, why?" My mother knew a bathing suit was the last thing I'd willingly wear. I didn't even own one, hence my request.

"I decided to sign up for a sweat, soak, and writing retreat. We're to spend time in a hot tub and a sauna. It's supposed to be conducive to writing."

Mom looked at me in disbelief. "You're going to spend the day in a hot tub and sauna with a group of strange women?"

I let out a sigh. How did I explain that I was tired of being afraid of life? I am the least adventurous person I know. I plan ahead. I don't like surprises. I also don't like who I've become. "I just want to try something different," I muttered. My life was not going as planned. I had a broken engagement and a stagnant career to show for all my years of hard work. I wanted something more. I was hoping this retreat would be the motivation I needed to pursue my dream of becoming a writer.

"The thing that's making me nervous," I continued, "is that the invitation says we can bring a bathing suit if we want. That implies there could be some women not wearing bathing suits!"

When I arrived at the retreat, I parked the car and prayed for some courage. I grabbed my purse and bag of necessities with one hand and the salad I'd made for the potluck with my other. This event was hosted by a well-known local author who holds several writing classes each year. The only rules were anonymity and that we were not to discuss anything another participant shared. It was freeing to be to be able to share our innermost thoughts with a group of strangers with no repercussions.

The nine of us spent the morning on writing exercises. We were baring our souls with every word, even if only on paper. We were invited to share our words, but I wasn't brave enough. Changing one's life takes time.

The next step in the day's journey was spending time in the sauna. A selection of filmy wraps were made available for those not wanting to enter the sauna *au naturel*, but bathing suits were actually discouraged as they did not allow the body to properly breathe. Umm, what? I couldn't wear my bathing suit?

The homeowner said we could change clothes either in the one-roomed yurt where we had spent the morning writing, or in the privacy of her bathroom. Without running anyone over, I promptly made my way to the bathroom. Feeling so very exposed, even with the sarong wrapped tightly around me, I followed the others into the sauna.

Nine women in an eight-seat sauna is a very tight fit. Soon a jar of salt scrub was passed around. We were told to all turn to the left and wash the back of the woman in front of us. It's very hard to breathe deep, calming breaths in a sauna without passing out. So instead I just went to my happy place in my head until it was all over. I'm sure the woman sitting next to me was a wonderful person. At the moment all I knew was that she was a naked stranger who I was currently massaging, while another naked woman was touching my back in return.

I was so out of my comfort zone.

Not able to spend great lengths of time in the sauna, we took breaks, out on the patio either lying in the sun or sitting in the hot tub. I opted to sit in a lone chair and cling desperately to my soaked sarong. I was pleasant to anyone who spoke to me, but inside I was one deep breath away from a full-blown panic attack. I had to keep reminding myself that I was there to make a change.

It took me most of the afternoon to work up the courage to join a few women in the hot tub. This was our final break before we were to go back in the yurt for dinner and more writing. Since I had come this far, I figured it was only right to push myself a little farther. I dropped the wrap onto the chair and casually made my way to the steps of the hot tub. As I climbed to the edge of the tub it occurred to me that there really is no graceful way to get into a hot tub, especially not if you're uncomfortably naked. Not wanting to draw attention to myself, I slowly stepped forward, slipping only one foot in the water. With my other foot still on the outside of the tub I did the most spectacular splits in my life, sliding halfway across the water, landing dead center in the group of women I had been hoping wouldn't notice me. With my dignity gone, I laughingly told them all I was fine, while I frantically tried to figure out how I was supposed to get back out of the tub without any more gymnastics.

Thankfully that portion of the day came to an end. Once again I was fully clothed and back in the yurt. There are no tables in the yurt, only rugs, blankets and chairs, meant to create a welcoming environment. As I knelt on the floor, assembling my salad for dinner, the class moderator wandered in and began to dress a few feet away from me.

"So, did you learn anything about yourself today?" she asked. Before I could come up with a socially acceptable platitude, I blurted out, "I learned I'm a bit of a prude."

She laughed as she pulled up her underwear. "Not comfortable being naked? I guess you weren't around in the 60's."

I agreed, saved from further conversation as the rest of the group joined us.

After dinner and a few more writing exercises, we prepared to end the day. The moderator said she knew the day had been calming and relaxing for everyone. She hoped we were not all so relaxed we'd fall asleep on our way home.

I laughed silently. I was the opposite of calm and relaxed. After the day I'd had, I was wound so tightly it would take a week in the fetal position just to relax enough to breathe normally.

As I pulled out of the driveway, the moderator's final words were still in my head, "Ask yourself, where do I have room to grow?"

After that day I realized my potential for growth was limitless. But one thing was certain—the next time I decided on a growing experience, I'd be keeping my clothes on.

~Rebecca Olker

From Corporate to Carrots

Don't ask yourself what the world needs; ask yourself what makes you come alive. And then go and do that. Because what the world needs is people who have come alive.
~Harold Whitman

A t age fifty I was stuck in a job I hated, working for an international corporation that provided real estate advice to non-American investors. The corporate culture was paternalistic and downright offensive to women working there, despite my title. But it had taken months to find a decent paycheck, and many friends my age said they weren't finding anything at all after years of looking.

Then we got bad news. Rumors swirled that the company might close because of the 9/11 attacks. I began immediately looking, but after six months had nothing, not even an interview. Why hire me, when there were others half my age willing to work for half the price? I began to panic.

Just before Christmas, HR confirmed we would definitely be closing the following March. They knew I had been looking and were willing to provide a good reference. I held back my tears until I escaped out the door. I was the sole support for my preteen daughter and had stupidly run up many bills, believing I would continue to flourish in my career. With unemployment paying only twenty percent of what I was taking home, we were facing poverty, homelessness and possibly bankruptcy fairly quickly.

We were told we could quit at any time. I didn't understand why. Our doing so would only make closing the company much more difficult. But I didn't have that option — there was no place for me to go! The last week the company was open, HR called me back in, and reluctantly advised me that since I had stayed on with the firm, I was entitled to severance. Severance? Whoopee! It wouldn't be much, but at least I wouldn't be out in the street immediately.

Driving home I realized I had a choice. I could keep trying to find a replacement position and run out of money within six months, or I could do something different. I didn't know what that alternative path might be, but I had suffered through nearly five years of continuous depression while being unappreciated and overworked. Different began to sound better — much better, actually.

Hour after hour I pored over the Internet. What had other seniors done after being laid off? I didn't feel old, but apparently I was. I had two choices: to somehow make myself seem younger; or quit trying to convince employers of my value and earn a living another way. I chose the latter. I figured that if I worked for myself, I might be more in control of my destiny and maybe even enjoy the benefits of doing so, instead of turning it all over to someone else. There was the risk of failing, but since I couldn't find a job anyway, in my mind I was already a failure. I had nothing left to lose.

The severance we received wasn't huge, but it was large enough to offer me some options. Since I had to come up with a new life, I also looked at what I might be receiving later from Social Security. Not a lot — certainly not enough to continue living in one of the most expensive areas in the U.S. I had seen how Mother had been treated while living in Los Angeles as she entered her seventies, and it had been ugly. Merchants had cheated her when she didn't see well; drivers harassed her because she drove too slowly; and punks threatened and harassed her, making her life miserable.

We needed to move from the most expensive area to one of the least, but where? I had only worked on the coasts, and whatever income

I could drum up wasn't going to be enough to live there. Since my life needed to change, I also decided that in my new life I would have a job that gave me time to spend with friends and family and where I didn't have to sit all day.

I ended up choosing a new location based on what we could afford. It was 1,800 miles away from home in Southwest Missouri—a land full of open range, woods, critters and long drives to a city of any size—an area I'd never seen and my ancestors had left many generations before. We sold most of our possessions. Everyone thought we were crazy. I thought so too. But this was exactly what my great-great-grandmother must have done when she moved west looking for a better life.

Once in Missouri, we found a foreclosure. It was nine acres of rundown land with a beaten-up old barn partly converted to live in, next to a pond, and surrounded by thousands of acres of forest and cattle ranches. It was also five miles to any business and thirty miles to the smallest town. Yikes! However, it was peaceful and had been planted at one time. Most importantly, the payment for it would be even lower than I had budgeted. If I were completely unable to make a go of a business, I could keep it going on what little unemployment I was to receive, part-time minimum wages, or my future retirement income. I went straight into developing an organic farm selling vegetables, with hopes of expanding.

A number of years have passed. I'm glad I changed from corporate life to farming. We have also planted fruit and nut trees that should produce shortly. There's room to let our rescued dogs run and play. I don't have to listen to next-door fights or sirens going off incessantly. Despite an occasional bout of loneliness (since neighbors are few and far between) I wouldn't trade this lifestyle for anything. I don't have the income or the "stuff" I once did, but the peace of mind, true friends, and freedom are priceless.

~Kamia Taylor

365 Envelopes

The world is a book, and those who do not travel read only a page.
~St. Augustine

I sat cross-legged on the beige carpet of my bedroom floor surrounded by half-packed boxes and hundreds of white business-sized envelopes. What had I gotten myself into?

In a few weeks I would be moving from Chicago to Germany, so I should have been packing. Instead I was working on a goodbye gift for my boyfriend—one envelope for him to open each day of the upcoming year, when we'd be living six time zones apart.

The decision to accept the job in Germany hadn't been easy. David and I had been falling in love for a year, and we'd begun discussing marriage! But I had dreamed for years about living abroad, and David had encouraged me to pursue my dream. So there I was, stuffing envelopes with things that would make David smile and think about me throughout the year: favorite quotes, articles, comic strips, photos, personalized crossword puzzles, a 3x5 card with plastic googly eyes glued to it and a note saying "I miss seeing your face."

Into envelope 178, I put a photocopy of an article that I had come across years earlier. It was a story from *Chicken Soup for the Traveler's Soul* called "We Almost Did That." The author, Steve Gardiner, wrote about the regret-tinged comments that he heard over and over as he and his wife were preparing to quit their jobs and travel around South America and Europe. "We almost applied to teach overseas once," people would say. "We almost quit our jobs and traveled." The end of Mr. Gardiner's story embedded itself in my mind: "After eighteen months overseas, we arrived home with no money. In fact, we were in debt. But our riches include a shelf of ragged guidebooks, a trunk of well-worn maps, two minds filled with memories and no urge to say, 'We almost did that.'"

I highlighted those last three sentences and jotted a note to David: "Proof that marriage doesn't have to mean settling down."

That year living apart was tough. But the envelopes helped, and so did David's visits. We traveled all over Germany and Spain, and we talked about the idea of living abroad together someday, like the couple from envelope 178. On his last visit before I moved back to the States, David proposed. Four months later we were married and happily living together.

Throughout our first few years of marriage, we continued to talk about living abroad. We schemed and dreamed, researched and planned. We took a scouting trip to El Salvador, but it didn't pan out. We investigated jobs in Guatemala, Spain and Costa Rica. For one reason or another, nothing worked out. Then an opportunity came up for David to work as a doctor in a chiropractic clinic in a city called Arequipa in southern Peru. We visited and fell in love with the city and its glittering white buildings made from volcanic stone. We gawked at the three towering volcanoes that ring the city, and we dreamed of climbing them someday. The job seemed ideal, and we gave the clinic owner a tentative "yes." We went back to the States and began making preparations to leave. But when the buyer for our own chiropractic practice backed out, we knew we couldn't pull things together in time to take the job in Peru. The day we sent an e-mail to tell the clinic owner we couldn't come, we both lay on the bed and cried.

As the years passed, we talked about our dream less often. We stopped telling friends and family about every latest scheme. "I wonder what they think of us," we'd often say to each other. "Do they roll their eyes behind our backs every time we talk about moving overseas?" From time to time, one of us would say to the other, "What if that Peru opportunity came up again?" But it didn't. And our lives were comfortable. We enjoyed our jobs and our house on two acres in upstate New York. On weekends we did projects around the house and spent time with David's parents and sisters, who lived nearby. We took weekend trips to the Finger Lakes and New York City. We visited my family in Chicago. Once in a while, we would stand in front of the world map that hung in our home office and dream. Or we'd Google "overseas job opportunities."

Our dream to live abroad began to seem just a little irresponsible. Unrealistic. Childish. Perhaps, we thought, it was time to let it go. "We have a really good life," we'd remind each other. I even contemplated buying a KitchenAid mixer, in my mind, the epitome of settling down.

Then one day, we got an e-mail from the owner of the chiropractic clinic in Peru.

> Hi David and Karen,
> The clinic in Arequipa is looking for a new doctor at the end
> of the year. Are you still interested?
> Dr. Rick

We considered the e-mail for about sixty seconds and then sprang into action. I quit my job. We got rid of a car. We hired another chiropractor to work in our practice in New York. We found renters for our house. We took carloads of stuff to the Salvation Army and threw away armloads more. We hung a big piece of white paper on our kitchen wall: THINGS TO DO FOR PERU. We marked up the daunting to-do list with colored Sharpie markers: blue for house-related tasks, orange for the business, brown for things to bring to Peru.

The to-do list took a long time. From the day we got the e-mail to the day we stood by the single luggage carousel in Arequipa's airport waiting to collect our two fifty-pound duffel bags, it had been eight months. But we never doubted that it was well worth the effort. That year in Peru was without question the greatest experience of our life together so far. We trekked through the jungle and explored deserted Incan ruins. We awoke beneath mosquito nets to the sounds of monkeys swinging through the trees outside our bungalow in the

Amazon rainforest. We hiked to the top of Arequipa's tallest volcano and learned how it feels to try to breathe the sparse oxygen at 20,000 feet. We learned Spanish. We made great friends.

Most significantly, we spent Saturday afternoons hanging out with a group of kids who lived at an orphanage near our house. Almost every weekend, after another day at the park or outing to the mall, we joked about wanting to bring home some of the kids. Then somewhere along the way it stopped being a joke and started to seem like our destiny.

We began the adoption process as soon as we got back to the States. It's been almost two years of working our way through another daunting to-do list, but we're nearly finished. We just recently got final approval to travel back to Peru—and this time we'll be bringing home four teenagers from the orphanage in Arequipa.

That year in Peru was an incredible adventure, but it was only the beginning. As we prepare to go from being a family of two to a family of six, we know our life may not be comfortable again any time soon. And that's okay. At least we'll never have to say we almost did that.

~Karen Martin

Jumping Fences

Fear is the highest fence.
~Dudley Nichols

'm good at making excuses. I came up with a new one every time the idea of returning to college presented itself.

I had enrolled at Tennessee Tech right out of high school. I stayed a year and didn't do well, probably because deciding what to wear took priority over preparing for class.

As the years passed, I regretted not finishing my English degree and pursuing a career as a writer. I comforted myself with excuses—I'm planning my wedding. I have three little ones who need me at home. I'm busy with the children's school activities. I work full-time. I can't go back to school at the age of fifty. Old dogs can't learn new tricks.

The truth was that I was just plain scared to go back to school. What if I needed remedial courses? What if I walked into a classroom and there was nowhere to sit? What if an 18-wheeler blew me off the interstate? What if my phone rang during class? What if I tripped and fell? What if a professor called attention to me? What if I stood out in a sea of young faces?

After my children finished college, they insisted it was my turn. I called Dalton State College and set up a time to take the Compass Test to see if I needed remedial courses.

A few days later, I pulled onto the interstate and pointed my red Honda towards Dalton, Georgia. The phone in the cupholder rang. Rachel, my middle child, was calling from her home in Los Angeles.

When I revealed my destination, I heard the pride in her voice. "Oh, Mama, are you driving on the interstate?"

That was all it took. Hot tears tumbled down my cheeks as she spoke words of encouragement to me. Two hours later, I called her with the news. "I scored 99 on the English/Writing portion of the test and 96 on the Reading."

"Great! How about the Math section?"

"Um, 13. I'll need not one but two remedial courses to prepare for Algebra." But I didn't care. After decades of excuses, I'd finally thrown my leg over the high fence of fear. I couldn't wait to register for classes.

My first course was U.S. History. I've never been good with dates, but the professor calmed my jitters. "I don't care about dates, but I expect you to know the names of significant individuals. For instance, who was the first person to set foot on the moon?"

"Neil Armstrong," chorused several students.

"Does anyone know when that event took place?"

The professor didn't expect anyone to know the answer, but I did. Since it might be the only question I could answer all semester, I sheepishly raised my hand.

He peered over his half-glasses. "You know when Armstrong walked on the moon?"

I nodded. "July 20, 1969."

"How the hell do you know that?"

In a near-whisper, I explained. "The landing took place on my husband's fifteenth birthday. He mentions it every chance he gets."

"I bet you don't know any other significant dates."

"No, sir. None."

At home that evening, I told husband, "The first night in class and I drove the professor to profanity!"

Other fears turned into reality. I walked into rooms with no seats available, my phone rang during a class, and once I fell outside the library in front of a crowd. As with the history class, none of them proved fatal. The trucks didn't get a chance to blow me off the interstate, because a friend told me how to get to the college on back roads. And, after surviving two grueling remedial math courses, I passed Algebra with a big, fat, beautiful B.

As for my fear of standing out in a sea of young faces, I'd forgotten all about it until I met Delores. She entered the Southern Women Writers class with a rolling book bag and stopped at my table. "Hey, you look like me," she said.

Delores wore her steel-gray hair cropped close to her head. Even though she was at least ten years older than me, I looked more like her than I did the other students. She suggested we meet for coffee and "join forces against these young folks."

Just then, my friend Leah was laughing at Elisabeth's latest tale about her rowdy children. Jessi tossed her head to show off her Batman earrings. Adela adjusted her Middle Eastern head covering and Brent eased down the aisle with his walking cane.

I had worried my age made me too different. An outsider. Me against them. Instead, the students—each with his or her own distinctions—welcomed me to their lunch table, "friended" me on Facebook, and collaborated on class projects. Each one, from Delores with her steel-gray curls to Jessi with her superhero earrings, brought unique perspectives about the world to classroom discussions and something of value to my life.

Thanks to those unexpected friendships, I decided to walk across the stage to receive my Bachelor's degree rather than having my diploma mailed to me. Hundreds would be watching, but I wasn't self-conscious about my differences anymore. Besides, I'd already experienced most of my fears. What else could happen?

Sporting a black robe and balancing a mortarboard on my head, I marched into the auditorium to the tune of "Pomp and Circumstance." As I filed down the row behind Jay, a budding screenwriter with a dapper goatee, something didn't look quite right. I compared the graduates to the number of chairs and sucked in a breath. We were a chair short. I'd be left standing at the end of the row.

Just then, Jay turned and whispered, "Arlene, I don't think there are enough chairs. Here's the plan. You'll step past me and take mine.

I'll squat at the end of the row until I can get someone's attention for another chair. It's going to be fine."

And it was.

~Arlene Ledbetter

Laying Myself Off

A ship in harbor is safe — but that is not what ships are for.
~John A. Shedd

When the economic downturn forced my company to lay off some of our employees, it fell to me, as the human resources manager, to choose who would stay and who would go in my department. My own life had taken a downturn, too. My marriage had ended five years earlier, and I was raising my daughter alone. We lived in a small Midwestern town where most people were married, and dating prospects were slim. My own job was solid, and I had steadily climbed the ladder. But something was missing. My enthusiasm was gone. I could see years of the same routine stretched out before me.

I had an idea. What if I let myself go instead and gave someone my job? I had no debt, a good amount of money in the bank, and a sister I could stay with if I wanted to make a move to thriving Texas. Praying all the while, I created an organization chart and a proposal. The decision was made. It was time for a change in my life.

Right after I turned in my proposal, my boss announced he had taken another job. The president of the company asked me to stay and fill my boss's job. This threw me for a loop. It was a good raise and a great career move. But was it a great life move? My heart said no. Instead of taking the job, I helped them interview and fill it with someone else.

Weeks later my little girl and I were on our way to the heart of

Texas. We pulled over at the Texas state line and stopped to put on cowgirl boots, literally "rebooting" our lives.

A month after arriving I made a new friend whose husband was a commander at nearby Fort Hood. She started talking about a handsome lieutenant who would be perfect for me. The thought of dating made me nervous.

"Lord," I prayed, "I am a jerk magnet. If you ever want me to be married again you have to pick him." My friend persisted, and cautiously I went on a blind date. I was so nervous I barely talked. I decided maybe he wasn't for me. Still, my friend was so sure he was right for me, she kept asking us to go on another date. I gave in, and that night I saw something very special in that man.

We continued to date. I continued to pursue a new life, landing a job at a division of a Fortune 500 company in Austin. In the year that followed I started to realize we were fitting together like hand in glove. I watched closely to see what kind of man he truly was. Was he genuine? Did he have integrity? Did we share the same faith and values? Most importantly, how did he feel about my little girl? He seemed to be checking out just fine. My love for him was growing. Maybe in another year we would see where this might lead.

Suddenly I was faced with choices again. My new company merged two divisions. Then they did some more restructuring. They were excited to tell me they were going to move me to another city hundreds of miles away. At the same time, that special man in my life was getting orders to move to Fort Knox, Kentucky in a few months. And another friend called me about sending my résumé for a dream job in Chicago.

"Would you really go?" my lieutenant asked.

"If I have to I will," I told him. "I have a little girl to support."

What would happen to our relationship? Would we date long distance? We were nudged out of our comfort zone. He added another question to the mix.

"I know we said we would date at least two years before deciding to get married. But I already know I love you. You don't have to take a job. We don't have to date long distance. Will you marry me now and go with me to Kentucky?"

I kept thinking about the quote by Scott Peck I had taped to the back of my bedroom door. "If someone is determined not to risk pain, then such a person must do without many things: having children, getting married, the ecstasy of sex, the hope of ambition, friendship—all that makes life alive, meaningful and significant." Would I choose the security of a job over someone I knew I loved? Would dating another six months just to make it to my two-year mandate really lessen the risk? I was older. I knew what I had hoped for in a man, and I had talked to God about it countless times. I even had a list of what I longed for if I was ever to have a husband again, and only God knew what was on that list. This man seemed to have been brought to me, being the man all my heart—and head—desired. I took the risk.

We've been married twenty years. I've had several other good jobs. Our family grew with another daughter and a son. We have even been given the gift of two extra daughters God brought into our lives who needed a loving mom and dad. Loving, we've discovered, is what we do best.

How grateful I am that I traveled that road to Texas and took a risk.

~Sharron Carrns

25

The Life of the Party

The only thing we have to fear is fear itself.
~Franklin D. Roosevelt

I used to be the wallflower who camped out by the dried-out veggie platter at social and business events. You know, the jittery one who needed to be rescued from her isolation by others with enough guts to initiate a conversation.

I panicked just thinking about saying "Hello, what do you do?" to a stranger.

My inability to socialize resulted in a slew of unfair, hurtful labels: conceited, cold, aloof.

It wasn't true. I wanted to be friendly, but something in me refused to cooperate. The problem surfaced after being bullied in school by a classic mean girl and her cadre of friends. They used to stop me in the hallway on my way to the bus. "Where do you think you're going?" they'd say. Or they'd invite me over to their table in the cafeteria to eat lunch and then throw mashed potatoes in my face.

To overcome my shyness, I took a class called "How To Make Small Talk." The instructor told a room of frightened introverts to break off into groups and practice his suggested icebreakers. We eyed each other with apprehension as we dragged our chairs into circles and asked: "Who do you admire?" "What have you been up to?" and "What's your favorite book?" He also suggested we talk to ourselves in the mirror each morning.

And so I began each day conversing with my reflection, concocting sassy, witty lines. "Isn't this party just wild and wooly?" I laughed while tossing back my long, wavy hair. "Aren't you digging it?"

Unfortunately, once I left the safety of my bathroom I lost all confidence. I could not start a conversation with a stranger. This became financially debilitating a decade later when I opened my own graphic design business. I had to learn to schmooze if I wanted to put food on the table.

Not long after I founded my graphic design company, a friend invited me to a political fundraiser. My first thought was that I could make some serious business contacts. My second thought was there was no way I was subjecting myself to an uncomfortable party with strangers. I envisioned myself cowering in the corner with the baby carrots while everyone around me socialized with ease.

"No," I said.

A few days later, she asked me again. I wanted to be a good friend, so I bit the bullet and agreed to go.

But I gave myself one scary task: "You must speak to everyone in the room."

The day of the event, I regretted my decision. I drove into the event parking lot and sat there for fifteen minutes, unable to get out of the car. I finally summoned up enough courage to look into the rearview mirror and say to myself, "Giulietta, get out of the car and go face your fear."

I entered the meeting room and instinctively headed toward the ranch dip. When I saw my first victim, an intimidating male wearing a grey power suit, I extended my hand and faked confidence. "Hi, I'm Giulietta. Where do you live?"

He responded with a big smile. "I live in Holliston. And you?" We chatted easily about our adjacent towns before bidding adieu to meet others. I continued scoping out new folks to engage, some more talkative than others. Surprisingly, the more I reached out to converse, the easier it got. I learned to ask questions that engaged the other person's interest or revealed common ground.

Later that evening, I met a man, who like me, had an Italian last name, so I queried, "Have you been to Italy?" We talked about his visit to Milan to see "The Last Supper," my visit to Rome to see the Trevi Fountain. Not long after, I found myself running around the large, rectangular room introducing folks standing alone to other folks in need of company. They seemed relieved. I felt useful in my new role as social matchmaker.

The night was going really well until I ran into a man I'd spoken to briefly at a party a year earlier, when a mutual acquaintance insisted on introducing us. "Hi, remember me?" I said, recalling the promise I made to myself to speak to each person in the room. "I'm the one who knew the capital of every African country."

"Oh, yes," he nodded without cracking a smile. "Quick, what's the capital of Angola?"

"Luanda," I answered proudly. "It's also the name of a maximum-security prison in Louisiana." Pumped up by my newfound courage, I continued to run with the prison theme until I unexpectedly blurted, "I love prisons." I knew within seconds I'd made a fatal conversational error. He grimaced. "You are a very strange person," he said.

Watching him back away shaking his head, I felt rejected, ashamed and embarrassed. What compelled me to say I loved prisons when it wasn't even true? I began beating myself up for not clarifying that I loved prison movies with gutsy main characters like *The Shawshank Redemption* and *Cool Hand Luke* and for not apologizing when I offended him. I wanted to disappear and began inching towards the exit.

I stopped. It didn't matter if he liked me. It mattered if I liked me. I brushed myself off emotionally and stood tall. He was the judgmental one. So what if he didn't approve of something I said. It's not the end of the world to say something stupid.

I continued to relationship-build around the room with positive results, no longer imprisoned by my fear. At the end of the evening, I felt powerful, connected and free.

In the months that followed, I sought out weekly opportunities to start conversations. They existed all around me: I spoke to wait staff, employees at my town hall, and small business owners. It resulted in a kinder, warmer, and happier place to live. Occasionally, I still struggled to make the first social move, but that too disappeared with time and practice.

Now five years later, I can walk up to anyone at any kind of event and start a conversation with ease. Giving myself permission to be friendly has allowed me to grow my business, start a creativity group that benefited my community, and make more friends than I thought possible.

Recently, a business acquaintance introduced me to others at a local networking group as "the woman who everyone knows in town." I'd become that fun person across the room who I always wanted to meet but didn't have the courage to approach.

~Giulietta Nardone

Chicken Soup for the Soul

Safely Stuck in a Rut

All changes, even the most longed for, have their melancholy;
for what we leave behind us is a part of ourselves; we must die
to one life before we can enter another.
~Anatole France

'm not afraid to admit it; I am absolutely terrified of losing my rut. People talk about being stuck in a rut as if it's a bad thing, but I don't see it that way. A rut is safe. A rut is a straight line. A rut allows you to see where you're supposed to be going. The future is laid out in front of you and you can reasonably assume that if you follow your rut, it will take you to the end of the road. It's predictable. It's comfortable. It's safe. I'm about to lose my rut whether I'm ready for it or not and I am absolutely terrified.

For the last five and a half years, I have been an aircraft mechanic in the United States Air Force. Before that I was a CNC machinist in a fabrication plant. Before that I was a box office cashier at my local movie theater. And before all of that, I was a fifteen-year-old kid who wanted to become a writer, but also knew that I was going to have to get a REAL job if I wanted to earn a decent income.

My point is that I have never before been unemployed for any considerable length of time, but in five months that is exactly the position that I will find myself in. My safe, comfortable rut is going to disappear.

To be fair, I am losing my rut for a good cause. Seven months ago, my husband and I became the proud owners of a positive pregnancy test. Or rather, he was the proud one and I was the absolutely terrified recipient of unexpected news. Even before we sat down and discussed what needed discussing and made our decisions about the future, I knew that my predictable, steady, SAFE rut was disappearing.

We decided together that with a new baby joining our little family it wouldn't be feasible to continue with the military lifestyle. There is no law or regulation telling me that I cannot be a military mom. There are thousands of women out there who can pull it off and they have my respect. But the truth is that we do live a hard lifestyle. My husband and I belong to a particularly vigorous unit that has been in a constant deployment rotation since 2001 and the tempo has never slowed down. During our first year of marriage, we were separated by our mutual deployment obligations for longer than we were actually together. It was hard, but we managed to get through it. We knew the risks and pitfalls before we got married.

But now we are having a baby. According to regulation, a mother is not allowed to deploy for the first four months after having her baby. But after that, if the mission requires it, she must go. The chances of it happening are slim, even in our chaotic, deployment-happy unit, but the thought of leaving a four-month-old baby behind is too awful for me to take the risk. Mike and I are tough enough to get through the separations, but our baby shouldn't have to be tough. So I made the decision to part ways with my rut.

I haven't decided which makes me feel more selfish, deciding that I need to stay home with the baby, or being terrified by abandoning my self-sufficiency. My husband is completely supportive of me becoming a stay-at-home mom, but I can't help feeling that I'm no longer going to be carrying my weight in this family. I have always had an income.

Twenty-four weeks into this venture, we learned that we were having a boy. It is easier to work for a cause when it has a name. My new cause is going to be named Theodore.

Instead of being anxious about the future, I'm going to embrace it. I've been saying for as long as I can remember that when I grow up, I'm going to be a writer. It is difficult to be a writer when you're stuck in a rut, even if it is a rut that you're content with. When I joined the

Air Force I thought I would make a career of it. Now I'm trading in that safety net for the sake of a little guy I haven't even met yet.

Today, my husband and I arrived at the clinic for an ultrasound and I saw Theo's face for the first time. Or at least, I could have if I wasn't crying so much.

The good news is that it's a different sort of crying than I did when I was away from my husband for so long. This time I'm scared, but happy.

~Tanya Rusheon

The Tuesday Night Ladies League

Keep your fears to yourself but share your courage with others.
~Robert Louis Stevenson

Bowling? My jaw dropped when my friend Sherry invited me to join the Tuesday Night Ladies Bowling League. She'd been bowling for decades, but I hadn't picked up a bowling ball since high school. When I told her I didn't even know how to tally scores anymore, she laughed. Apparently a computer takes care of that now, which further demonstrated how far removed I was from the bowling world. The thought of doing something so far out of my skill set seemed ridiculous.

"Don't worry," she told me. "You get a handicap based on your bowling average so it all works out. Anyway, we just bowl for fun."

Still, I hesitated. In addition to being clueless about bowling, after getting home from work, the last thing I wanted to do was go back out. I knew I should say no, but I surprised myself by saying, "Okay, I'll try."

Sherry wrote my name on her team roster while I chewed my lip and thought about sitting in front of the TV with my feet up.

The next evening I went to the pro shop. Bob, the man in charge, must have sensed my lack of enthusiasm. He gave me a pep talk on how addictive and exciting bowling would be for me. All I needed to do was throw the ball at the pins and make sure I followed through with my arm. Bob handed me a ball and I nearly dropped it on my foot. When I asked for a lighter model, he frowned and informed me that a bowling ball should be about ten percent of the bowler's body weight. After a quick calculation, my eyes widened. I opted for the ten-pound ball instead.

On my first night of bowling, I slipped into the building feeling like an imposter. The scent of fried food and old shoes immediately assaulted my senses. I saw ladies everywhere. Some were young enough to be my daughter and others old enough to be my mom. Each one took a turn hurling a ball down the lane. Pins crashed as strikes and spares were tallied. The game seemed simple enough. Perhaps bowling wouldn't be as tough as I feared. I found my new teammates and pulled on a pair of bright white bowling shoes.

My palms were damp when it came time for me to bowl. I picked up the ball and walked to the line. My back prickled with the sense that dozens of eyes were on me as I took aim, walked forward, and let the ball fly. It didn't go anywhere near where I wanted it to go. In fact, the ball curved right into the gutter. Face flaming, I tried again. Another gutter ball.

I sat down and my teammates flocked around me. Their bowling shirts made them look like brightly colored birds as each one gave me advice.

"Don't drop your shoulder."

"Focus on the arrows, not the pins."

"Hit the sweet spot."

I understood why they were eager to help me. My performance didn't exactly contribute to the team total. I felt sure everyone in the place had pegged me as someone who didn't belong. I wished I was back home in my comfy chair. If I quit now, surely it wouldn't be hard to replace me with someone who could actually hit those stubborn pins.

After the third game of the night, my only consolation was that at least my best score was higher than my age. I slumped in the seat and removed my shoes, wishing the bowling alley had a dark corner so I could slink off to hide. My teammates provided consoling pats on the back. Even women from other teams came by to chirp a few words of encouragement. They told me everyone starts somewhere, and if I kept at it my game would surely improve. In the face of such generosity it seemed small of me to announce that I'd rather call it a day. So I dusted off my bruised ego and went back the next week.

And as it turns out, they were right. After a month I began to understand the best way to hold my arm and when to release the ball. On the night my score finally broke 100, it was high fives all around. I couldn't stop smiling.

It would never have occurred to me to join a bowling team if my friend hadn't suggested it. The Tuesday Night Ladies League helped me step outside my circle of comfort and exchange a stale old routine for a vibrant new one. In the process I've gotten to know a wonderful group of women who comfort me when I have a bad game and cheer me on when I do well. Bowling is a night out with the girls. We talk and laugh and once in a while send a ball spinning down the alley. Though I'll never be part of any pro tour, that's okay. A few hours of bowling makes me feel much better than sitting at home.

The next time an unlikely opportunity comes along, I won't hesitate a minute. You see, my Wednesday nights could use a little excitement, too.

~Pat Wahler

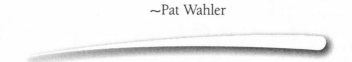

Moments of Clarity

Being miserable is a habit; being happy is a habit;
and the choice is yours.
~Tom Hopkins

When I was twenty-two I realized I was on the fast track to nowhere. Life was a constant string of bar nights and alcohol-fueled parties funded by my part-time job as a grocery clerk. Pressure was building and since "bar star" wasn't a legitimate career, I started to do some careful thinking about finding a real job and starting my life.

Lots of kids have that one thing they want to be when they grow up, and mine was always a writer. I pictured myself signing books for lines of adoring readers, going on book tours all over the country, having a shelf full of books with my name on the cover.

But everyone always told me the same thing: There's no money in writing. Be realistic and get a real job. The writing will be a nice hobby on the side.

So I wracked my brain, trying to think of a "real" job that I would enjoy.

Maybe I could be an English teacher. Wait, that would mean I'd need to take courses in math, which was basically the bane of my existence. Could I open a bookstore? No. Bookstores were a dying breed, and not any more practical than being a writer. My ideas began to get wilder. I could move to Italy and breed dogs. Or ship myself off to sea and become a sailor.

Again I felt that sense of aimlessness. There was nothing I wanted to do.

One day my mother came back from the spa glowing with excitement. She'd talked to the esthetician doing her facial, who had raved about how much she loved her job. I did some research and discovered it would take ten months of school and then I could be out in the world and making money. There was no math involved, so how hard could it be?

I signed up and put myself through ten months of beauty classes. Before the year was out, I hit the streets looking for work. In less than a week, I found the ideal job at a swanky spa complete with tinkling waterfalls, massaging footbaths and moisturizers with French names I couldn't pronounce.

I'd done it! I'd graduated from esthetics school with top grades and obtained the ultimate real job.

There was only one problem. I hated it.

I hated everything about it. From touching people's smelly feet all day, to the eye-watering smell of nail polish, to the fussy rich ladies who made me feel that I couldn't get anything right. I would drive to work every morning, stomach churning, feeling like I was about to throw up.

But I couldn't quit. This was a real job, damn it, and I'd paid a lot of money to learn this stuff.

Over the next three years I tried other things—working for myself out of my basement suite, getting a job at a tiny hair salon where I waxed people's legs in a cramped little back room. Often I would pause and stare at the sticky wax pot or the rows of colorful nail polish and think to myself, "What on earth am I doing here?"

All could think about was how much I missed my writing. Between the salon and taking waxing clients in my basement, I had barely any time for it. I longed to sit down and write all the stories in my head.

One morning my boss at the salon pulled me aside and said, "We have to talk."

What she said next shattered me. "I'm afraid I have to fire you."

I was devastated. Outraged. I'd never been fired before. How could she do that to me? I started to break down right there in the back room. My ex-boss gave me the world's most awkward hug.

Then she said the words that would change my life. "Maybe this isn't what you're supposed to be doing. I don't think you're happy here."

Lots of tears and self-pity followed, along with more chocolate than was either necessary or prudent. It wasn't until later that I remembered her words, which along with my relentless urge to write again, were the only true moments of clarity I'd had in the last three years.

Weeks later I opened my secondhand laptop and began writing my first real novel, resolving that this time I would get serious. No more putting writing on the back burner, no more pretending it was a hobby instead of an all-consuming, burning passion.

I began querying literary agents, and it was like a fire had been stoked inside me. Rejections piled up, but I didn't care. I was fiercely happy to be doing what I loved at last.

Four years later I've had my successes and failures. Ups and downs. I've had a story accepted and then watched the magazine go under. I've jumped out of bed at five in the morning shrieking my head off when I got "the call" from a literary agent.

I may not sell my first novel. I may end up in a drafty apartment eating ramen noodles and barely paying the rent. But I'm happy knowing that when those moments of clarity come, when I step back and ask myself, "What am I doing?"

The answer is always the same: Exactly what I'm supposed to.

~Erin Latimer

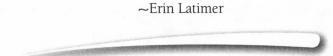

Moving to Hong Kong

Take risks: if you win, you will be happy; if you lose, you will be wise.
~Author Unknown

"I'm ready to change our lives," I told my husband Dave. "We've only got a few years left till we both retire from teaching. Let's do something exciting."

Our youngest son was a high school senior enrolled in a study abroad college program for the coming fall.

"We could plan our own overseas adventure," I suggested. "We've never traveled outside of North America."

I'd just had the two most challenging years of my career. My classes had been packed with nearly forty students, many with severe behavioral challenges. This was the first time in my life I hadn't looked forward to going to work every morning. I knew Dave was a little disillusioned, too. He'd applied for an administrative position for which he was perfectly suited, but they'd hired someone younger.

"We're not too old for new jobs," I said. "We're talented and experienced."

The next month, I saw an advertisement posted by an international school in Hong Kong. "Should we apply?" I asked Dave.

"Let's go for it," he said.

I emailed our résumés. Around 2 A.M. we were jolted out of our sleep by the phone ringing.

"I'm calling from Hong Kong," said an administrative assistant. She'd forgotten about the time difference with Canada and wanted to know if we'd be prepared to do a phone interview with the school headmaster.

We had a lengthy middle-of-the-night conversation right then. "We'd appreciate you signing contracts within two weeks," the headmaster requested at the end of it.

"I'm so excited I'll never fall back to sleep," I said to Dave.

"We'll be moving to one of the biggest cities in the world," he said, "and I've heard it's easy and cheap to travel to lots of places from Hong Kong."

"Will most people speak Mandarin or Cantonese?" I wondered. "Just think of the interesting new things we'll get to teach. And our students and colleagues will come from so many different countries. Doesn't it seem too good to be true?"

It was. One month later, the SARS epidemic hit Hong Kong.

"What are we going to do?" I asked Dave. "The news reports sound so scary and they've closed all the schools."

"I talked to our Hong Kong headmaster today," he said. "Some teachers they hired for next year have broken their contracts. He hopes we won't."

"But do you think we should?" I wondered. "Everyone keeps asking me if we still plan to go. My parents are worried."

"Mine are, too," admitted Dave, "and someone at work today told me we were just plain stupid to go to Hong Kong in the middle of a deadly epidemic."

I was practical. "We really can't turn back now. We've already rented out our house and resigned from our jobs here. We'll just have to hope the schools in Hong Kong reopen in time."

We stuck to our plan. The SARS epidemic was over before we left Canada to live and work in Hong Kong. During our school holidays, we traveled to nearly fifty fascinating destinations. We grew to love the people and places of Hong Kong.

When I'm asked about how the experience changed our lives I say, "We learned we could live happily in a small apartment with few possessions. We managed without a car, walked many miles, ate healthy Asian cuisine and got into terrific shape. Dave and I grew closer, because without our extended families nearby we had to depend on each other. Our children were able to visit several times and we had some great family adventures in Asia together. Teaching our hardworking and gifted Hong Kong students turned out to be the most rewarding professional experience of our careers."

We are retired and back home in Canada now. Our years in Hong Kong enriched our lives and expanded our horizons immeasurably.

~MaryLou Driedger

Running Away to Join the Circus

Damn everything but the circus.

~E.E. Cummings

I n March, when the weather is damp, chilly and unpleasant, I'm diagnosed with yet another respiratory infection. Despite the ache in my chest, the fatigue, the shortness of breath and the painful coughing fits, I'm thrilled, because it means that I don't have to go to work.

Perhaps this should be an epiphany for me. After all, when you've reached the point where incapacitating illness is preferable to your workplace, it's probably a glaring sign that you need to find a new job. When it comes down to it, my work is more hazardous to me than my lung infection.

On paper it should be a dream: I work evenings, I make a decent salary for the hours I put in, and I can take time off when I need to. However, in reality, it's eating me alive. The work has a customer service component, and the patrons tend to be belligerent and rude. More taxing, though, are the majority of my co-workers, who engage in the sort of catty name-calling and bullying that most of us left behind in middle school, if we ever did it at all.

I know that when my colleagues are ornery, it's a reflection on their character, not mine, so I don't give their remarks a second of my time. I ignore them and go about my assigned tasks. I don't talk about my activities outside of work so they don't have anything to mock. Still, spending every evening in an unpleasant environment takes its toll, and the negative energy drains the life out of me. Every night when I begin my two-mile walk to work I feel fine. By the time I reach my workplace, my head hurts and I'm nauseous. As I walk through the door, I'm tense and ready for combat. It's toxic.

However, I don't resign. After all, the economy is unstable and people are struggling to find jobs. Under the circumstances, I feel it would be foolish to give up steady employment. In addition, if I were to quit, my awful colleagues would win. Win what? I don't know, but I can't help but feel that to leave would be to concede defeat.

When my lung infection calms down a little, I return to work. I'm still sick and weak but I think I can handle it. I don't even make it through a week. The supervisor doesn't even ask how I am; she simply throws me into the busiest section with the most demanding clients. My colleagues sit in the corner and talk, since they don't have patrons to handle.

As I struggle along, it dawns on me that I'm overthinking things. I don't want to be there. Why can't I leave? Because it's foolish? Because quitting has a negative connotation? What I'm currently enduring is bad too, isn't it? When every moment is fraught with stress, I'm not in a healthy environment. I finally decide that the only thing holding me back is me. It's hurting me more to stay than it would to leave.

I call out sick again.

I resolve that I need to find another job, so I start surfing through employment listings online. To my surprise, I find an ad for a touring human-only circus. They're going to be in town for a few months and they need help. The work is basic and completely below my capabilities. I could have done it when I was in high school. I would love a chance to learn more about the circus arts, so I submit my résumé anyway. A few days later I score an interview and end up getting hired.

I present my resignation to the toxic job, but the bosses at the head office don't accept it. I've put it in writing, but after three weeks, they e-mail me to ask when I'm coming back to work. Two months later, they write to me again to ask if I'm ready to return from my leave of absence. I get suspiciously friendly e-mails from formerly hostile colleagues who wish me well and fish for information on my current whereabouts. I tune them out as much as I can.

The pay at the circus is less than it was at my former job. The hours are longer; the work is more physically taxing. There are a few blistering summer days where we have to spray ourselves down with ice water to keep from passing out. The difference is that I'm in an environment where my bosses and colleagues are decent, so I'm neither tired nor drained when I clock out at the end of the day. It takes a while for this to sink in. For the first few weeks of work I'm jumpy, I'm tense, and I'm always looking over my shoulder. I'm reluctant to befriend my co-workers; for fear that they will turn on me later. Nonetheless, I begin to notice that I'm smiling and laughing at work. That my colleagues and I look out for each other. That when problems arise, we talk them through instead of slinging mud. I don't mind eating lunch with them. When we get stuck on the train together on the way home, I'm happy about it. It makes me realize more than ever that the problems at my old job weren't about me. I smile because I'm not there, and I wonder why I waited so long to leave.

I don't think of my old co-workers with bitterness any more. I realize that they're going to be stuck in their web of petty cruelty for the foreseeable future, and I honestly feel sorry them. They're dedicating all their time to being hateful. I, on the other hand, am devoting my energy to improving and enjoying my life.

Lesson learned: on occasion, the best way to win a war is to leave the battlefield... and join the circus.

~Denise Reich

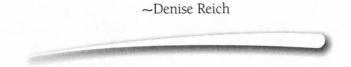

Chapter 4

Reboot Your Life

Find Your Purpose

What's Your Story?

Storytelling is a very old human skill that gives us an evolutionary advantage.
~Margaret Atwood

When my daughter joined her brother at college the year I turned fifty, I was finally an empty nester. My husband and I had been working from home—he on investments and various business ventures, and I on investments and several corporate board memberships. So this should have been our time to scale back our workloads, travel, exercise, and enjoy ourselves.

But no. Crazy us. We had learned earlier that year that Chicken Soup for the Soul was for sale by its founders, Jack Canfield, Mark Victor Hansen, and his ex-wife Patty Hansen. We loved the brand and thought that we could take the company to the next level, bringing the books back to their old level of popularity and relevance, and expanding into new areas where we could add value to people's lives.

The second half of 2007 and the first few months of 2008 were devoted to due diligence, and in April 2008 we and our business partners became the proud new owners of Chicken Soup for the Soul. We kept a couple of key people from the editorial staff in Southern California and opened our new headquarters in Cos Cob, Connecticut, in a tiny office over a CVS drugstore.

I had read 100 of the old Chicken Soup for the Soul books in preparation for the acquisition, and somehow I thought I knew, really knew, exactly what to do when we took over. It was like Chicken Soup for the Soul had been inside me all along waiting to come out. I hit the ground running as publisher, editor-in-chief, and author of the books, with a clear vision of what I wanted to accomplish and how I wanted to tell positive, uplifting stories to our readers.

Thus, at ages fifty-five and fifty, respectively, my husband and I returned to the world of full-time work, just when we should have been planning our exit strategy! It has been non-stop excitement ever since. The first "excitement" was that we managed to time our purchase perfectly for the start of the deepest recession since the Great Depression, one that led to Borders shutting down, independent bookstores closing, and consumers scaling back on discretionary purchases. But we survived that, managing to redesign our books and increase our sales and have a number of bestsellers among the 100+ new titles that we have published. We've also updated our popular pet food products, launched a new line of delicious food for people, created a new website, started a television production business, and signed to have a major motion picture made by a big Hollywood studio, using our stories as inspiration. And we've grown a lot, taking over more and more space in our little office building and creating a large staff of passionate, talented, friendly people who work as hard as we do.

The first thirty years of my career were all about business and finance. I was a Wall Street analyst, a hedge fund manager, a corporate executive at a high-flying public telecommunications company, and a director of several publicly traded technology companies. I must admit I was the "writer" in all those positions, writing the annual reports and press releases for my companies, writing voluminous persuasive investment recommendations, even doing whatever writing was required on my corporate boards. After all, everything in business is really about telling stories, whether it's explaining a company's mission, or leading an investor through recent results, or describing a new technology or product in a way that is understandable.

I wrote a lot of great stories in business and finance, as I made the complex understandable and passionately explained the reasoning behind my buy and sell recommendations. But it seemed like the two main emotions I dealt with in the world of public companies were the classic stock market ones: fear and greed.

Now, at Chicken Soup for the Soul, I get to deal with the whole panoply of human emotions, and it is a real treat. And reading and editing the stories submitted for our books has also made a difference in my own life. I've learned how to have better personal relationships, how to focus on what's important, how to stay fit, how to look for the positive in every situation, and how to put in perspective the daily ups and downs of life.

There is a saying that in order to be happy you should return to what you loved doing when you were ten years old. When I was ten I loved to walk in the acres of woods behind our house, wrote stories just for fun, and read books. And now I have a job where I read and write every day, I go for long walks in the nature preserve near my house, and I occasionally get to read books that I did not have to edit. So despite the fact that I am working seven days a week and am constantly in crisis mode, I am truly doing what I have always loved doing.

When I started at Chicken Soup for the Soul, it took me a little while to realize that I had actually done this before while in college! During my junior and senior years of college, I researched and wrote a thesis about popular, spoken-word poetry in Brazil, which involved living in Brazil for several months, traveling throughout its impoverished northeast region, and meeting with poets and writers to collect their stories. These stories were about every aspect of their lives, usually told in the form of chanted poetry, and were printed up as pamphlets and sold at marketplaces. These *folhetos* were the "literature" of the masses in Brazil. I'm delighted to have come full circle in my writing career—from collecting poetry "from the people" in Brazil as a twenty-year-old to, three decades later, collecting stories and poems "from the people" for Chicken Soup for the Soul.

Maybe "rebooting" our lives is not just about starting something entirely new. Maybe it's about returning to our core passions, to what makes us tick, to what we have always valued. My "reboot" feels a lot like coming home.

~Amy Newmark

Making a Difference

If there are no dogs in Heaven, then when I die, I want to go where they went.
~Will Rogers

It was a crisp fall morning when I suddenly awoke from a deep sleep. I looked over at my husband, snoring slightly, and nudged him not so gently. "I was thinking about starting a Labrador Retriever rescue."

"Why?"

That one-word question made me stop and think, really think, about where this crazy notion had come from.

"I think I'm being called to do it." It was as honest an answer as I could give.

"Then go for it. Can we talk more when I'm fully awake?"

That was eleven years ago. As I reflect back on all that has happened in my life since then one thing remains constant. I saved lives and I will forever be changed because of it. In 2000, I founded a Labrador Retriever rescue. I had never visited an animal shelter and had no clue that Labs were one of the breeds of dogs most likely to be euthanized. Who would want to give up a Lab?

I was pretty clueless as to where or how to start this venture, so the computer became my friend. I Googled and searched and then made more phone calls than I care to remember.

One call I made was to our local animal shelter. I made an appointment to meet with Cheryl, the head of the Humane Society. Her job was to pull as many animals from death's door as she could. I was excited about meeting her and seeing the dogs.

When Cheryl and I met, I noticed an edginess about her, even a slight distrust. I assumed correctly that this saving-life business was just a short-term interest for most volunteers. They would start out strong, last a couple of weeks, and then get too busy. I think Cheryl had already me sized up in her head. I'd prove her wrong.

The first time I walked down the corridor of the kennels, I was in shock at the number of dogs in this high-kill facility. My excitement quickly turned to disbelief at these conditions. It was staggering to realize that most of these potential pets would die on what became known as Terrible Thursdays, when the gas chamber was fired up.

I walked a little further and happened upon kennel #25. What I saw took my breath away. There he stood, a gentle giant of pure chocolate love. The look on his face was so full of hope, I couldn't turn away.

I asked Cheryl for a leash and we took the big guy outside. I'll never forget how he stopped to sniff the flowers and lifted his head to the air as if to absorb those moments before harsh reality came back. We continued walking around (well, he was walking, I was just trying to catch up) and came upon an old stump. I sat down on it, and this beautiful chocolate boy sat down right beside me. He was just precious. Those velvety triangular ears that only a Lab can have were sheer perfection. Any passerby would have thought we were long lost friends.

I was stunned that a dog this gentle and loving would be stranded at a place like this. I knew one thing—he wasn't going back in there. He'd just have to come home with me.

I made my decision and filled out the paperwork. As we stood to go in, a family pulled up and parked. Without one moment of hesitation a little girl threw open her car door and rushed over to us.

What's his name?" she asked.

"Hershey," I said. I had no clue what his name might be, but I couldn't let him go nameless.

"He is so sweet, and I like his name." The little girl and Hershey were drawn to each other.

The little girl's parents came over, and we were all gathered around oohing and aahing over Hershey.

Cheryl came out to observe the scene. She gave me a thumbs-up. I realized I had just made my first save.

"Are you a Lab rescuer, ma'am?" the father asked.

I hesitated for just a moment before answering. "Why, yes, I am. And it appears you have found yourself a new addition to the family."

The father chuckled but there was sadness, too. "It appears to be love at first sight. Our daughter, Olivia, has leukemia, and she has wanted a dog for so long. She loves dogs and chocolate, so I think Hershey is just what she needs."

Tears began to well up in my eyes. I turned away before anyone noticed. Olivia and Hershey explored the grounds together. Unlike the way he'd tugged when I held the leash, Hershey was very gentle with Olivia. If she stopped, he stopped. It was truly magical. Only once did Hershey look in my direction. Already, he was completely devoted to that little girl.

The family adopted Hershey on the spot, loaded him up, and prepared to go home. I cried like a baby. Hershey's tail never stopped thumping. He had found his Heaven.

I can't describe the feeling of rescuing an animal. It is addictive and selfless in the same breath. I went on to save nine hundred and ninety-nine more Labs in the two and a half years I was blessed enough to have my rescue. A divorce left me no choice but to close my doors and dream of one day opening them again. It is a calling. When you wake from a dead sleep to embark on a dream you never even knew you had, you don't ignore it, you simply take that bull by the horns and go full force. There isn't a day that I don't think back and smile and tear up remembering details about each experience. It is hard to say who comes out on top, the rescuer or the rescued. Each gains something so special in the process. I used to tell people that a little piece of my heart went with every Lab I rescued and every one I couldn't.

Olivia died two years later. She was nine years old. Her parents told me Hershey never left her bed those last few weeks of hospice, and he was there when they buried her.

We can all make a difference if we hop on a wing of faith and let it guide us to where we are supposed to be. I learned to make the most of every situation, even those that seemed too difficult to handle. This lesson was taught to me by a precious little girl who knew her time on this earth was limited, and by a chocolate Lab who had every reason to give up on the goodness of people, but didn't.

~Lisa Morris

Finding My Happiness

The torment of precautions often exceeds the dangers to be avoided. It is sometimes better to abandon one's self to destiny.
~Napoleon Bonaparte

I found myself dreaming about retirement even though I was only forty. When my alarm went off at five in the morning, I would lie in bed yearning for the golden years. I was exhausted and felt trapped. I was teaching History to 180 high school students that year, the most I'd ever had. A request for an additional teacher for the next year had been denied, and enrollment wasn't declining.

I was also a mom with four kids ranging from elementary to high school. As a working mom, I kept a tightly managed schedule to meet my responsibilities for classroom and family. Teaching over one hundred students meant bringing home piles of papers to grade every night. I took my grade book with me to sporting events, practices, even church events. After putting my own kids to bed, I'd stay up making instructional plans for the next day, channeling my energy into creative lessons to make History come alive. I was on top of my game professionally, but I was physically and emotionally exhausted.

I felt like a hamster on a fast-paced-wheel that never ended. I daydreamed of being in my house with nothing but silence. I longed for time by myself, but didn't want to wish away the years my kids were at home. I was in a rut and saw no way out. I longed for the ability to work part-time or find a job where I could leave work at the office. I loved teaching more than anything, but it took all my energy.

Over time, my stress levels affected our family. While I held things together on the outside, I was a mess inside. I was chronically irritable, tired, and would easily snap at my kids and husband.

Changing professions never occurred to me until a neighbor reached out for some informal counseling. After meeting with her a few times, I wondered what it would be like to counsel professionally. But changing careers mid-life with a large family to take care of seemed out of the question. When I shared my internal struggle and exhaustion with my husband, he gave me the go-ahead, and I began to pray about doing something different. Suddenly, I didn't feel so trapped.

After prayer, research, and weighing options, I applied to be a full-time graduate student in a three-year master's degree program. It was a hard decision professionally, financially, and personally. But when I left the interview for the counseling program, I felt a peace and calm I hadn't felt in years, and I knew it was the right thing.

It wasn't easy. Going back to school in a technology-based environment required learning new skills and mastering the Internet, discussion boards, and APA formatting. I was in grad school when my oldest began her first year at a university. We tightened our belts. I cleaned houses to pay for lunch money. It was all worth it. Three years, two internships, and thousands of driving hours later, I currently work part-time as a school counseling professional and have a small private counseling practice.

I've also developed new hobbies, like writing. I attend my children's school activities without a briefcase in hand. I occasionally meet a friend for coffee, and at times, have empty mental space. I sleep better and laugh more. I'm only forty-five.

The greatest thing I've learned from choosing to get out of a mid-life rut is how my countenance affects my kids. I recently heard my teenager say, "My mom loves her job and is happy." When children know their parents are happy, they're happy, too.

~Brenda Lazzaro Yoder

A Happiness Throttle

checked the clock on the bottom right corner of my office computer. Only ten minutes longer. I sent another e-mail, then checked the clock again: only nine minutes now. Eight minutes later, as the clock struck 5:29, I closed my office laptop as quickly and quietly as possible, wished my team a good night, and scuttled off the fifth floor.

There should be a survival kit for navigating your twenties. What no one ever tells college students is how little they'll be prepared for the real world once they get out there. Many will not get the job they wanted. The job they do find will be different than the job they dreamed about.

On top of that, friends will be moving to opposite ends of the country, romantic relationships may end, and unless you're in the small minority of twenty-somethings, life will become about surviving paycheck to paycheck, in a world of unpaid internships and night jobs where college degrees mean squat.

Phew. At least I had a job.

The elevator, taking five minutes too long, took me down to the first floor, where the desk attendant tipped his hat goodnight. Trudging two blocks to my car, I shoved my heavy briefcase onto the back seat. I climbed into my Honda CRV and peered at my hair in the rearview mirror. It was frizzing from the humidity as usual. I sighed. Curly hair problems.

I had been one of the lucky ones. After graduating with honors, I'd packed my bags and headed to the big city for a well-paying internship with good job potential upon completion. I hoped this would be my opportunity to expand my professional résumé, enjoy the culture Washington, D.C. had to offer, and figure out what I was supposed to do with my life.

Boy, was I wrong.

Before I knew it, I was swept into the entry-level job world: long hours behind a computer screen, customer service calls from rude clients, horrible commutes, carpal tunnel syndrome, and robotic work I didn't give a darn about.

I had studied the liberal arts: Psychology, English, and Sociology. I was supposed to be working in a job that allowed me to use my passions, not ignore them. This was not at all what I had signed up for.

A dark wave of depression floated over me. This was hell.

Well-meaning opinions from parents and friends did not help. I couldn't help rolling my eyes at their attempts to console me.

"Everyone hates their first job."

"You just need to adjust to the professional world."

"Just give it time."

"You're only twenty-two. You don't know what you want."

But I did know. At least I knew that I didn't want this. Doing what every twenty-something was supposed to do wasn't working for me. Following the path most traveled felt like the fastest path to my self-destruction.

So I decided to turn in my notice.

The next morning, as the alarm shrieked me awake from a peaceful slumber, instead of dragging myself out of bed, I jumped. This was the beginning of the end. As I stepped into my knee-length skirt, black flats, and gray blazer, I was overcome by a sense of calm, the likes of which I hadn't felt for months.

When I arrived at work, I even grinned at the desk attendant.

"Good morning ma'am," he said, a twinkle in his eye.

My smiling co-workers were grinning, too, as they brought fresh toasted bagels and coffee from the kitchen. We made small talk and then settled into our morning tasks. Somehow, the snippy client seemed less angry this morning. The market research less draining. My carpal tunnel syndrome less painful.

As the clock struck 5:29, I approached my supervisor. I calmly shared my action plan.

"Thank you for your hard work," she replied. "Let me know if you ever need anything."

I trudged the familiar path to the parking garage. I paused for a moment and smiled.

Two weeks later I packed my bags and moved back to my college town. I found a job working with kids with special needs and began a part-time freelance writing career. And I found out special needs kids are the greatest and writing is transcendent.

Money is not worth it if you hate your job. The key to happiness may very well be doing what you love. Sometimes all it takes is a spontaneous life decision to bring back your joy. In order to live a truly authentic life, it becomes necessary to throw away the rulebook and answer to one person and one person only: yourself.

~Alli Page

Lost and Found

Help us to be ever faithful gardeners of the spirit, who know that without
darkness nothing comes to birth, and without light nothing flowers.
~May Sarton

loved my hair salon, and when I was forced to retire at the age
of thirty-eight due to a health crisis, I was completely lost. It
seemed I was living someone else's life. I went from being surrounded by clients and co-workers to being totally isolated and cut
off from the life I once knew. I was clueless as to how to move on.
That I was physically limited after failed back surgery made everything much harder to figure out. It's one thing to lose your career and
still have your health. It's a whole other animal when you have to
navigate a new livelihood while lying flat on your back.

I didn't want this new life, but I had to make the best of it. So I
read while lying down. I read every motivational book I could get my
hands on. I visited the library twice a week and scoured the shelves
for everything uplifting, spiritual, and funny. The librarians got to
know my routine so well that when I walked in they'd just point and
say, "Hi Marijo, there's a new book we think you'll like."

Day after day, week after week, year after year, I read. Three years
to be exact. All I did was read, lie on the floor, and wonder how the
heck I could get out of this cycle, this life of nothingness. What could
I do to change my life? How could I be of use this way? I asked God,
the universe, and anyone else who would listen.

I started to write. First, I wrote about how desperate I was for something new to happen to me. Then I wrote about all the people I was mad at, all the bad things that had happened to me, and all the things I hated in my life. Before long, something shifted. I started to find my own answers. Once I got all the garbage out on paper, I was left with a clear mind. I was able to understand myself better—to see myself, possibly, for the first time.

I used two notebooks initially. One notebook I named Garbage Out, and the other I named Wisdom In. I put all of my woes and heartaches in my Garbage book and all my positive insights in my Wisdom book. After a while, I didn't need the Garbage Out journal, because my Wisdom In journal had become my mainstay.

I started my Wisdom journal with prompts like: I have no limits because…I have learned… My purpose is…

And then I wrote until I had exhausted the possibilities. I knew that journaling was supposed to be cathartic. I had read that it helps you clarify your life if you're feeling lost. It's even been proven to ease chronic pain conditions. I realized firsthand that it can heal you on a deep level. After filling countless notebooks with my inner thoughts, I got to know myself pretty well. I got to know my strengths and weaknesses. I was able to step back and see myself objectively.

After releasing all my negativity in my Garbage Out journal, and realizing all the weight I had been carrying, I was left with pure inspiration. I could finally see some good in my life. I began writing about how I could inspire other people. I wrote motivational material that actually motivated me.

The very same journaling exercise that I created to get myself out of a funk is now being used by a leading heath plan company in their health promotions department. It's used to help people with chronic pain and cardiac problems. Writing out all the bad stuff on paper and then writing about all the good stuff was something I did by accident, but that technique is now helping many other people. Those years that I thought I was being nonproductive were actually a period of something larger at work within me.

It's what I had prayed for while I was going through those dark years. I hoped I would be a light to others who were going through hard times. I just kept telling myself that I needed to find a way when it looked like there was no way. I kept seeking.

Little did I know that my reading and journaling would turn into a new livelihood. The whole time I was struggling through a horrible rut, I was actually working on myself. I was studying for my new life. My rut was in reality a time of learning, evolving, and becoming my new self.

My old life as a hair salon owner allowed me to touch lives on a personal level. I got to talk with people and share stories with them. I loved that part of my life and missed it terribly.

I now think of the time that followed as the most fruitful, graceful, and enlightening period of my life. I learned what I was made of, and it's given me a greater confidence during dormant times. Ultimately, I found that being lost for a little while was just the thing I needed to find myself.

~Marijo Herndon

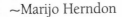

Restaurant Epiphany

You may not have saved a lot of money in your life, but if you have saved a lot of heartaches for other folks, you are a pretty rich man.
~Seth Parker

I didn't appreciate the joy of volunteering until after I completed a successful twenty-year stint as a college teacher and ventured into a sales and consulting career for four years. Then, at age forty-six, I returned to teaching and experienced an epiphany that forever changed my priorities and perspectives.

As a newly hired marketing instructor at California State University, I was asked if I would volunteer my services to an enterprise called Eden Express—a restaurant unlike any other restaurant in America. What made the eighty-two-seat, out-of-the-way eatery unusual was its status as a not-for-profit restaurant training program that provided on-the-job training to developmentally-disabled adults. Trainees' disabilities included schizophrenia, manic depression, brain injury, deafness, autism, cerebral palsy, and epilepsy. Eden's paid and volunteer staff offered concrete, experiential training with built-in rewards. During its nine-year history, Eden helped many of its 750 disabled clients learn how to work independently in the foodservice industry.

One sunny day in May 1984, I reported to the executive director, a remarkable leader named Barbara Lawson whose daughter Lori was so severely disabled that she could not qualify to participate in the training program.

Barbara put me to work immediately, asking me to promote the restaurant and help raise urgently needed funds. During the next five years I helped create ads, flyers, letters, training manuals, and other hardcopy materials, offered marketing workshops for five cities seeking to emulate the successful Eden Express program, and served on the Eden Express Board of Directors and as president of the Eden Institute of Education.

During those extraordinary years, I discovered a "new me"—learning what "normal" really means (or what Eden clients perceived as "normal"), learning how important it is to be patient with people who are "different," and discovering that, if you give, you get.

I learned that by making a real commitment to help others (who had given up on themselves), I could help them rebuild their lives to become positive, participating members of the community. And I learned it was a "no-no" to coddle clients who had fallen through the cracks—just wanting to be "normal."

During my five years as marketing director and occasional stand-in counselor for Eden Express, I became part of a nationally acclaimed vocational rehabilitation program that helped rescue many developmentally disabled adults from a life of hopelessness.

None of my other, succeeding volunteer activities ever quite rivaled the Eden Express adventure. But, importantly, I'd been bitten by the volunteer "bug," subsequently serving as a volunteer for food banks, animal shelters, senior centers, the Private Industry Council of Contra Costa County (CA), and director of a college community outreach program. I served as a board member or officer of four nonprofit corporations and earned some personal accolades along the way.

But it's Eden Express that remains most memorable. I'll never forget the Eden Express venture. I'll remember clients like Gina, brain-damaged from birth and functionally retarded, who told me that being "normal" was working eight hours a day, living on her own, taking care of her cats, and doing things that made her happy—not a bad definition of "normal."

I'll remember Paul, a UC Berkeley honor student who suffered a severe mental breakdown in his senior year and took to the streets until Eden Express came to his rescue. Paul advised me that without

Eden Express he might have successfully committed suicide (after one previous unsuccessful attempt). He said the Eden Express staff helped him focus, find some real purpose, and discover a path to independence and productivity. When Paul completed the four-month program at the restaurant, I coached him for his job search and actually walked him to his first interview. Positive and determined, Paul landed a good steady job at a nearby Burger King, remaining at the job for several years. To this day, I'm convinced that Paul's accomplishments had more to do with his pride than his paychecks.

And how could I forget such a delightful client as Peter? One day, when I visited the restaurant to see if I could help out, the manager pressed me into service as a stand-in for a counselor who was ill. She asked me to check in on Peter, who was washing dishes in the kitchen. (At Eden, every new client started in the laundry room and kitchen, eventually advancing into bussing dishes, taking orders, serving, and cashiering.)

Peter was talking to the bubbles, as dishwashers at Eden often did. I asked him: "Who are you talking to?" "God," he answered. Taking a stab at some real "counseling," I replied, "Talk to the bubbles on break time, Peter. Right now, wash the dishes." It worked. Peter smiled and continued to wash dishes. Eventually, Peter advanced to the top restaurant position—cashier.

My volunteer work with Eden Express helped me value and practice empathy and to always remember that old maxim, "Only the wearer knows how much the shoe pinches." My Eden Express experience also made me, an experienced college teacher, less of a "sage on the stage" and more of a caring person, who now wears his heart on his sleeve. I'll always value the "new me" launched by that little restaurant—from the first time I walked into it.

~Robert J. Brake

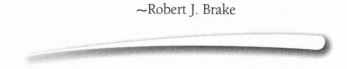

37

Family of Rejects

A teacher's purpose is not to create students in his own image,
but to develop students who can create their own image.
~Author Unknown

Growing up, the first day of school had always been exciting—new clothes, supplies, and classes. Now, at twenty-three, the first day of school had me in a panic.

I was the new teacher.

This was not the beginning I had planned. I had just celebrated my birthday, the new year, and my divorce. Unloved and unneeded, the rejection of a failed marriage still hurt.

I'd graduated in December, and a school more than sixty miles from my apartment had hired me. I would start the semester with a class of twenty-two fifth graders.

As I entered the school, stale carpet assaulted my nose and the aroma of cleaning products stung my eyes.

"What happened to the last teacher?" I asked the principal as she walked me to my classroom.

"Well—" The warning bells cut him off. "She left a week into the year. There have been thirteen substitutes in this class since then. But don't worry, we have a substitute the students are familiar with as a co-teacher for you."

This did little to calm my nerves.

The substitute was friendly enough, and the kids seemed happy to see her as they entered. They were wildly curious about me, clamoring to ask questions, talking over each other, and showing off. Before the end of first period, I had a headache.

The kids sat wherever they wanted, talked whenever they pleased, and only a few paid attention to the substitute. As she attempted to lead the class, I watched the kids fixing their hair, drawing, passing notes.

One girl crawled under her desk, and I spent the next half hour trying to coach her out. She only smiled.

One boy raised his hand, crying, while the students around him began screaming and complaining. As I approached him, the smell hit me.

"Go to the restroom," the substitute instructed before calling the office for cleanup.

The bell rang a few minutes later, dismissing the students for fine arts class—my conference period. The substitute led us to the room.

When the door closed behind them, she looked at me.

"Things you need to know: Tracy is the girl under the desk. She barely knows her letters, and can't read at all."

"Why is she in a regular class?"

"She goes to a special needs class for reading and language, but the school doesn't offer anything for her when it comes to math, science or social studies."

"What does she do while she's in our class?"

"Just leave her to herself, and make up a grade."

"Are you joking?"

"No, Paul is the same. He sits next to her. You'll only see them half a day. If you leave them alone, they'll leave you alone."

"What about Kyle?" I asked, referring to the boy who'd had an accident. "Shouldn't we check on him?"

"No, he'll get a change of clothes and be back later."

We entered our room to find a man cleaning Kyle's desk.

"Hi, I'm Sylvia." I said, offering my hand. He looked at it, then at the substitute, before turning back to work without a word.

"One more thing," the substitute said. "Conference period is personal time. I usually leave campus for a few minutes. I'll be back."

She didn't return, and neither did Kyle. I found out later that his mom had come to pick him up.

The custodian never said a word as he finished cleaning the desk. He began emptying trashcans, vacuuming, and washing the chalkboards. I got the feeling teachers didn't show him a lot of respect. Or maybe he just felt that way.

He finished by putting his supplies back in his cart and pushing it to the door. I crossed my arms on my desk, lowered my head, and wondered what I had gotten myself into.

"They didn't tell you, did they?" said the custodian.

I lifted my head and asked what he meant.

"Most of this class has been kicked out of others. They are the rejects, the students no one else wants."

"What's wrong with them?"

"Depends on who you ask."

The bell rang and he gave me a small smile as I rose to meet my students. "My name is Willie. I hope you stay."

Twenty-one students entered and immediately noticed I was now alone with them.

"I told you she would be gone," one yelled.

"I'm sure she'll be back any moment," I replied.

"Yeah right," said a girl brushing her hair.

"Even if she isn't, I'm still here," I said.

"Not for long," a chorus rang out.

Then it hit me. They were used to rejection, to seeing others walk away. The sting of my divorce was so fresh I knew how that felt. They deserved more.

"I'm your teacher for the remainder of the year," I informed them.

"Sure you are."

"You'll be gone soon," another student said.

I spent the rest of the day breaking up fights as I tried to get to know them. Many refused to answer me. One threw his desk at me. Another stood in the back of the room slamming his head into the wall repeatedly.

The minutes crept by until the final dismissal bell.

As the last child left, I sank into my chair, wanting nothing more than to curl into a ball and weep. If this was how tired and hollow I felt after one day, how much worse must it be for them every day?

That first week was mentally and physically exhausting. Gradually the students realized I cared, and that I wasn't leaving. By the end of the first month, I no longer fought for order in the classroom. They sat at their assigned desks. Most were following directions as well as completing work.

Since the school didn't supply work for special needs, and I refused to "make up a grade," Tracy and Paul were working from preschool level workbooks I purchased at Walmart. I thought the other kids would make fun of them, but they didn't. The kids had become a unit, a family of rejects.

By spring, I loved each of them as if they were my own children. I knew their moods, needs, fears, and dreams. At the end of the school year, nineteen of my students passed state testing, and all but one passed the fifth grade.

The last day was full of celebrating and fun. We played games, ate junk food, and watched a movie. When dismissal time arrived, every one of them gave me a hug and said they would miss me.

When my room was quiet, I began to cry. I would miss them too.

"You did it," Willie said, as he pushed his supply cart into my room. "You stayed, and you saved them."

"No," I said. "They saved me."

~Sylvia Ney

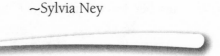

38

The Confidence to Change

Success comes in cans, not can'ts.
~Author Unknown

Before my senior year of high school, I'd already planned out the next two decades of my life. My future would include a doctorate degree in psychology, a cozy therapy practice, a successful husband, and a beautiful house to call my own. After that, I planned to start a college fund for the kids, and, of course, have kids.

I began my journey as a very busy college student. Along with being a full-time student and working part-time, I was volunteering at a local outreach center, participating in psychology-related campus organizations, and spending time with my professors so I could benefit from their mentoring.

By my junior year, I was tired. By my senior year, I was exhausted. The best part of my day was my job. An English tutor at the university's tutoring office, I loved helping struggling students understand and love literature and writing as much as I did. No matter how tired I was, working with the students always perked me up.

By the time I finished my master's degree, I was drained. Physically, emotionally, spiritually. When I wasn't in class or studying, I was working full-time at a counseling job I'd landed at an inpatient facility.

My work hours usually lasted well into the night, and I spent every Saturday and Sunday pulling at least ten-hour workdays.

My dream of getting my doctorate started to feel like a nightmare. After a long night of gut-wrenching deliberation, I finally made the decision to take a break after I finished my master's degree. I had enough credit to get my licensure to practice therapy, so I told myself all was not lost.

For the next seven years, I was a therapist. One day, during lunch with a friend, I found myself venting as usual about how therapy wasn't a good fit for me. She leaned over and asked, "What would you do if you weren't afraid?"

Without taking a second to think about it, I answered, "I'd teach at a college."

For the rest of our lunch, I told her about my college days as a tutor, about the students whose faces and names I still remembered, about my excitement at witnessing a student's "a-ha" moment.

On the drive home, I reminded myself about all the roadblocks to teaching. I only had a master's degree. College teaching gigs were hard to come by. My friends and family would be confused by my career change. There were few colleges nearby.

I began to think I didn't have what it took. I hadn't made any of my long-term goals happen. I was a failure, a quitter. I didn't know anything about teaching, and I didn't have any experience. What college would want me? I told myself that even if I did find a teaching position, I probably wouldn't be any good.

By that evening, I was drowning in self-doubt. I told myself to focus on more practical things—like working more hours at a job I didn't enjoy. To try and re-motivate myself about my job, I sought out retreats and workshops. I read self-help books. I tried to pursue a new hobby.

A month later I received an e-mail from a woman I'd never met. She was the Director of Student Effectiveness at the local community college. She asked if we could meet and chat.

When we met she said the college was looking for someone to teach a College Success course. She said a couple of people had tossed out my name because I had a lot of energy and excitement. From what she'd heard, my personality sounded like a perfect fit for the students.

I was in shock but I didn't hesitate. I immediately agreed to teach the course.

At first, I was excited. Then, I grew anxious. Instead of seeing this as my chance to kick-start a new career, I worried about all the things that could go wrong. Finally, I picked up the phone and called my friend.

"What would you say to a client in your situation?" she asked.

What a great question! I knew exactly what I'd say to a client in my situation. I'd ask her to jot down all the reasons why she'd probably be great at teaching. Then I'd ask her to list all the reasons why she might not be.

Minutes later, I was making two lists. I scribbled down every thought that came to mind. When I finished, I realized there was a much higher chance that I would be a good teacher than a bad one. More than that, I realized that most of the reasons I'd listed for not being a good teacher were related to my low self-confidence, not because of any concrete evidence that I wouldn't be good at it.

I decided to come up with ways to battle my self-doubt. I read books about teaching by leading researchers. I read articles written by students about what they wanted and needed from instructors. I talked to friends who taught and asked for their advice.

The class felt like a hit. I felt great about my prep and delivery, and the students seemed engaged. When the dean gave me my class's end-of-the-semester evaluations, I was beside myself. Students wrote that they'd felt inspired, hopeful. Many said the class gave them confidence and made them feel like they could be successful in college.

The department asked me to become a regular instructor for the course. After that, I made the decision to pursue teaching. Starting small, I began introducing myself to other faculty members as we passed in the hallways and around campus. Then I heard about an opportunity to join a faculty committee. Whenever people asked me where I worked, I told them I was a therapist but that I was interested in pursuing teaching.

Word got around, and my networking paid off. Within a year, two other departments on campus asked me to teach in their areas as well. After quitting my job as a therapist, I accepted.

Teaching has been so rewarding that it's given me the energy to pursue other interests, including taking violin lessons, which is something I'd wanted to do since I was a child. I also began writing fiction, playing the piano, and training for a marathon.

Today, I don't ask myself what I'm afraid of. Today, I ask myself what exciting opportunities lie ahead.

~Angela Ogburn

39

Unexpected Changes

Don't simply retire from something; have something to retire to.
~Harry Emerson Fosdick

"Y ou aren't going back to work," my husband Jeff stated as we left the doctor's office. I'd been feeling miserable since September when I'd returned to teaching. Now, at the end of October, my doctor had said that I'd better walk out of the school before I needed to be carried out. My blood pressure was dangerously high. It was time to terminate my twenty-eight year teaching career.

"I can't quit now," I argued weakly. "I only have two more years to go and I can collect my full retirement."

"You heard what the doctor said. You won't be around to get any retirement if you don't get out now. I know it's hard, but there really isn't a choice. You have to leave."

That night I thought a lot about my life. Teaching had been all I'd ever wanted to do. My first job was as an elementary special needs teacher in a small town in the western part of the state. I drove nearly an hour each way through back roads to get to the school. But I'd enjoyed my work. On weekends, Jeff and I would often pick up some of my students and take them to Fenway Park or some other attraction.

Life went on. We bought a house. I began working on my master's degree. With the arrival of our first son, Eric, I quit teaching. Second son, Greg, arrived three years later. Another teaching job would come along at the right time, I was sure.

With the help of a friend who was home with her own children and willing to babysit, I did some substitute teaching while the boys were little. Eventually, they were both in school and I found a job at a local junior high school. From there, I moved on to a high school. I'd just received my twenty-five-year pin from that high school a month before we received the news from my doctor.

Of course, teaching had changed during those years. But I really enjoyed working with the older students who had learning disabilities, preferring classes of juniors and seniors. It wasn't easy. Special education teachers are certified to teach all areas of the curriculum and I had fourteen classes of various subjects and various students over each two-week period.

Often, students questioned the contents of lessons and would ask, "How will this help in the REAL world?" I felt comfortable that what I was teaching was applicable to the daily life of an adult and answered them with confidence, giving them relevant examples. I enjoyed spending time with these young adults and felt that I was making a difference in at least some of their lives.

But big changes were on the horizon. The state stepped in. Our lifetime certifications were revoked and had to be renewed every five years. Vacations were spent at workshops, taking courses or rewriting curriculum to meet state specifications. Unfortunately, most of the course and workshop content was exactly what I'd learned years earlier and curriculum revisions were merely, to me, an exercise in semantics and an extensive waste of time and paper. Meetings became more frequent as more special needs students were placed in mainstream classrooms but still needed extensive help. There were times when I was literally supposed to be in three places at once! The paperwork on students I had in class and those being monitored increased considerably. I was spending as much time on secretarial work as I was on teaching.

Mandated state testing on material I considered irrelevant to daily life was the proverbial last straw. I no longer believed in what I was doing each day. I knew that what I had to teach to students with limited learning abilities so they could pass the test was not what they needed in the real world. They needed to know how to balance a checkbook before being taught how to solve algebraic equations. They needed basic reading and writing skills, not daily repetitions of questions and unfamiliar words that were basically useless but had appeared on previous tests. Now when they asked me about the relevance of the material, I could only answer that they needed to learn the material to pass the test. I thought I was handling the situation, but obviously my body knew differently. My teaching days were over.

The next day was difficult. Jeff and I went to school and arranged for my early retirement. I signed papers. I was in such a state of shock about the change in my life that I felt like I was watching someone else sign them. Jeff had retired the previous June after more than thirty years of teaching. He'd planned his retirement for a year. I'd had less than a day.

I stayed home for the next few months, following the doctor's orders and taking medication. Jeff found a part-time job booking rides for the elderly at our local senior center. Our son and daughter-in-law moved in with us for several months while their house was being built. While they were all working, I was taking care of the house and cooking meals each night.

Eventually, Kim and Greg moved into their new home. My blood pressure returned to normal, even without medication. I was now faced with a challenge. What was I going to do with the rest of my life? I began painting again, something I hadn't done in years. I redecorated the house, did some reading, had an occasional lunch out with friends or spent weekend time with family. And I started writing again. But I needed more. I wasn't ready to completely retire. If teaching was out, then where did I go from here?

I decided to volunteer at the Fitchburg Senior Center where Jeff was working. I began by offering a writing class once a week. The response was good and I soon found myself involved in teaching once again. But this time with a much older, and more appreciative, group of students.

A few months after my volunteering began I was offered the job of program coordinator. I accepted immediately. This was an entirely different type of work than anything I'd ever thought of doing. I was responsible for scheduling the activities for the center, advertising, coordinating events and writing a monthly newsletter of eight pages. My computer skills improved out of necessity. But there was so much more!

The huge building which houses the senior center is a former armory located off Main Street, across the street from City Hall. Part of the building had been used to house vehicles during training in WWII. Because of its size and location, the center is a perfect place for large group meetings and entertainment. I soon knew the area entertainers and politicians. I even had the opportunity to meet the late Senator Ted Kennedy.

Advertising was done in local newspapers. I began submitting stories and pictures of the senior center members to one local newspaper along with the schedule of events. The editor invited me to write a regular column, usually humorous, about my own life. Strangers recognize me from my newspaper picture, and I'll admit that I am extremely happy when I'm told how much my column is enjoyed.

At the center I've met some wonderful people, many of them from the WWII era. I enjoy hearing their stories and spending time with them.

I started a craft shop called the Closet Boutique. All items are handmade and it is an ongoing fundraiser for the center. My writing group still meets every Tuesday. We are about to self-publish our eleventh book, with proceeds also going to the center. These two ongoing fundraisers have provided money for everything from new coffee pots and furniture to helping with a new sound system in the large hall. Most importantly, the programs have given people a worthwhile purpose. Many dedicated, hard-working people have made the success of these programs possible.

Bingo is played at the center. I found that, while I don't enjoy playing the game, I do enjoy being the caller. Health and wellness fairs are scheduled along with many other informational meetings. The list of activities is endless. There is something for everyone.

And so the end of my teaching career wasn't the end of my working life. I've simply moved on and the move has been a good one.

~Jane Lonnqvist

Express Yourself

When we are no longer able to change a situation,
we are challenged to change ourselves.
~Viktor Frankl

he snap of something in the vicinity of my right ankle resounded like a shotgun blast and I crumpled to the ground. "You've torn your Achilles tendon," said the doctor as he examined my MRI, "and it's a bad one."

My stomach clenched into a hard knot. "Can you fix it?"

"I'll do my best," he said, patting my shoulder. "But it's going to be a long road to recovery."

He wasn't kidding. I was absent a full two and a half months from the classroom where I taught fourth grade.

Confined to a wheelchair, the interior of my house became my entire world. I wore a groove in my bedroom carpet, clear down to the backing. And while I tried to function as normally as possible, being housebound was not something I accepted easily.

As the weeks wore on, I spiraled into a deep depression.

Friends began disappearing. I couldn't blame them for not wanting to spend much time with someone totally consumed by doom and gloom. By the end of the first month, I often had days go by with no visitors, and no one called.

I kept the TV going constantly, not caring much about what was on and not even bothering to change the channel. One day I saw some version of the same news broadcast four times: morning, noon, evening, and late night.

And oddly enough, that was what saved me. The fourth time around, I actually heard what was being said. Quality literature was being banned in certain public schools, and such censorship of reading material pushed my teacher buttons.

I flashed back to a time in high school when the school board had forbidden a certain headline on an article that had already been printed in our school newspaper. The journalism class was directed to physically cut the "offending" headline off the paper before distribution.

Although it took hours after school, the journalism class did as told. And then they took all the little strips of paper containing the headline and pasted them on all 1200 student lockers throughout the building.

I sat at my computer and wrote that story, connecting it to the type of censorship that continued to plague our public schools even twenty years later. Then I sent the story to the local newspaper. They published it.

I enjoyed seeing my name in print. The following week, I wrote another article that also appeared on the "Opinions Page." After my third submission in as many weeks, the editor called.

"We've received some very positive feedback about your writing," he said. "Would you like to be a regular columnist for the paper?"

"I'd love to! How often? How many words? What does it pay?"

My mojo came rushing back. My depression vanished. I'll never again underestimate the true value of expressing my opinion!

~Jan Bono

Reboot Your Life

Start Over

A New Model

We must be willing to get rid of the life we've planned,
so as to have the life that is waiting for us.
~Joseph Campbell

It was September 2009. I was visiting Manhattan, not realizing it was Fashion Week. As I taxied toward my bed and breakfast, passing through the Meatpacking District, I noticed a group of people gathered outside a rebuilt warehouse. Fashion people. I dropped off my bag in the B&B's floral and paisley room, I threw on a cute but reserved dress, ballet flats, and ran out, hoping to be part of it again, even if it was just for the night.

Rounding the corner toward the party, I realized I had been on this block before. Fifteen years earlier, I shot my first film on this corner. This street had changed. Blood no longer ran from under slaughterhouse doors. Tenements had been converted to designer stores and high-priced eateries. New York had once again embraced this old street and filled in the cracks.

I scanned the people outside the fashion event, gauging who would be best to approach, settling on two tall guys, both beautiful. We chatted. They invited me inside. Back when I had been a working model in the '90s, Kate Moss made it sexy to be 5'7" and models, not actors, graced the covers of magazines. I, too, had been on my share of covers such as *Sassy* and *Maxim*.

Now, wearing simple ballet flats, the new models towered over me. I drank champagne, giggled and danced with my male hosts.

People turned to look. "Who's the girl in flats?" I heard. It made me shy but proud to still be noticed, that my spirit could override what had happened since I'd left the entertainment world. If I had appeared at this party in a bikini, the looks in my direction would have been of shock or pity. The large scar, in the shape of a wishbone, running from my breastbone to my belly button and across is surprising to see on someone so young.

I was twenty-six when they found the mass.

One night I felt a strange ache in my side. My then-husband, Alex, and I had been to LA's famous farmers market earlier that day, and I joked that I had a crepe stuck in my appendix. When the pain didn't subside, we went to the emergency room. For the rest of the night I was poked, prodded, hooked up to different machines. I had goo rubbed on my belly, and iodine pumped into my veins. Twelve hours later, a doctor came into my echoless room and said, "Well, the good news is they are benign."

For four years we went to from doctor to doctor, sending my films to places mentioned on all the best websites. I did not have cancer, but a large mass called a hemangioma, a balloon of blood attached and growing on my liver. No doctor wanted to touch me. They just waited. They watched as the mass grew and grew. It grew until I had trouble breathing.

It was a risky surgery. After four years of waiting, a surgeon at UCLA finally agreed to try to remove the growth. "Jennifer, you know that there is only a 50/50 chance that I can remove the tumor," Dr. B said. "Either way I am going to cut your chest open and if I can't take it out, we'll try to get you a new liver in the next six months."

I nodded. "Yes, I know. I need you to try, please." My quality of life had gone down so much that I chose this huge risk over continuing life as it was. I made peace the best I could. I had lived an extraordinary life. Traveled the world. Been on covers, in movies. I'd had dinner with Michael Jackson and been to Skywalker Ranch. My family loved me and I had found a great and profound love in Alex. I counted my many blessings and took the chance. We passed Bob Barker walking his dog in the early morning on my surgery day.

In the cold, white pre-op room, Alex sat next to me, holding my hand. We shared his iPod—one ear bud for each of us—and listened to the special mix he had made for this day until they came to take me away.

Six hours later, Alex appeared next to me. Through the intense pain and subsiding anesthesia, I heard him say, "He did it, Jen. He removed the tumor. You don't need a transplant."

That day, half my liver was cut away and I received five blood transfusions. The tumor they removed was the size of a large grapefruit and weighed ten pounds.

While I recovered in the hospital, Alex was at my side 24/7, sleeping on a tiny, rollaway bed. He held my hand, my head, and changed my bandages. Between his trips to get me more ice and ginger ale, he wrote songs on his laptop, quietly humming in the corner of the room while a stranger's blood flowed through my veins.

I had survived the surgery. But now I had a large scar, a jagged pink line that I could not easily camouflage. The acting parts I usually played were sexy, the vixen with a heart of gold. My body was my tool. Even though the large wound would heal, I was now a liability for any company that hired me. I had a pre-existing condition, and in 2009 that made me uninsurable for producers who must insure every person who works on their set.

A month after I got home, my manager called to say he was dropping me as a client, since I was no longer actively bringing in commissions. At twenty-eight, I retired from the career I'd had since I was fifteen. Like a ballerina whose ankles eventually weaken, my body had had enough. I was done.

It was impossible for me to view myself as anything other than a failure. Depression and anger took over my daily life. What was I going to do? I clung to Alex as my only source of joy and missed the signs that he was cracking: his growing need to travel and spend time away from the house, away from me. One night, I found him crying alone in his studio. I hadn't seen the hints or heard the stress in his voice, but after helping me through my long illness, he just couldn't give any longer.

Three weeks after our divorce was finalized, Alex was engaged to a pretty twenty-one-year-old. After the initial shock, my first thought was that it didn't seem fair that he could move on so easily while I was left with the scars.

Now, outside the Fashion Week party, the air was soft and fresh. I took a deep breath and looked around. I observed the newest players in fashion. I smiled at my new friends standing on this old corner. Like this street, my past had been cleaned out, the cracks filled in, and I had been replaced with a new model.

Six months after this party, I moved to New York to go to college—something I never had time to do as a model or actor. In March 2012, I received my bachelor's degree with honors. I am now in graduate school. I have been in a loving relationship for two years and I work as a professional writer.

These are all things I never would have had the opportunity, or the courage, to do if my old life hadn't been cut away.

~Jennifer Sky

A Long Walk

A journey of a thousand miles must begin with a single step.
~Lao Tzu

The worst kind of English weather had set in, the kind when you look at the dark, grey sky and think, "How is it possible that there is still any liquid left up there?"

I chased the soccer ball down the touchline. Then it stopped suddenly in a puddle, and I tried to slam on my brakes before I overran it. My left leg shot out in front of me and my whole body weight fell onto the right leg that had remained bent beneath me.

Then came the horrible sound. The sound that shattered a dream.

The coach looked at my knee in the changing room and said, "Put some ice on it — I'm sure you'll be fit to play again by tomorrow." Just a week earlier, he had told me that if I worked hard I could go all the way. That was what I had wanted for as long I could remember.

But I wouldn't ever play again. I had three operations on The Knee and spent months at a time on crutches, but nothing worked, at least not for long. And each time I went back into the hospital, surrounded by people many decades older than me, I lost a little bit of the ambition that had burned so brightly in me.

Eventually I didn't even bother to do the exercises the doctors gave me, and gradually the muscles on my right leg wasted away until I could hardly even run, let alone kick a ball.

Feeling defeated and hard done by, I started drinking heavily.

Eventually, it would be something as trivial as a picture that changed it all. Years after my accident, a friend of mine posted an old picture on Facebook of a bunch of us school friends on summer holiday, standing on a beach with the sea sparkling in the sun behind us. The photo was taken just a month or so before my injury. I looked at myself. I was so tanned, fit, strong and healthy. So happy and full of hope.

In the years since my injury I had become a little overweight, a little cynical, and completely unfit. I had done countless menial jobs, none of which I had stuck at. All I really knew was that I wanted to get as far away from England as possible and start afresh, but I kept blowing most of the money I made on alcohol. I was going nowhere fast, and somehow that old picture made it all too clear. That was all it took, but it was like a lightning bolt. I had to stop the rot.

Then later that night I started reading a book about the Congo. The author meets an old man who walks around 900 miles once every few months to sell palm oil in the nearest town.

My mind began racing. I could do that. There was nothing to stop me. I could do it all for charity and raise enough money to finally get out of England, enough to go somewhere in Africa and do something different, worthwhile—maybe coach football for a sports-based NGO (non-governmental organization). Perhaps I could even raise enough money to help fund an NGO project. I would get fit again. I would see parts of my country that I had never thought to visit before. Maybe I would even fall in love with my country a little bit again before leaving it all behind. It was perfect.

I went home and told my dad about my big plan. He looked at me with tired eyes. "But you've never walked anywhere. You don't even walk to the shops. You'll never make it. Not a chance."

That was exactly what I needed to hear.

Three months later, I had raised over £3,000 and chalked up at least a hundred miles in practice walks. The knee was feeling stronger than it had for years. I was ready to head off with my tent, sleeping bag, a small gas cooker and my clothes all on my back.

I left Land's End, Britain's most southerly point, on a perfect summer day. The road was flat and I felt good. I covered fifteen miles comfortably that day, then pitched my tent and slept like the dead.

But it wouldn't always be so easy. For the next two weeks, it rained almost incessantly. I got lost, almost drowned wading through a river, and had a close shave with a very angry bull. I had agonizing blisters on my feet, and my bag seemed to dig into my shoulders more every day.

But I kept going.

Soon the weather improved again. Having given my body no time to wallow in the pain it was feeling, it had no choice but to mend itself on the move.

After a month, walking twenty miles every day.had become comfortable. As I sat down on the grass next to my tent in the evening to eat whatever simple food I had made or went to wash in a nearby river or stream, I gradually became aware that I felt happier and healthier than I could remember feeling for years, if ever. I was accomplishing something. It was so simple and so rewarding. And England was more beautiful than I had ever imagined.

Autumn was already in full swing when I crossed into Scotland. My tent was covered in frost in the mornings, and I dreaded getting undressed and washing and shaving. The landscape had changed too. It was less hospitable, darker, wilder, more stark and striking. The closer to the end of my journey I came, the more I felt as if I was walking towards the end of the world.

After a little over two months, having covered 1,076 miles, I arrived at my destination in John O'Groats, the land having finally run out. I ceremoniously threw my walking boots into a dustbin. As I looked out to sea, I felt that I could do anything I put my mind to. Feeling hard done by for so long had just been the easy way out.

A few months later I boarded a plane to South Africa. I spent the next twelve months travelling around Africa working for a variety of sports-based NGOs. Then I came back to Cape Town to take up a job as a journalist for a news platform that focuses on development and social entrepreneurship in South Africa. I'm still here, writing about the things that matter to me most, and still coaching some soccer from time to time.

My dad came to visit me recently for the first time and meet my South African girlfriend. We have found a way to be close again even with this great geographical distance between us.

"Well, that was quite a journey," he said when I met him at the airport.

"Yes," I said. "It sure was."

~Christopher Clark

43

I Should Thank Him

Don't compromise yourself. You are all you've got.
~Janis Joplin

The night the knock came at our door, I was unprepared. I was at home with Jason, my boyfriend of two years. I had moved from Maine to Florida to be with him. He was my first love and my first real relationship. We had been talking about possibly buying engagement rings. Jason had been acting a little strange lately, and we had been arguing a bit. But couples have their ups and downs, right? It was just a rough patch, and we'd get through it.

The knock came at 7 P.M. Jason answered the door. I came downstairs just in time to see him get hit.

"Stay away from my wife," the guy said to Jason. And then, before he left, he looked at me and said, "Your boyfriend has been sending e-mails to my wife."

I was in shock. What kind of e-mails? I kept asking Jason what he was talking about, if he was involved with this man's wife. He denied it over and over again. Finally I asked him for her phone number so I could talk to her husband. He gave it to me and I called. The husband answered and I arranged for him to bring copies of the e-mails to me at work the next day.

That night I couldn't sleep. What if it was true? What would I do? Jason was my entire life. I'd given up everything for him, even to the point of putting myself in debt in order to get him out of debt. I didn't have enough money to move back to Maine. Other than a few friends at work, I didn't know anyone else here at all. And even worse, I didn't have a driver's license. Jason was my sole means of transportation.

Reading the e-mails the next day made me sick to my stomach. Jason wrote about how much he wanted this girl and how much chemistry they had, about kissing her and having her over to our house, about skipping work with her so they could be together. He wrote about nights that I'd stayed up and how sorry he was that I did, because it meant that he couldn't talk to her that night. Over and over again, I read about how wonderful he thought she was, and how he didn't care for me at all. I cried so hard I was physically sick.

I had to make a choice. Did I stay with Jason and give up my self-esteem? Or did I remove him from my life and try to make it on my own? It was not an easy choice, but in the end, there was only one thing I could do.

The lease for our apartment was in my name. I called him from work that day and told him to take whatever he needed for the night and to be gone by the time I got home. That weekend I packed up all his stuff and left it for outside for him.

It was scary being on my own. In the beginning, I took a taxi to and from work or bummed rides from people. Eventually I figured out the bus route and took that instead. It was lonely, but some friends at work stepped up and helped me. A cousin moved down to help me with the rent, and it was nice having family around.

Then came a time I had to be at work on the weekend and didn't have access to a ride of any kind. Because I worked as a vet technician, I had to be there to feed the animals, and let them out to go to the bathroom. So I walked. I was overweight and thought the walking would be hard, but it was actually pretty easy with my headphones on. When I later mentioned this to my cousin, he said, "Why don't you walk all the time? It's good exercise."

His comments changed my life.

From that point on, I walked eight miles home from work each and every day. As I walked, I felt better about things and my outlook improved. They say exercise is good for your soul. I agree. Music doesn't hurt either.

I was alone in my life without anyone to take care of or to take care of me. And you know what? It felt pretty good. And as the pounds started coming off I felt like a new person. A happier person, maybe happier then I'd ever been. I tried to share my happiness with others. My motto became "Practice random acts of kindness, and senseless acts of beauty."

I became more confident, more outgoing. People began to notice, especially a client around my age, who'd been bringing his animals to the vet clinic for years. It wasn't long before we were dating. But, this time things were different. I stayed focused on improving myself and helping others, instead of just fixating on the guy and the relationship.

I'd learned a big lesson and, boy, did it pay off. We were engaged a year after we started dating and married six months later. By then I had lost seventy pounds. I looked and felt the best I ever had.

Right before we got married, my fiancé and I bumped into Jason at a bookstore where he was working. We talked for a little bit. Jason told me how he was living with the girl he'd e-mailed. I told him I was engaged. I wished him well, and I meant it.

After all, I had a lot to be grateful to him for. Our breakup was the best thing that ever happened to me.

~Heather Ray

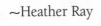

44

The Adventure of Starting Over

Courage is the power to let go of the familiar.
~Raymond Lindquist

"Bob, our loan was approved. We got the house!"

"Pat, there isn't going to be any house. I just got laid off at work. We're going to be leaving Denver."

I couldn't speak. After our daughter Jeanne was born, my husband and I had spent months looking for a house. The red brick bungalow with the built-in bookcases on each side of the fireplace, close to a park, was everything we wanted.

A month later we left our beloved Colorado mountains to start over in Missouri, where my husband found a job teaching at a junior college.

Two weeks after arriving in Kirkwood, Missouri, I was surprised to discover that I was expecting another child. While my husband was preoccupied with his new teaching position, I had plenty to do as I unpacked in our new apartment. This one had two huge bedrooms, central-air, and even a wonderful swimming pool and play area out back. I rekindled a close friendship with one of my favorite cousins who also lived in the area, and before long, starting over didn't seem so bad after all.

In January that year Julia bounced into the world. Seventeen months later, we welcomed Michael. With three children under four years old, our family was complete. But unfortunately, over the next few years, our lives fell apart because of my husband's addiction to alcohol.

After spending the day in divorce court, my mother and father helped load the moving truck, and my three children—ages three, four and six—and I left Missouri, crossed the Mississippi River, and drove to my hometown of Rock Falls, Illinois.

That was how my single parenthood began—near the love and support of my parents who were into their thirtieth year of a happy marriage.

Every morning before work mother stopped in for a visit. The children loved having their grandma around for the first time in their lives. Mom and I drank tea and talked about my job search and about how nicely the house was shaping up with my various rummage sale purchases. The tension that had permeated our lives in Missouri was gone.

The next month I found an interesting job at a radio station and, once again, starting over wasn't nearly as scary as I thought it would be. In fact, it was the best time of my life.

A year later, when I was broadcasting a parade for the radio station, I met a man who had come from Wisconsin to judge the high school band parade competition. Even though my mother warned me about the seventeen-year difference in our ages, Harold and I continued to see each other every weekend for the next two years.

When Harold talked about getting married, I wasn't sure I was ready to start over again in another marriage, especially in another state. But Harold persisted. We were married in my hometown church and Harold began a commuter marriage.

The previous winter, during the happiest and most active time of my mother's life, she and dad were taking ballroom dancing lessons, downhill ski lessons, and trips around the country. Mother noticed that she was becoming uncoordinated, even tripping and falling down for no reason. After months of tests she was diagnosed with ALS, Lou Gehrig's disease. She died after suffering with the disease for just sixteen months.

My best friend, confidante, and grandmother to my children was gone. I was devastated that she would never even see or get to know my fourth child. I was five months pregnant when she died. Andrew was born the following December while I was still under a cloud of missing my mother so much.

Harold continued his commuter marriage for nearly three years, even after the arrival of baby Andrew. Finally he insisted we move to Wisconsin so he could end his weekend commute. And so, once again, we started over, this time without my mother, who had always been my biggest cheerleader.

Once again, I prayed monumental prayers, turned over all the trust I could muster to God, and in a caravan of cars and a rental truck, the four children and I headed north to Wisconsin.

The children thrived in their new school. I found a part-time job at another radio station. Harold was happy that he didn't have to commute anymore, and we all loved our new sprawling home.

And so we lived happily ever after, right? Well, not quite. Unfortunately, this older man I'd married did not thrive in a household with three preteens and a baby. It was different than the carefree fun and romance we'd enjoyed for the past three years when Harold was still making the weekend trek to our home in Illinois.

The next five years of our marriage were a roller coaster. Before long the unbearable times were the norm. I suggested we separate for a year, enough time to figure out how to make the marriage work.

Two months after we separated, I thought everything was going great. We were about to make another appointment with a marriage counselor. A stranger came to the door and served me with divorce papers.

Not again. I just couldn't start over again. Not with four children and a two-day-a-week job. By this time I had fifteen years worth of starting-overs under my belt. Somehow each new start had brought wonderful people and experiences into our lives.

The day our divorce was final, Harold married his girlfriend. Within a month, my part-time work at the radio station became a four-day-a-week career. With the help of child support, some extra writing jobs, and the various jobs my teenagers had, we were able to keep going financially and stay in the house we'd grown to love. Amazing how the power of prayer comes to your aid when you need it.

The children and I laughed and cried together, created adventures for ourselves, made a home for each other, and figured out ways to get the three oldest through college at the same time.

I suspected that starting over as an empty nester just might be the most exciting new start of all. It was. I sold my house in Wisconsin and two-thirds of my possessions and moved to Florida. I married Jack. This mother of four, stepmother of six, grandmother of nine, step-grandmother of eleven and wife of one is loving every minute of life!

~Patricia Lorenz

45

Rewriting My Story

The world is round and the place which may seem like the end may also be only the beginning.
~Ivy Baker Priest

I had heard the old adage that insanity is doing the same thing over and over but expecting different results. In fact, I was getting tired of my own "insanity." I knew I needed to do something different in order to achieve a different outcome.

The solution came to me while driving to a conference in Philadelphia during Friday afternoon rush hour. I had been reciting a litany of frustrations — the traffic, the other drivers, the road repairs — when a light came on in my heart and soul.

"Okay," I said to myself. "It is a lovely day. I am headed to a conference I want to attend. I have an entire weekend to learn new things and enjoy myself. I am safe. All is well here. I choose to see this situation differently, right NOW!"

I relaxed, and traffic inched ahead. At that moment, my life began to change for the better.

I'd had inklings in my long years of marriage that my husband was not as committed to our relationship or to me as I was to him. After the children were born, late in our life together, this became more apparent. But still it shocked and wounded me deeply when he announced he was leaving me for a new life with someone else.

I tried to pick up the pieces of my life, parent my two young children, grieve for my marriage. I also mourned the loss of my father, who died right around the same time. My children and I moved to a new town. After several years at home, I went back to work. With depressing regularity, I ran through all these emotions and more: hurt, betrayal, fear, anger, sadness, loneliness, despair.

Friends who had known us as a couple said the usual supportive things to me, things like they had never liked or trusted him anyway. These comments were intended to help me, but they only made me feel more like a victim. I was able to tell the story of his shortcomings, although this never made me feel any better. Most of me blamed him. Part of me blamed me. Either way left me feeling hurt and angry, and did nothing to enhance my life in any way.

Suddenly, I realized that sitting in Friday rush hour traffic was a metaphor for my life. I couldn't change my circumstances, but if I could tell myself a different story, I could have a different outcome. And if I could rewrite the story of urban traffic, why couldn't I rewrite the story of the end of a marriage, and tell a story instead that ended with my own rebirth?

The traffic was simply an obstacle I needed to overcome to get to a wonderful weekend of learning. The end of my marriage was, in truth, a huge gift to me. When I stopped blaming, I could see the possibilities ahead of me for my life.

Instead of focusing on my former husband being the villain and me being the victim, I could rewrite my story to make myself, or even BOTH of us, into people simply trying to travel the road of life as well as we could. It was as if I had found the key that unlocked my heart, and just like the Grinch's once did, my heart grew three sizes that day. I felt compassion for myself as well as for the man I had been married to for so long. We had never been well matched, and so eventually the marriage ended. It no longer mattered who left whom.

As I told a different story, in which I chose to be uncoupled from someone who made me feel small and unloved, I grew larger and more empowered in my own story. My marriage ended because we were headed in different directions, with differing values and goals. I could let this be okay. In fact, it could be fine. *I* could be fine.

Now that I have let go of my old ending and focused on my

new beginning, I feel hopeful and I've become happier. In my new story, I am not carrying around with me the slings and arrows of old wounds. In this story, life is rich with possibilities. I have discovered I am capable, strong, adventurous, smart, and I have a quirky sense of humor. I have made new social connections, found new interests and hobbies.

Since that day when I was stuck in traffic (in more ways than one), I've turned my life around. I feel empowered and optimistic. And life reflects this back to me at every turn.

~Deborah K. Wood

Finding Me at Fifty

When we cannot bear to be alone, it means we do not properly value the only
companion we will have from birth to death—ourselves.
~Eda LeShan

You can go either way when you turn fifty—you can slide downhill or you can look at it as the halfway mark and a chance to shake things up a bit. I chose to shake things up. To anybody who would listen, I boasted, "I have spent the first half of my life learning how to live my life, and now I am going to live it."

My birthday was in early March. I threw a small party for close friends and family. I wanted a meaningful, reflective kind of gathering. My much younger boyfriend mostly distanced himself from the affair. We had been together for a couple of years, but problems were creeping in and the age difference was becoming an issue.

A month later, over a cup of coffee on an ordinary day, out of nowhere I blurted, "This relationship isn't working for me anymore." I wasn't fully aware I felt this, but as soon as I said the words, I knew they were right.

There was silence, while we both absorbed what I had said.

"I guess I will go then," my boyfriend said. He grabbed his guitar, a few records, his jacket, and he walked out the door. No protest, no asking what was wrong, nothing. He just left.

I cried. I couldn't stop. It was out-loud crying, the kind of wailing I never did. I don't remember the rest of the day. The following day he came over and found me in the bathroom crying. He looked alarmed and hovered. He offered to stay. I sent him on his way again.

Nothing in my world made sense. My crying confused me. Ours hadn't been a big love affair. We were good friends. Our relationship had been easy and we always knew it was meant to be short-lived. I shouldn't have been this thrown by our breakup. I stayed home from work for a week. I saw a counselor and went for a massage.

I came to understand I was crying for the loss of the relationship before this one. I'd joined Al-Anon to learn to cope with that partner's alcoholism, after ten years of a roller coaster existence where I enabled and endured and in the end had no sense of who I was or what I felt.

And I was crying for the marriage to the father of my children before that relationship. I'd buried my feelings and spent the final few years like a zombie, afraid to move a single foot the wrong way.

I had gone from my childhood home to marriage, to divorce with kids, to another relationship, and finally to this young man. Through it all, I was proud of my calm and restraint. I never shed a tear.

This crying was necessary, finally. I was crying for all the lost men, for all the lost dreams, and most of all, I was crying for my loss of self.

I went back to work to a job I had grown to despise, the atmosphere made toxic by the threat of cutbacks. I had never lived alone, and I hated coming home to any empty house. Depression set in. This was not part of my plan. Where was my bravado? Having a breakdown was not how I expected to reinvent myself at fifty.

I had struggled with postpartum depression with the birth of each child, and I'd learned some strategies that I put into use now. I forced myself to leave the house, to commit to doing something on the days I felt good.

As a child I used to count in a magical sequence to give myself the courage to speak up to a teacher, or to make myself walk on dangerous log crossings over gaps in the rocks at the beach, or to lower my feet to the floor at night to go to the bathroom, even though there was a monster under the bed. But this current monster was much bigger, and counting wasn't enough to overcome these feelings of despair.

I recalled that creating ME collages in group therapy in the 1960's had made me happy. I'd filled my collages with orange marigolds and hot yellow sunflowers, and these sunny flowers were meant to represent the inner me. So my new mantra became Marigolds and Sunflowers. I recited those two words in the morning when I woke up, dreading going out into the world. I chanted them as I drove my car to work, and as I parked and walked in. I said them when the black dogs of my depression closed in.

And then one day, I noticed I was happy. It happened as suddenly as my discontent with my young boyfriend had just a few months before. I was in my kitchen stir-frying something on the stove. A bottle of wine was chilling in the fridge, music was playing, and I had forgotten that it was a Saturday night and I was alone. The table and candles were all for me and I was happy.

I discovered that I loved living alone. I went back to university part-time, hosted casual dinner parties for friends. I dyed my hair pink and blue, loving the shock factor. Buyouts were offered to anyone at work with the right combination of age and years, and I took one. By the end of the year that I turned fifty I had my dream job, looked forward to going to work each day, had a great group of friends and a brand new bright red Volkswagen convertible. I had learned to get in touch with my feelings, to state my boundaries, to have healthier relationships and most all know that I had value and liked myself and could exist very well on my own. I was on top of the world.

The year I turned fifty, I found myself. I am now in the final quarter of my life, or as I prefer to view it, halfway through the second half. I share my life with a man who makes me happy, but more importantly, I am living each day exploring my creative self and still following my dreams. The days are filled with possibilities, and I wake up most mornings full of excitement for the day ahead.

~Liz Maxwell Forbes

The Power of Positive Pigheadedness

*A dream doesn't become reality through magic; it takes sweat,
determination and hard work.*
~Colin Powell

"I'm too old," I wailed. "No one wants to hire a middle-aged woman. I'm doomed. What am I going to do?"

As dramatic as it sounded, I was dead serious. After my divorce, I felt so defeated and hopeless I really believed I would end up destitute.

The jobs I qualified for wouldn't pay enough to support a household, and I was past the age where moving up the ladder was a likely option.

"You should start a business," a friend advised.

"Doing what?" I was still mired in self-pity. During my married life, I'd focused on raising my children, supporting my husband's endeavors and publishing a few books and articles on the side. I knew I could write well, but even though I'd been publishing for decades, I'd never made any real money doing it.

She shrugged. I realized no matter how much she wanted to help, I had to find my own solution.

As I saw it, I had two choices: wallow or get creative.

I tried wallowing for a while. It didn't suit me. Too passive.

So, I took an inventory. What did I have going for me? I sat down and made a list of my existing talents and abilities. I included my curiosity, love of learning and stubbornness. My pig-headedness was legendary. Silly me, for years I thought it was a fault. Little did I know it would be the secret ingredient that would take me from despair to destiny.

Personality assessments helped me identify my strengths. One test said that my smartest career move would be "any job where you're paid to be opinionated."

I looked in the paper but didn't see anything that met that criterion.

I could get paid for my opinions if I had my own business, but if I wanted people to listen, I had to have information worth hearing.

It wasn't a straight line from where I was to where I wanted to end up. My long-term goal required training, and the short-term goal, survival, demanded an income. Fitting both into my days wouldn't be easy.

I tried different combinations of paid work and study time. I sampled jobs the way Goldilocks tried porridge. One was too hot, another too cold. In the background, hungry bears hovered, ready to eat me if I didn't keep moving forward.

I tried real estate, then retail sales. The Christmas chaos renewed my commitment to make a change.

My marketing and advertising background was an asset, but times had changed. To catch up, I would dive into this new world, reading and doing research, taking online classes and soaking up knowledge. I got a job with a software company managing their social media. This was a while ago, when social media was still a new concept. It was a disaster.

The experience made me want to understand what went wrong.

If it's true you learn more from your failures than from your successes, I was on the fast track to becoming an expert.

I took a novice class on how to build websites.

Yikes! There was so much information. Most of it was over my head. I struggled, fell behind and dropped out.

At this point, my secret ingredient, politely referred to as tenacious determination, kicked in. I refused to abandon my goal.

This was not going to defeat me.

A few months later, I took the course again. This time I kept extensive notes and did every assignment.

Things were beginning to make sense.

I made websites for family members and for myself. They were pretty simplistic, but gave me a chance to practice. I experimented, crashing my own sites, then figuring out how to fix them.

Tackling and solving problems increased my confidence.

I took an advanced website development course. Again I found myself over my head, so I repeated it until I got it.

The next step required finding real clients.

Terrified and tentative, I forced myself to go to professional mixers and events, where I tested out my elevator speech.

Initially I led with my identity as a writer. This usually ended the conversation.

I reframed my introduction.

"I build websites," I told them. "And help companies and individuals with marketing and promotion."

People hired me.

I'd done it!

I built a business from scratch. Taking what I knew and expanding it, ignoring the negative little voices along they way that insisted I couldn't do it.

It's been five years now and I've settled into my niche. Websites and graphic design keep the hungry bears satisfied, and I write every day. I've found a balance doing work I love.

Rebooting a computer clears out the old cache, eliminating those things that prevent it from functioning well.

Rebooting a life does the same. It's a fresh start, bringing together who you are, what you know, what you're willing to learn, and where you want to go.

And don't forget the power of positive pig-headedness. It's the final ingredient that can make all the difference in your success.

~Lynn Kinnaman

Doors Wide Open

Falling in love consists merely in uncorking the imagination
and bottling the common sense.
~Helen Rowland

I could see the white sedan pulling into the driveway through the half-open blinds of my home office. My first instinct was to scream. I felt like a giddy sixteen-year-old schoolgirl instead of a forty-two-year-old mother of three going on a blind date.

I had agreed a few nights before at a moms' night out, glass of chardonnay in hand, to go out with Rob, the best friend of my friend Florence's husband. She passed along my number, and he called the next night. It was a surprisingly easy conversation. My children, ages ten, eight, and six, had just vacated for the weekend with their dad, and Rob was dead-on when he asked, "What did you do first? Clean up or catch your breath and relax?" From there we shared lighthearted stories about our kids (he had two, ages seven and five) and dangled tidbits about our failed marriages—enough that I was curious about how a man could be as relieved and positive about his divorce as I was.

It had taken me almost a year to get to this optimistic place. At first, when my husband moved out on the notion that he needed "a break," I felt defeated. I'd already gone through the pain of caring for and losing both of my parents within eighteen months, and now my husband was leaving me alone with three young kids.

I couldn't help feeling punished—like everyone except me deserved loving husbands and nearby extended families. At Back-to-School Night and on the soccer fields, I felt my singleness the most. And then right before the holidays, we got hit with lice (yes, all four of us had live bugs). As I picked nits out of hair for hours every night and waded through piles of laundry, I wondered if for the rest of my life I would have to tackle every obstacle alone. That included the thirty-six inches of snow that was dumped a few days later, the day after Christmas. I had to climb out my kitchen window to attempt to shovel, only to realize my kids had played with the shovels the night before and they were all buried. It was all too much, and I found myself paralyzed on the couch. (Later, I would say: "My mom died, my dad died, and my husband left, and I survived. It was the lice and snow that nearly killed me.")

So what changed? In February, as I approached my forty-second birthday, I went to one of those women's "change your life for the better" workshops, led by a woman I knew who had also gone through a divorce. I learned some important lessons that night from women who had come through way worse than I had, including breast cancer and abusive marriages.

I, Jennifer Chauhan, was the only person responsible for my happiness. Not my ex-husband. Not my children. Not my mom's six surviving siblings or my brothers who lived on the other side of the country. Not my friends.

Nobody owed me anything.

If I believed in my heart that my life could change for the better, it would.

Shedding my victim skin, I began reciting very Zen-like (slightly scaring all those around me), "I choose not to suffer. I choose to be happy."

I wrote down in my journal everything I wanted in my life: to sell my house for the asking price; for my divorce to go amicably and for me to get what I needed; to be successful professionally and do well financially.

I paused a moment before writing, "to find a true partner who loves me for me." Could this really happen?

The night Rob and I met was my thirteen-year wedding anniversary.

Exactly one year prior I had slid off my wedding rings and asked for a divorce (just one week after my husband had moved out).

So much had changed in a year.

Coincidentally (or not, as I'm more and more inclined to believe) Rob had moved out the same weekend Chris had. He'd been married just about the same length—twelve years.

We were traveling on paths winding toward one another.

We spent that first night together at an outside bar overlooking the ocean, talking and laughing as we shared stories about our kids and opened up about our marriages. We laughed until we cried as I realized my six-year-old son was obsessed with all-boy bands, namely Big Time Rush, and how I told my friends the best way for them to be my friend was to stop giving advice and "hold my hand and shut up."

Rob's given me a fairytale romance—strolling through Washington Square Park and kissing for hours on a park bench (serenaded by an NYU violin student), taking me to the ballet, sending me late-night love texts—that is still as passionate and romantic and real nearly three years later.

At times, I've been guarded. Having lost so much in such a short time, I have a fear of abandonment—I'm wired to expect people to leave me. But Rob shows over and over again that I can trust him. He wants me to open up and be real, share my fears, my concerns. He wants me to cry when I miss my mom and tell him when I think he's not doing enough.

There are no games. No lies.

Our kids have met, get along wonderfully, and even though we live an hour apart and are not sure how logistically we can get married anytime soon (there's alimony, I don't want to uproot my kids, etc.) we know we will always be together.

And because he believes in me and in us, I have gone on to do braver things than open my front door to a blind date in a white sedan. I've sold my marital home and discarded the belongings of my former life, including my favorite white everyday Williams-Sonoma dishes, the brand-new king-sized bed that was never shared, even my still-sealed-in-plastic framed wedding photo.

I've opened my own business, a writing studio, and offer creative writing workshops for teenagers and adults. And now I'm starting a nonprofit to help disadvantaged kids achieve academic success and personal growth through writing.

Most of the time, I have no idea what I'm doing and just plunge ahead, figuring it out as I go. Having been thrown too many curve balls, I know this is the better approach.

Life is messy; it's unpredictable. The only known is that we get to choose how we want to experience it. And I want live mine with doors wide open and believing that anything is possible.

~Jennifer Chauhan

Never Too Old

For 'mid old friends, tried and true,
Once more we our youth renewed.
~Author Unknown

My heart was racing as I put down the phone. What was I thinking? A male friend at my age? I scarcely knew what to say when my grandson asked me, "Grandma, do you have a boyfriend?" Yet, I could not deny that Ted made me feel special again. Talking to him on the phone stirred up feelings that I thought were dead. We had gone to high school together and then went very separate ways. Though we had never been close, a common bond of grief now brought us together with a new understanding of mature friendship.

We had both lost our mates.

We e-mailed each other almost every day. Eventually, gifts, cards, and flowers began to arrive. Then one day he showed up at my door and asked me out.

What would my children think? What would my friends say? My beloved husband of forty-eight years had passed away four years earlier. Though I loved him with every fiber of my being, I could not bring him back. It was time to let go. The past is lovely, filled with tender memories, but it is a desolate place to live.

I tearfully removed my wedding rings and put them away. It was not a one-time process. The action was repeated off and on for two years before I finally was able to be at peace with it.

"I have a decision to make," I'd explained to my children. "I can go on crying my life away or I can step out of my comfort zone and take a chance on living and possibly loving again."

Their immediate response had been, "Go for it! You have a right to be happy. Dad wouldn't want you to live in pain."

Another friend had said, "It is impossible to go forward if you are constantly looking back."

Even armed with that affirmation, the process of courting at seventy is a little like hunting with a dog that has lost his sense of smell. Ted had rented one of those hearse-sized, four-door trucks standing high off the ground. He apologized for the obvious overkill of the size of the vehicle, but it was all that was available from the local car rental. He gallantly opened the door and watched in painful silence as I struggled to make the leap inside. He flailed his arms at my clumsy attempt to get lift off, not knowing quite where to put his hands to boost me in.

Once inside we sat quietly trying to regain our dignity.

As we drove down the freeway to the nearest big city, where we planned to dine in style, I began to ponder the wisdom of riding in a vehicle with a guy who mentioned that he was considering cataract surgery. It was no comfort that he was still wearing the bright yellow sunglasses that covered most of his face, even though it was dark outside. I discretely suggested that we might be just as well served by dining at a restaurant close by.

He readily agreed, though it meant that the place would be full of locals, all curious to see who the widow woman was with, who he was related to, and why he was in town. Ted put up with all the gawking and probing with good-natured humor. I guess he thought no one could really see him behind those glasses and by the time they had him figured out he would be out of town. To his credit, he must have decided that I was worth the scrutiny, because he was back the next day and every day until he had to fly home.

We discussed many important topics, such as long-term health care plans, retirement funds, children, grandchildren, religion, politics—and fiber. We decided that love is not exclusive. It has many facets. It expands to fill the expectations put upon it and rather than diminish the past, embraces it.

He likes documentaries. I like feature films. He likes fish. I like steak. I am the land. He is the sea. There is much to learn, much to process, and much to gain. We have only begun this new journey but this I can tell you: Love at any age is sweet.

~Kay Thomann

50

Laid Off and Living the Dream

It is not true that people stop pursuing dreams because they grow old;
they grow old because they stop pursuing dreams.
~Gabriel García Márquez

t was just before noon on a weekday when I walked up to the front door of my home. I was carrying a box full of stuff from my office. I took a deep breath to compose myself.

I opened the door and looked to the living room where my wife was playing with our two little girls. She stood up, looked at the box and then my face, and knew instantly what happened. I watched as a look of fear flashed across her face. Then tears welled up in her eyes.

"What happened?" she asked almost rhetorically.

"I got laid off." I simply stood there watching her.

Then something happened. Her face changed. "You're not getting another job!" she said. "Jobs aren't helping us get any closer to our dreams. This is it. It's go time!"

Her words rocked me to the soul. She was absolutely right. In one stroke she single-handedly took away my disappointment and gave me hope. Deep down I knew she was right. It was time to go for it. It was time to live the life we'd always wanted to. At that moment we didn't know what we would do. That didn't matter. It just seemed right.

What followed next was a whirlwind of activity. Through prayer and inspiration, we made two very key decisions.

The first was to start our own business. Based on my own career experience, we formed a company that would help local businesses grow through marketing on the Internet. Because this business was based online, it would allow us to work from literally anywhere with an Internet connection.

This led to the second decision, which was to leave our home in Orange County, California behind and hit the open road. The goal was to see places we'd always wanted to see. Being tied down to a job never let us get out and truly explore.

Within less than a month, we sold most of the stuff we once held so dear. If it didn't fit in the car, it didn't go with us.

Part of us wondered if what we were doing was right. It was challenging getting rid of stuff we'd worked so hard to accumulate. It was also hard knowing we'd be saying goodbye to friends and family, at least for a while. But we held onto our resolve.

We moved faster than our fear.

Over the next two years we explored the Pacific Coast—the Puget Sound area and the San Francisco Bay area. We loved every minute of it. We were able to grow the business and make many new friends along the way.

The time finally came to make an even bigger jump, to go international. Our first stop was Cozumel, Mexico. Being a family of ocean lovers, living on an island in the Caribbean seemed like the right thing to do.

In fact, we're still here and we love it! We sometimes have to pinch ourselves just to make sure we're not dreaming.

~Sean Marshall

51

Chicken Soup
for the **Soul.**

Meeting Mom

Fortunately analysis is not the only way to resolve inner conflicts.
Life itself remains a very effective therapist.
~Karen Horney

"**S**o, what does poison ivy look like?" my mom asked with a nervous laugh. I could hear her picking her way gingerly through the bramble—over rocks, around prickly bushes. As she followed me over a fallen tree, I realized that some part of me was purposefully choosing the toughest, most overgrown path and, amazingly, she was following nearly without complaint.

As we trudged through the damp weeds and clambered over a jutting rock, I felt the years melt away... I was no longer an out-of-shape teacher in her late twenties leading her overweight fifty-year-old mother down into an abandoned ravine choked with debris and runaway weeds. I was twelve again and, for the first time ever I was sharing a childhood exploration with my mom.

A lump rose in my throat and I blinked hard, silently chastising myself: Don't cry now, she'll never understand. The tears came anyway and so I tucked my head down and pressed further into the overgrowth.

"What did you and Cyd do down here?" my mother puffed as she struggled to keep up.

"You'll see, if we ever manage to find the creek under all these weeds."

As a kid I had been as familiar with this ravine as I was with the path that ran from my house to Cyd's, but it hadn't been so overgrown then. It used to be so open and pretty, and when I had stood at the mouth of the ravine with my best friend and looked down, it was like staring into our own private Land of the Lost.

We had made it to the base of the ravine by now and I caught a glimpse of the creek's dark water beneath the branches of a fallen tree. I climbed out and balanced precariously on the limb that served as a tenuous bridge between the two banks. "See? I told you it was here."

I stepped off onto the other bank and slipped off my shoes. The water felt just like I remembered, so cold my feet were numb to the squishy mud between my toes. On her side, my mom leaned tentatively against the fallen tree and untied her muddied shoes, which only fifteen minutes ago had been as white as her linen sheets. Then she was in the water with me, her pants delicately rolled up halfway to her knees.

At first she fretted about getting her clothes wet or cutting her foot on a rock submerged in the dark water, but soon she was staring in awe at the untouched wilderness around her. I wished I knew what she was thinking—I could see her face lighten, the worries and stresses being carried toward the river on the creek's cool current.

She spotted a crayfish in a shallow pool near me. As she leaned toward the water for a better view, I couldn't restrain myself. I knew it would break the spell and ruin the moment, possibly the whole afternoon, but I just couldn't keep my hands from doing it.

Maybe I was trying to punish her for withholding this moment from me when I was twelve years old and desperately yearning for my mom's affection. Maybe it was just one of those childish pranks revived from my twelve-year-old mind, the ones that had irritated even Cyd.

Either way, it could not be stopped.

My hands did the unthinkable—they scooped up the ice cold water and flung it at my mom. It wasn't a lot of water—more than a splash, but less than a dousing. Just enough to soak her neatly pressed pants.

She looked up astonished. "What...?" Her voice trailed off and her eyes took on a strange cast, almost devilish. Next thing I knew, I was drenched head to toe, and my mother's look of surprise had been replaced with one of feigned innocence. I was flabbergasted. How could she do that? I knew I splashed first, but...

Then it occurred to me how we must look: two grown women standing knee-deep in a creek, fully dressed and dripping wet, make-up melting into rivulets down our faces.

My mom must have been thinking the same thing, because suddenly she tilted her head back and laughed, a sweet beautiful laugh rising from her heart and startling the birds from the treetops. It was a sound so foreign to the small dark house in which we had tiptoed around each other for all those years that now it collected in my throat like forgotten sadness and I swallowed until I could feel the weight of it in my chest. Her laughter, so light and sudden in the abandoned ravine, made me realize something that had never occurred to me before: Maybe it wasn't me who had been deprived all those years that she wasn't part of my life. Maybe while my mother sat alone in her dark room, locked within the prison of her depression, she dreamed of today and a daughter who would insist that she live... even if it meant dragging her kicking and screaming into the sunlight.

Later, as we trekked home trailing wet weeds behind us, I almost asked her. I could feel the heat of the unspoken question, the challenge I had carried for the last fifteen years: "Mom, where were you?"

I smiled as I realized that I didn't have to voice that question.

You're here now, Mom.

Thank you.

~Katherine Higgs-Coulthard

Chapter 6

Reboot Your Life

Mind Your Health

52

Chicken Soup
for the Soul

Who Would Have Thought?

Our bodies are our gardens to which our wills are gardeners.
~William Shakespeare

I heard screaming—a piercing, terrifying, series of screams. As I regained consciousness, I came to the realization they were my screams. I lay on the floor, screaming shrilly into the phone as my daughter, on the other end, told me to calm down. An ambulance was on the way.

Moments later I was surrounded by paramedics. I wondered how they got into the house. A neighbor showed up behind them. I was embarrassed to have her see my house, with all the messy piles around. Why hadn't I gotten my house cleaned? I vowed to never let piles get the best of me again.

I'd broken three metatarsal bones in my foot when I fainted from dehydration from food poisoning. I was in a cast, a boot. Months of physical therapy followed before life returned to normal.

The hospital did a bone density scan, and found mine was low. I was shocked. Why would I have low bone density? I always drank three glasses of milk a day, and took calcium pills.

The doctor put me on medication that was supposed to help aging women with this problem, to stabilize further decline of the bone mass. After a few years, he took me off it because he said new evidence showed it could produce problems in the neck. I went natural, hoping my bones wouldn't deteriorate further.

When I was sixty, I heard that First Lady Laura Bush had a physical trainer come to the White House to work with her on weight resistance machines so she wouldn't get osteoporosis. Weight resistance machines? I didn't know what they were. I'd never exercised in my life, but thought if Laura Bush knew how to ward off this debilitating condition, I'd follow her example. I joined a gym, and a whole new world opened up to me!

I'm now sixty-eight years old, and I love my biceps and triceps. When I see other women my age with, their lower arms flapping like the wings of a bird, I wish they knew about weight resistance machines. They don't need to look like that.

It's more than just looks. My husband is eighty-six years old, and because he doesn't go to the gym he can no longer physically carry heavy things. When we fly on an airplane, I'm the one who puts our carry-on luggage in the overhead compartment. I carry the logs to the fireplace. I carry huge cases of water from the car into the house. I wonder, if I keep going to the gym and working with the weight resistance machines, will I still be able to do these things when I am eighty-six? I intend to find out!

This year, I started taking ice skating lessons. I fell during the second lesson, really, really hard—spread eagle on my front. That fall taught me the ice is to be respected!

I decided I'd better get a bone density test, and see where I stood before I committed, long-term, to the sport. I didn't want to break my hip in a fall.

My doctor's office called. "Dr. Lo said your bone density test came out normal."

"Really? I'm not even heading towards a problem?"

"No, perfectly normal," the nurse said.

"Pretty good for a sixty-eight-year-old woman, isn't it?"

"That's what Dr. Lo said. He said you have the bones of a young adult."

Imagine that, I thought, as I hung up the phone. Thirteen years ago I had a terrible break in my foot. Today, I ice skate. At sixty-eight. Thank you, Laura Bush. Who would have thought?

~Esther Clark

53

Back in the Saddle Again

The essential joy of being with horses is that it brings us in contact
with the rare elements of grace, beauty, spirit, and fire.
~Sharon Ralls Lemon

Was this what menopause was all about? I'd known there would likely be hot flashes. A thickening waistline. Mood swings. What I hadn't figured on was falling into an ever-deepening funk as I moved further and further into my fifties. I'd scold myself when I'd become weepy for no reason. I had nothing to be unhappy about. I had a wonderful husband, three happy kids who are on their own, a roof over my head, shoes on my feet and no worries about where my next meal was coming from.

It wasn't that I didn't have enough to keep me busy. I had a too-big house to clean and a too-big lawn to mow. A garden to tend. Meals to cook and dishes to wash. I volunteered at church and at a neighborhood elementary school. On top of all that, my husband and I lived on a small farm. Though the cattle, goats and chickens that we'd once cared for were gone, we still had horses, cats, and Sophie, our three-year-old Boxer mix who clearly relished being a farm dog.

But Sophie's waistline was thickening, too, and I knew it was my fault. Did I feed her too much? Yes. (Somehow it made it easier to justify my own overeating.) Did I exercise her enough? No. (Most days, I had no desire to walk through the woods behind our house or around the pond in our pasture. Surely, Sophie didn't either.)

We did, however, climb the steep stairs to the hayloft in the barn every morning. I'd cut the rough twine away from a couple of hay bales and toss them, flake by flake, down into the horses' manger. Then Sophie and I would descend the loft stairs and make our way back to the house. We were both out of breath by the time we got there.

Pathetic. It was clear that Sophie and I needed to find something to bring physical fitness—and, along with it, zest—back into our lives. But what?

On a sunny morning in early April, we headed to the barn as usual. And as usual, our three horses stood in the pasture and followed us with their gaze. But on this day, they didn't sprint to the barn. Instead, they dropped their heads and tore at the new-green grass that had, seemingly overnight, begun to poke through the pasture's brown stubble. When I got to the loft, I saw that the hay I'd tossed out yesterday still littered the barn floor.

I knelt down and threw my arms around Sophie's neck. "It's spring, girl," I told her. "No more hay chores!"

Sophie wagged all over.

"How about if we take a walk?"

More wagging.

As we began our first loop around the pond, I noticed that Sunny, our palomino gelding, was following us. I stopped to scratch between his ears and discovered that his mane and forelock were matted with cockleburs. "You poor thing," I told him, "let's take you to the barnyard and get you cleaned up."

Sunny stood patiently as I combed the burs out of his hair. He lifted his feet so I could use the hoof pick to clean out the dried mud and rocks. He practically grinned when I began rubbing the curry comb over his coat. As he grew cleaner and I grew dirtier, I noticed myself humming and wondering how long it had been since I'd groomed this horse. More than that, how long had it been since I'd ridden him? Or any other horse for that matter.

Two years at least. Not so long ago, I had ridden almost every day. But I'd fallen out of the habit. Allowed other things to get in the way. Let myself and my animals get fat and lazy. Perhaps the time had come to change that.

Except that you can't just jump on a horse and ride him as if he's a bicycle. It's important to make sure he's in decent aerobic shape. Free of leg and foot problems. And safe to ride. (A horse that's used to being a pasture ornament just might morph into a bucking bronco!) I needed to work Sunny on a lunge line for at least a couple of weeks to make sure he was sound. He seemed to have no objection. In fact, he seemed to enjoy our daily sessions. As did Sophie, who romped and played the whole time Sunny and I were working.

When it was clear that Sunny was ready to be ridden, I lugged his tack out of the barn. I draped the saddle blanket over a fence rail and beat the dust out of it with a broom. I cleaned the saddle and bridle and reins with saddle soap and rubbed them with Neatsfoot oil until they gleamed. I polished the bit until it shone like new. Then I got Sunny tacked up. He looked beautiful. And, as crazy as it might sound, happy.

The time had come to untie Sunny from the fence post and climb onto his back.

My fifty-five-year-old heart was beating hard. Was I too old for this? Were my muscles still strong and limber enough to mount a horse? Could I keep my balance once Sunny started to move? Did I remember how to use my hands and legs and voice to make him stop and go and change directions? There was only one way to find out.

I put my left foot in the stirrup, grabbed a clump of Sunny's perfectly coiffed mane with my left hand, and sprang off my right foot into the saddle. It felt good. No, not just good. Wonderful. I relaxed my grip on the reins and squeezed Sunny's sides with my legs.

"Giddy-up, fella," I said.

And with that, Sunny and I headed for the woods, with Sophie following close behind. We rode for more than an hour that day, taking in the sights and sounds and smells of spring and having a perfectly marvelous time. I collapsed into bed that night with every muscle in my body groaning. They were groaning even louder the next morning.

But no matter. As soon as my housework was done, I headed straight for the barn.

I whistled once. Here came Sophie. I whistled again. Here came Sunny. Both of them ready—just like me—to put a little fun back into our lives.

~Jennie Ivey

54

No Smoking

The greater the obstacle, the more glory in overcoming it.
~Molière

"Oh I wish I had listened to my mom," I thought, as I paced around my living room. "I am so addicted. I hate it."

I was trying to create a more positive life, but smoking was getting in the way. I had recently been hired by a nonprofit society, and even the executive director was encouraging me to quit.

My friend and I had taken our first drags decades ago. We gagged and coughed. The smoke burned our lungs. The smell made us nauseous and our eyes watered, but we laughed and continued smoking because we thought we were cool.

My mom warned me about how easily she'd become addicted, and how she just couldn't seem to get rid of her cough.

"Don't worry," I said. "I'm sure I can quit anytime I want. Everyone smokes."

My mother's and my smoke circled above us, painting more yellow on the kitchen walls. Years later I would develop chronic bronchitis, often progressing to pneumonia, but I still continued to smoke.

Time changed the way society viewed smoking. It also changed the way I felt about it. I soon had no doubt I was addicted. Smoking seemed to consume me. And yet, sadly, I decided I could never give it up. I would just continue to smoke.

Circumstances in my life created an opportunity for me to wake up and explore more positive ways of living. I was able to let go of negative relationships and seek out a more positive work environment. I connected to my spiritual side and began meditating. I started to care for myself and to build a solid healthy side.

But I still continued to smoke.

"Oh, not again." I gasped as I felt the familiar severe pain hit my left side. "I think it's getting worse."

I stopped walking and waited for the pain to subside. As I stood there, I realized I had a choice. I could continue smoking, but if I did, my journey here would be cut short.

I made my choice. I would try quitting New Year's Day. Christmas was almost here, so it wasn't long to wait.

On Boxing Day, my daughter and I sat by the Christmas tree together relaxing.

"Tanya," I said, my voice low and unsure. "I have decided to try to quit smoking."

An amazing look of relief filled my daughter's face and tears filled her big blue eyes. "I am so scared I will lose you if you don't quit."

The next morning, I stood in front of the mirror and thought, "Yup, I am quitting New Year's Day."

I stopped. Suddenly, deep down I knew I would not quit New Year's Day.

Why wait? I would quit right then and there.

Within twenty minutes of my decision to quit, I felt the urge to smoke. The urges grew stronger. It felt like they were screaming as they relentlessly ordered me to obey. I found that writing down the minutes, then the hours, and finally the days I resisted helped me to survive the first difficult stage.

It amazed me how much power lived within my addiction. I prayed, paced, and meditated through the first few nights when sleep was almost impossible. I felt like I was just barely holding on. Everything in my life stopped.

Thankfully, my supportive work environment helped me through some tough times, as did my friends. My daughter was incredible. As time passed, I realized I was not my addiction. I was so much more. I decided to keep concentrating on building my healthy side.

When I felt like I couldn't last much longer without a cigarette, I found my spirituality was there to help me. "Let go. Let God," I would whisper.

Finally, I felt my addiction grow weaker. Eventually the urges came less often and with less power, but they were always there waiting. When I was tired, down, angry or vulnerable, my addiction would be ready to take advantage of the situation. It would tempt me: "Oh come on, have just one cigarette. You deserve it! You should be able to have just one now."

Thankfully, I knew that one cigarette could easily lead to another and another. My list of emergency strategies came in handy. I also knew that relapse can be part of recovery and if a relapse did happen, the best thing I could do was learn from my slip and get back on track.

Fortunately, I did not suffer a relapse. The light grew brighter.

At times though, I felt sad, like I was losing a good friend. Smoking had been part of my life for so long. A quick fix whenever I needed it, which was often. It took care of many needs, in an unhealthy way, but it did take care of them. Now I realized the consequence of my smoking was the exact opposite of what I needed.

Self-love, increased awareness, and spirituality were the most powerful tools in my recovery and relapse prevention. I took one day at a time. I also realized my addiction was only sleeping and all it would take was one cigarette to awaken it.

A few years after I quit, I completed addiction counseling training. The nonprofit society where I worked offered me the opportunity to work with various addiction programs in the community. For over a decade, I was privileged to help men, women, and youth find their own power and path to freedom.

Sadly, my mom never did quit smoking. She lost her battle with lung cancer long ago. As my own health improved, I felt motivated to volunteer in cancer research. I have been part of the Lung Health Study for many years.

It has been almost a quarter century since my last cigarette. I have received many blessings and privileges, but none as valuable as loving and being there for my family and watching my four grandchildren grow.

All these years later, I still believe my addiction is only sleeping.

~Elizabeth Smayda

A Kick in the Keister

Vision is not enough, it must be combined with venture.
It is not enough to stare up the steps, we must step up the stairs.
~Vaclav Havel

"So how did you do it?" my girlfriend Teri asked.

"Do what?" We sat outside on lawn chairs in the warm summer sun. Slices of lemon floated on top of our glasses of ice water.

"You know what I'm talking about." Teri sipped her drink. "You've lost forty-five pounds and kept it off for three years. What's your secret?"

I wondered if I should tell her how hard I'd hit bottom, and I wasn't talking derrière. The day the scale registered the highest number I had ever seen was a real eye-opener for me. I was sick of the ups and downs.

"Come on," Teri prodded. "Tell me."

"Well, first you have to know that it's not just one thing, like joining a Weight Watchers group or buying pre-packaged prepared meals."

"Okay, what then?"

I thought back to that day on the scale and how I found my purpose and resolved to change my life. I was tired of not being the me I wanted to be. Oh, sure, losing weight was not the cure for all my problems, but it sure would help with my self-esteem. And my physical ailments too — the doctor had told me to lose weight to keep my blood pressure under control. I didn't listen to him and went about my regular lifestyle of eating burgers and fries.

Then came that day on the scale. It was time to get a handle on things, especially when I took a look at my backside in a full-length mirror. It was time to give myself a swift kick in the keister.

"I did lots of little things," I said to Teri.

"Like what?" Teri stared at me over her water glass. "I can stand to lose some weight."

"Okay, where do I start? First, I hate the word "diet." It conjures up images of deprivation. Definitely not a good feeling. And on top of that, what I was going for was a lifestyle change in my eating. A weight loss that would be forever, not a temporary loss and then gaining it all back again."

Teri nodded her head. "Been there, done that."

"I don't say that I can't have something. Now I say I choose to have this or that. It makes me feel empowered and in control of myself."

"What else?"

"Oh, gosh, there's so much more." I sipped my water and thought about all the things I'd learned over the last few years, like how eating is affected by what I keep in my cupboards and refrigerator at home, what I choose when I'm in a restaurant, and how family gatherings can be a minefield of emotions that can trigger overeating.

I looked up. "Okay, here's something quick and easy to do. Switch to fat free, use a small plate and small fork, and stop eating when you feel three-quarters full. It lets your head catch up to your stomach." I paused. "Oh, and portion sizes are key. Remember when a small soda was really little? The sizes they serve today are way too much."

"So do you ever blow it?" Teri smiled. "I can't believe you haven't had a juicy cheeseburger with fries."

I laughed. "You know what? When I was working so hard on losing the weight I only ate lean and healthy. Nothing fried or greasy. Now, if the scale says I'm within a pound or two of my goal weight, I occasionally eat a burger and fries."

"Ah ha. I knew it. You can't stay away from those things forever."

"You're right, you can't. But, and this is a big but, no pun intended because I have always tended toward a big butt," I paused to laugh at my own joke. "If I eat a meal like that, I ride my exercise bike an extra thirty minutes."

"What about chocolate and candy bars and glasses of wine?"

"Oh, I have all those things, but in moderation, and in small sizes. Did you know Snickers have little minis?" I got up and grabbed my water glass. "Do you want some more?"

"Thanks, I'm good."

In the kitchen I refilled my glass with fresh ice and added another slice of lemon and then I rejoined my friend outside. "I didn't give up my favorites. I just eat them in much smaller sizes and not so much. Like root beer floats. I love those."

"How is that on your diet?"

"It's not, because I'm not on a diet, remember?" We both laughed. "I have this tiny glass that holds three ounces. I put a small scoop of ice cream in it, a splash of root beer that foams up just like in a big glass, and I eat it with a small spoon, savoring every bite."

"And that's supposed to be satisfying? I'd want a giant one in a jumbo-sized cup," she answered.

"Just that little bit satisfies my cravings. And when I look in the mirror, I like what I see much more than how a giant float tastes for five minutes." I settled into my chair and laid my head back.

My girlfriend was quiet for a while. "Well, you look good."

"Thank you, and better yet, I feel good. My blood pressure came down and I'm not winded going up a flight of stairs. I had a friend, Tracey, who was there for me while I struggled through the weight loss. She was great. She held me accountable, plus there were times that no matter what I did, the scale just didn't show what I thought it should. That's when I needed my friend to talk me down off the ledge."

"So is that it, though? Is that all you did to lose the weight?"

"Well, I added exercise, of course, and squeezed it in where I could, like doing deep knee bends when picking up stuff around the house and forward lunges and squats when blow drying and curling my hair. Sounds weird, huh? But it works. I also took my dog for a walk all the time, and I rode my exercise bike every night for thirty minutes while I read the newspaper."

"Geez, that's a lot."

"Not really. All the little bits add up."

She was quiet for a while. Me, too.

Then she said, "So, will you help me be accountable?"

"You bet I will," I answered.

~B.J. Taylor

56

Made to Order?

Love yourself. Forgive yourself. Be true to yourself. How you treat yourself
sets the standard for how others will treat you.
~Steve Maraboli

T he summer before eighth grade was life changing. I discovered exercise and fell in love with it. Before that, I was always chubby and the last one picked for team sports. After school each day, I'd just park myself in front of the TV to watch old movies.

I'd been taking fun courses in summer school for the past two years. With home economics and art behind me, the only elective left was P.E. so I checked that box. I don't know what I was thinking, because P.E. had never been a pleasure for me.

The night before summer school began, I had a nightmare. I saw myself standing on the sidelines while the skinny kids played ball for two hours. I had to force myself to get out of bed that morning. I trudged to class filled with dread.

My teacher was a pleasant surprise. Not the drill sergeant I expected, he was around thirty, trim, dark-haired, and friendly. Best of all, he seemed fair to each of us regardless of our weight or physical abilities. Day one established our three-part routine: calisthenics, track, then team sports. Relief swept over me with the knowledge that the majority of each day's class would not involve being picked or, in my case, being passed over.

My regular school had P.E. just once a week for a half hour. Here, the first thirty minutes, the calisthenics, was just the warm-up. Following the jumping jacks, sit-ups, toe-touches, etc., I felt invigorated for track, though it was more of a walk than a run for me. Finally, miracle of miracles, I was accepted, and not ostracized, for softball, volleyball, badminton and every other sport we played.

After my first day of fear and uncertainty, I woke up eager to get to class for the rest of that summer. Each day I returned home with newfound energy. Along the way, without ever counting a calorie, I lost fifteen pounds.

In September, when I began eighth grade, I was bombarded by compliments on my weight loss. I weighed 115 and everyone told me I looked good. I started to think I'd look even better if I got down to 100 pounds.

Then I became obsessed. I started giving away my lunch every day at school. I fed my dog under the table when I was home. I counted every calorie. I kept lowering the number I'd consume, until I got below 500 calories a day. Apples and celery became my staples. I derived my enjoyment of brownies and cookies vicariously as I watched friends and family devour them.

By Christmas, I was down to 100 pounds and not looking healthy. During her annual visit, my Aunt Julia was shocked by the change in my appearance and told my mom that I looked like I'd been in a concentration camp.

Mom was busy with my sister's wedding, planned for January 27th. She was sewing all the bridesmaids' gowns and making their hats as well. Her fuse was short and when she'd yell at me to come to the table for dinner, I'd hide under my bed or in the closet.

I continued dieting. By eighth grade graduation, I was down to 89 pounds. My arms were like toothpicks. I had so little energy that I was usually leaning against something rather than standing up straight.

Freshman year, I met Richard, a sophomore, at my first high school dance. Though pale and gaunt, I thought I looked like a model. His interest in me reaffirmed my new confidence in myself.

I was stunned when, a month into our relationship, Richard told me I was too skinny and ought to put on some weight. I thought I was in love and wanted to do whatever made him happy. In this case,

I decided eating fries and drinking shakes would do it. It didn't seem like such a bad idea.

Eating what my friends ate was fun, and soon I was back up to 100 pounds. I wasn't able to stop there though. Once I began eating, I felt better, less moody, and happier. It was as though I'd been mentally ill while I starved myself and now I couldn't go back to that deprivation.

My tiny clothes were replaced by larger sizes. Richard started criticizing my weight for being too high. He'd look at me in disgust and say, "You're getting fat!"

After games and dances, while everyone devoured hamburgers, fries and hot fudge sundaes, Richard would humiliate me by ordering me a side salad and a Diet Coke. I never protested, hoping that his efforts to control me would go unnoticed.

My rebellion would strike right after he dropped me off. I'd raid the kitchen. We didn't have much to munch on in the way of packaged cookies or chips. Instead I'd make cookie dough and eat it raw. Or whip up a bowl of frosting and eat it without any cake. The pounds kept piling on. When I surpassed my previous all-time high, I quit stepping on the scale.

Sophomore year I surrounded myself with supportive people, most decades older than me, in a Weight Watcher's class. I learned about sensible eating. It worked until I lost enough weight to earn the compliments I longed for. As soon as I looked good, I stopped following the program. Soon I was back to my out-of-control binge eating.

Junior year I skipped both breakfast and lunch, which led to my biggest weight gain. I started eating at 4 P.M. and didn't quit until I fell asleep. Jeans were out and I replaced them with long, baggy dresses that I used as cover-ups.

After high school graduation, I attended our local state college. Parking was expensive and sparse. I rode my bike to school out of necessity, but found myself feeling firmer and more energized as well. Eating breakfast was a must if I was to maintain my focus in my early morning classes, especially statistics. I carried apples and bananas in my backpack to snack on between classes.

Without counting calories, I got back down to 140 pounds and made the final break with my always-critical boyfriend. Free of his control, I realized I'd never felt as self-conscious about my weight as I did when he was demanding me to be a certain size and ordering my food. Without the outside pressure, I took charge of my food choices and fitness level. I felt reconnected to my body much like I had at the end of my P.E. summer. This time I dropped another ten pounds and maintained the loss while enjoying swimming and dancing.

The urge to binge lessened. I wondered how I'd downed all that cookie dough and frosting. I didn't beat myself up over it though.

The last time I ran into Richard, he asked why I never looked this good when we were together.

I shrugged. "I guess I'm just not made to order."

~Marsha Porter

57

Running for My Life

The real purpose of running isn't to win a race;
it's to test the limits of the human heart.
~Bill Bowerman

"I ran 62.5 miles over the weekend," one of my co-workers announced.

"That sounds awful," I said. "Did your car break down? Aren't you a AAA member?"

Levi laughed and told me about participating in the Ultimate Race of Champions, a 100K race in the Appalachian Mountains of Waynesboro, Virginia. He described it as extremely challenging, a race that pushed his body and mind to their absolute limits. It was something he wanted to cross off his bucket list.

I immediately thought of my own bucket list: visit Tahiti, publish a novel, and sing with a band. Nope, none of my items had anything to do with running. In fact, they had nothing to do with exercise at all.

I do not like exercising. To be perfectly honest, I despise it almost as much as my biannual trips to the dentist.

When asked if I run, I typically respond, "Only when chased." But recently, instead of laughing at my sarcasm, Levi said, "Maybe you should practice. Then, if you are being chased, you might not get caught."

I thought about the truth of his remark. Maybe I would never need to outrun a mountain lion or an armed criminal. But obesity and hereditary diseases are chasing me. Those are the things I need to outrun. So Levi is right. I do need to get faster.

Since we don't live close to a gym, my husband and I purchased a treadmill. I have been exercising regularly now for a little over three months. I want to lose weight for an upcoming wedding I will be in. More importantly, I want to improve my health and outrun the demons of high blood pressure, diabetes, and obesity.

I am still in the very early stages of my lifestyle change, but I have already noticed some differences. My clothes fit better. I have more energy, and I am usually in a more positive mood. Plus, I am actually getting faster.

I still cannot say that I enjoy exercising. I would prefer a thirty-minute nap in a hammock swing to a thirty-minute jog any day.

But I am tolerating exercise better and incorporating it into my life more frequently. Each week I continue to increase my speed and degree of incline on the treadmill. My relationship with running has also improved from one of hatred to one of respect. I am hoping to establish a true friendship sometime in the near future.

Last month, we took our annual family trip to the Outer Banks of North Carolina. Typically, the most physical activity I engage in is a walk along the beach or a stroll through the outlet mall. This year, however, I took full advantage of the community fitness center. I exercised between thirty and sixty minutes on the treadmill, five out of seven days of my vacation. I didn't always enjoy it, but I did appreciate how I felt afterwards.

There are days when I get moving on the treadmill and I don't think I will last more than five minutes. My legs feel like lead, and I don't feel motivated. That's when I think back to something Levi said: "Discomfort is like a door you have to pass through to get to somewhere new in your life."

That is exactly what I want to accomplish. I want a new level of fitness that my body has not seen in years. So, if that means tolerating a certain degree of discomfort, then I am game.

Levi finished his ultra-marathon in sixteen hours, fifty-two minutes and twenty-eight seconds. He was the last person to finish under the elite cutoff. He met his goal.

I will probably never run a marathon, but next year I am going to enter a 5K. It will be my very first race, and I intend to finish it.

As I run for my life, I try to keep in mind everything that is chasing me.

~Melissa Face

58

My Big Wake-Up Call

The world breaks everyone. And afterward,
some are stronger at the broken places.
~Ernest Hemingway

My wake-up call happened five years ago on the scale at my doctor's office. Normally, I'd make small talk with the nurse by way of distraction. I'd step off the scale with no knowledge of just how much I weighed. The nurses would quietly write down the mysterious number while I made my way back to the examining room.

For years, my strategy of number avoidance worked beautifully to keep me ignorant of just how much I'd gained. But on wake-up call day, I put down my purse and stepped on the doctor's scale to find a very different experience with a very different kind of nurse.

I stepped on the scale with my usual darting eyes and light conversation about the weather. All of a sudden she announced my weight. Aloud! I'm not saying she shouted, but I'm saying every staff member and doctor and patient in the building knew my weight.

Worst of all, I knew it. Honestly, I can't remember the exact number (my subconscious is protecting me from the shock), but I do know it was more than I weighed going into the hospital to give birth.

I was shocked. Embarrassed. Completely in a tizzy over this number. And although I don't remember why I was at the doctor's that day, that cataclysmic event sent me on a mission to get healthy. It was the shove off the cliff I needed to get my body moving.

I called my dear friend, Amy, and took her up on the standing invitation to join her kickboxing class. It was the best decision I could have made.

The first day of kickboxing, I about passed out (quite literally). But I'd made a die-hard commitment to get in shape, and soon I fell in love with it. Kickboxing for exercise revived a childhood dream of becoming a black belt. Two years after starting, I started training at our local mixed martial arts school along with our two sons.

Last May I tested for my first-degree black belt, earning the Best Tester award in my category.

Five years after my wake-up call with the number-yelling nurse, at forty-four years old, I tested for my second-degree black belt. I fulfilled a dream while working my way into a stronger and healthier woman. I feel like I'm just getting started. It's true; some of the best things in life are just beyond our biggest wake-up calls.

~Lori Lara

59

Chicken Soup for the Soul

The Comeback

To give anything less than your best is to sacrifice the gift.
~Steve Prefontaine

I t was New Year's Eve 2011. I sat on my couch with my two dogs and was reflecting on the year. I had turned fifty in February and was taking some time to learn about myself. I was learning to embrace solitude and I was discovering peace.

As I sat on my couch, I recalled the joy I had experienced back in my glory days, running ultra marathons, winning National Championships, representing the United States at the World Championships. I thought of all of the friends I had made in the sport.

It had been a decade since I had entered a competition. Strangely, tears began to roll down my cheeks. Then, for the first time in many years, I wept openly. I tried to compose myself and walked to the bathroom to wash my face. It was there that I took a good, long, hard look at myself in the mirror.

I was no longer that ultra marathon runner. I had to confront reality. I was a middle-aged man in decent enough shape to sit behind the desk in my office for the day. Sure, I could still go out and run easily for an hour or go down to the gym and lift weights. I still worked out every day, but I was not the same person, the same athlete that I was in the late 1990s.

In the time away from competing, I'd raised my daughters and developed my law practice in Vermont. I attributed it all to growing up. It was easy to tell myself that. I had grown content in my life and appeared comfortable with the increase in the size of my waistline.

When I took a serious look at myself, I knew it was time to change. I lacked discipline and had no readily identifiable goals.

I shut off the TV. I began to contemplate what it was that I wanted in my life. Did I want to remain in my present state? Had I grown so old that I could no longer imagine a better me? Could I see myself transforming back into a competitive athlete? Did I have it in me? What was I made of? Was there something in me that desired more? Did I dare to dream?

A strange quiet came over me. I was going to transform my life. It was time to reinvent myself, to become all that I could imagine. I had to see it. I had to believe it. I began to think of myself as that thin, super fit athlete that could accomplish anything he set his mind to. This was not just about diet, exercise, and my routine. This was much deeper. It was going to be a complete transformation—mind, body and spirit.

I saw the end result as I sat there that night. The only things in the way of my desired result were effort and time. I asked myself one more question: "What are you willing to do to make this dream a reality?" The answer was a very simple one: "Whatever it takes!"

I slept well that night and was prepared for Day 1 of my metamorphosis. I gulped down a couple of cups of coffee and visualized my results. I was going to do this, but I was going to accept and forgive myself. It was time to be kind and loving to myself. It was going to be one day at a time. Day after day, doing whatever was required to reach my goal. I had not deteriorated into this condition overnight, and I expected it was going to take some time to achieve my ultimate goal. I understood the level of commitment that was needed and prepared myself for the battle that was ahead.

The first few days, I was filled with enthusiasm and it was easy to stay on track. I expected some plateaus and prepared myself mentally for the difficult days. As the days went by, my newly discovered discipline developed into more discipline. I vowed to abstain from alcohol and to remain true to my restricted diet of 1,200 calories per day. I was running for an hour every morning and lifting weights for another hour three or four days per week. Weight began to disappear. I lost approximately three pounds every week. This was feeling good. I was gaining momentum and strength as each day passed. There was no doubt in my mind that I would get down to my desired weight. I was planning a return to ultra marathons by the end of 2012. It was all going to happen.

By the beginning of June, I was down to my desired weight. My health was good and I was running well. I was running faster and my efforts were getting easier. It was time to up my mileage and forge ahead. I would start increasing my mileage by adding time and distance to my Sunday runs until I could run for four or five hours.

In my down time, I would read and study anything that I could on a wide range of topics. I was reading two to three books each week and increasing my knowledge base. My life was transforming. As my waist shrunk, my mind expanded. I was transforming myself in mind, body and spirit. It was as if a spark inside me had burst into flames. I became passionate about inspiring others, sharing what I was learning and helping others to grow in areas that they sought.

I would often remember Ralph Waldo Emerson's words: "Make the most of yourself, for that is all there is of you."

I decided to run a six-hour race in October and diligently trained for it. As race day approached in late October, I could feel those old feelings of excitement and anticipation. It was now time to come back and experience the joy that I always felt while competing in the sport that I loved so much. The results would not be nearly as important as the journey. The journey is, after all, the most important part. That is where we find success.

The six-hour race was a wonderful event. It was there that I shared my passion with fellow runners and experienced bliss for the entire event. Since that race, I have competed at numerous ultra marathons at distances ranging all the way up to 100 miles and timed races of up to twenty-four hours.

What has become abundantly clear to me is that it is not the achievement of our goals that define us, but rather what we become in the pursuit of those goals. As Ernest Hemingway stated, "It is good to have an end to journey toward; but it is the journey that matters, in the end."

~Brian Teason

How I Became
a Muddy Girl

*Nourishing yourself in a way that helps you blossom in the direction you
want to go is attainable, and you are worth the effort.*
~Deborah Day

A
t thirty-six, you're supposed to be in the prime of your
life. Boring, lazy, and antisocial should not be the words
that describe you. But they were for me, along with
unhealthy, overweight, and insecure. My weekends consisted of staying home, hanging out on the couch, watching TV, and of course,
eating. Because you can't watch a twenty-four-hour marathon of *Law
& Order* without stuffing your face, now can you?

As a child, I was shy and introverted. After years of bullying as a
teen, I became an insecure adult who was too afraid to try new things
for fear that I would fail. As soon as something got a little too difficult,
I would cut and run. I became an expert at avoidance.

Now here I was, in my thirties, and life was passing me by.

I decided to do something about it, starting with my weight. I
was over 200 pounds and miserable. I never considered myself a gym
person and I dreaded the idea of walking into an exercise class. So I
searched for something that would get me active and help me shed
the weight, but would also be fun. I'd loved running as a child, so I
thought a 5K would give me a goal to shoot for and some motivation
to start working out.

In my quest for a 5K, I stumbled upon something I had never heard of—a mud run. The specific one I came across called itself "an adult playground." Needless to say, this piqued my curiosity.

I learned that a mud run is an event at which participants not only run, but also crawl over and under obstacles—all in the mud. Lots and lots of mud.

I have no idea why I thought it was a good idea for an overweight and out-of-shape girl like myself to register for something like this. I was going to have to climb over walls, swing across monkey bars, walk balance beams, and crawl through mud, all for four miles.

But I thought it sounded like fun. Some women scurry in fear over just the mere thought of getting dirty. Not me. I grew up on a back road, surrounded by woods. Mud and dirt were a part of my childhood.

Through Facebook I met a lady who was doing the same event. She invited me to join her team. At least now I wasn't going to have to do this alone.

It was an experience that totally changed my life. I had to skip some obstacles because I had no upper body strength. My team and I walked the four miles instead of running them. As it turned out, most of them were also doing this for the very first time. I did what I could and had a blast. Not only did I have fun in the mud, but I made friendships that day with a group of women who were on similar journeys to get in shape.

In the year since, I have done four more mud run events, including one that was over six miles, in the mountains, and at night, with only a headlamp guiding my way. I went from skipping the walls to climbing over them all by myself. I have dropped more than forty pounds and my life has completely changed.

My self-esteem has skyrocketed. I've made so many new friends, all of whom have encouraged me to continue challenging myself. I have done things within the last year that I never imagined I would do. I started training in Mixed Martial Arts; I've gone zip lining, although I am deathly afraid of heights. I joined a gym and actually love it. I've done four 5Ks, and I am always on the lookout for the next crazy event o sign up for. I no longer have cable television because there's no point to it. I seem to have something going on almost every weekend. No more time for TV!

I am no longer afraid to step out of my comfort zone. I no longer fear the opinions of others or worry about failing. Now, when I try something new and don't quite succeed, I want to try it again with only three words in mind: BRING IT ON.

~Maggi Normile

Reboot Your Life

Overcome Adversity

From Homeless to Happy

If you want others to be happy, practice compassion.
If you want to be happy, practice compassion.
~Dalai Lama

I stared down at the $14.86 left in my hand after paying the weekly rent for the grimy motel we'd found. We had only a small amount of food in our kitchenette. I wondered how I could have gotten my eight-year-old daughter and me to the point where, we were this close to homelessness.

They say that poverty is a downward spiral, and until that day, I hadn't understood why. Just make one or two wrong assumptions about being able to find new employment, or think that a financial expenditure makes sense when it doesn't and you can find yourself in a real life version of the game *Candy Land*, on a ladder sliding downward, with no end in sight.

It did no good to ponder whether or not I should have left my ex-husband and the job I had then, because returning to either wasn't an option. Nor could I gain back the lost savings or the time spent looking for new employment without success. I had returned to our old neighborhood with my tail tucked between my legs. I was desperately trying to figure out what to do, so that my eight-year-old daughter and I didn't have to move into our van—the final act of desperation.

Our motel was an apartment house that had been converted to

weekly rentals. Staying there were druggies, single moms trying to escape from abusive marriages, seemingly happy gypsies, alcoholics, and people who just seemed to have a hard time fitting in.

I felt normal, so what was I doing here? More importantly, was there something these people could teach me about surviving until I could climb out of this pit?

I swallowed my pride and began to knock on door after door. Single parents or travelers, I always asking the same things. How are you doing? And what are doing to keep going?

I was told how to donate blood to earn a bit of money. How to apply for emergency food stamps and housing assistance. How one family worked at a local temp agency that paid daily. It was humbling, but doing everything they recommended allowed me to keep going. Then one mother told me about a program that would accept my daughter back into school, on a subsidized basis that gave her free breakfasts and lunches, which meant two less meals a day for me to worry about.

The whole time I continued to go on interview after interview in search of a regular job. I was grateful that living at the hotel allowed me to give a "real" address. So many homeless people don't have that and therefore can't find employment.

But I knew I couldn't stay there much longer. The management allowed no leeway, and I wasn't making enough money to pay rent.

I signed up for every temp-to-perm agency I could find within a reasonable distance. I worked so many mind-numbing jobs that it's painful to remember them. The experience reminded me how lucky I had been to have a job that provided a reasonable income and even interesting work. It also reminded me that if you want to get ahead you need to be a worker who stands out in the crowd, one who is willing to go that extra mile.

I landed a job as a receptionist. I saw all the partners as they came and went. Whenever I had an opportunity to make any kind of a positive impression, whether offering to return calls, making reservations, recommending a solution to a callers' problem, or anything else, I did so. I tried not to be obnoxious, but I wanted to appear both helpful and knowledgeable.

The effort paid off. My temp-to-perm job was extended for another two-week period. I was moved from the reception desk to the second assistant for one of the partners. This gave me the opportunity to see even more of what went on in the firm. I offered the executive assistant help in completing her work so that we could both go home at a more reasonable time.

Even though I knew it was rare for this firm to move anyone from temporary to permanent, I decided I'd do my job as if it were already mine. I organized the files. I set up a follow-up calendar. I made sure whatever was needed for meetings was there beforehand. I planned lunches and anything else I could think of to make myself indispensable. I figured that if I could keep working there for over four months, I might have a chance.

I had been working there eight weeks when my boss's executive assistant became ill and was hospitalized. Since she was expected back shortly, I offered to step in and do what she had done as well as my own tasks. It was hard work, and it kept me away from the motel longer than I would have preferred. Fortunately, one family there welcomed the extra babysitting money it earned by taking care of my daughter.

Sadly, the executive assistant never did fully recover from her ailments. After working six of the hardest months of my life, I was permanently offered her position. It provided benefits, stability, and eventually the opportunity to move into a better, closer apartment.

From time to time, the partner I worked for would try to get me to discuss my past. I was never willing to disclose that I had been homeless and panic-stricken. It was simply too embarrassing.

I worked for that firm for almost five years. I eventually took over the operation of a legal department and was promoted to the position of manager. Who would have imagined?

My time as a homeless person had given me a new compassion for people in trouble. Instead of simply evicting everyone who couldn't pay, my department developed an award-winning program for allowing them to work off past-due rents by providing needed services, such as cleaning, gardening, or painting, somewhere in our portfolio of apartment buildings.

Because of that program, our apartments became the most profitable of any firm in the area, and received the Mayor's Award of Excellence.

I went on to have other corporate jobs, and I now live on my own farm. But that stint with the druggies, hippies, and hopefuls made the biggest impression on me. It taught me never to take any of life's blessings for granted. The saying, "There, but for the grace of God, go I" really is true.

Whenever I see a person who needs help today, I wonder what their story is and how they got onto the *Candy Land* slide. And I try to offer them at least a warm cup of coffee or something to eat. Who knows, some day it might be me again. I'd like to think that someone would help if they could.

~Kamia Taylor

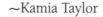

Jersey Shore Promises

Find joy in everything you choose to do. Every job, relationship, home...
it is your responsibility to love it or change it.
~Chuck Palahniuk

t was unseasonably cool that August day, almost sweater weather. Thick layers of stratus clouds stretched out overhead but my boys, ages eight and four, didn't seem to notice. With their little blue suitcases clutched tightly in hand, they bubbled with excitement as they climbed the steps of the magnificent hotel in beautiful Cape May.

It was the first time they would see the ocean, the first time any of us had visited the Jersey Shore. Even the three-hour drive from our Maryland home had been an adventure. My husband Jeff and I hurried to keep up with our sons, relishing their delight. But beneath it all, we both knew that the purpose of this long weekend was far more sobering than we had let on.

We had come to Cape May to save our marriage.

It had started to unravel the year before, when a car accident on my way to work had re-ordered life for me. Things prior to that had been pretty stressful, too. Jeff and I were working opposite shifts, shuffling the boys back and forth to school and daycare, and I was going to class at night to finish my college degree. As a computer systems analyst, I was part of a team tasked with taking over some existing computer applications from another company. I disliked the work and didn't feel very good at it, not to mention that the company from which we were migrating the computer applications wasn't happy about the takeover. To say that it was a hostile work environment was an understatement.

Jeff was experiencing work complications of his own. He had just accepted a job at IBM as a third-shift computer operator and while we were thrilled with this new opportunity, third shift was taking a toll. Jeff scarcely slept, and when he was home, I wasn't. We talked just enough, it seemed, to juggle schedules. My car accident added a whole new layer of misery to our lives, and the attendant pain, surgeries, and doctor appointments often left me cranky.

As summer approached that year, I was depressed and worried. We had somehow fallen into a rut and were fast becoming a statistic. Having wed shortly after high school, we'd had our first son by the time we were twenty. I knew many teenage marriages didn't survive, but I'd never before envisioned that outcome for us.

It was Jeff who came up with the idea of traveling to the shore. He'd heard about Cape May from a friend and booked us a room. "A lifesaver," this friend of his had said. "You'll think you've gone back in time."

As I stood on the hotel's expansive front porch, I couldn't help feeling skeptical. The going-back-in-time part I could definitely see. The hotel was an elegant lady dating back to the 1800s. It boasted shared bathrooms, no phones or TVs, and no air-conditioning. We were also required to dress up for meals, which convened at set times and with assigned tables that we shared with other hotel guests, most of whom were senior citizens. My skepticism grew.

But there is something magical about the Jersey Shore. And even though the next day dawned cloudy again, little by little the sun began to peek through. It was as if the present was unfurling, wrapping me within its sweet embrace. There was no past and no future. There was only this moment, this hour.

Maybe it was the sea that ultimately moved me. Like the hand of God caressing my ravaged soul, its ebb and flow seemed to cry out for transformation. Every ray of light struck me anew, every deep breath expanded my heart. The very salt air whispered revival.

Maybe it was the way one of the elderly women patted my hand at dinner. "In forty years, dear, you'll come back here and wonder where the time went." Her gentle words told me things that I am only now beginning to fathom. They told me that life is fleeting. They told me that the world can change in a heartbeat.

Maybe it was the joy my boys radiated at every turn, their little faces as bright as morning. Everything held fascination for them: the arcades of Wildwood, the sand castles we built, the incoming tide that tickled their tiny toes. Their smiles reminded me that the bond between parent and child is eternal and so very precious.

Maybe it was the way Jeff said, "How can we make things better?" and really listened as I explained how trapped I'd started to feel. He confessed that he sometimes felt trapped too.

He asked me about my dreams and I told him I'd always wanted to be a writer. "Let's see if we can make that work," he said.

It was also there, beneath those Jersey Shore skies, with the sun finally achieving full breakthrough, that we vowed to recapture another long-held dream: to adopt a child from a foreign country. In Jeff's soft brown eyes I suddenly saw that change was doable. I saw that he still believed in love. He still believed in me.

That was thirty years ago.

As I look back now, I marvel at how we could ever have been at that impasse. Our marriage today is strong. I like to say it is Jersey Shore strong. The changes we crafted back then took some implementing, but steadily we set them in motion. Jeff soon left third shift but stayed at IBM, and he has just retired from a distinguished thirty-year career. Nearly two years after our Cape May outing, we adopted not only one child, but two, five-year-old twin girls from Korea. And as for me, well, I'm still plugging away at the writing thing.

There's just something about the Jersey Shore. I was a stranger the first time I visited yet somehow it became part of my family, part of my heart. It is in my blood, in my very sinew. I can still hear my sons' voices calling on the sea breeze, as tender and free as the memories we made. I can still feel the beach, smell it, and every time I imagine it, I am at peace.

Yes, we went to Cape May to save our marriage, and over that long August weekend, we did just that—and so much more. The Jersey Shore promises we made have lasted us a lifetime.

~Theresa Sanders

The Café de l'Espérance

Life is either a daring adventure or nothing.
~Helen Keller

I stood in my raincoat with my two suitcases in front of a locked courtyard gate in the 9th Arrondissement. The airport taxi vanished, leaving me alone on the deserted street. The code I had been given before I left Los Angeles didn't unlock the big double doors of the eighteenth-century apartment building. In a moment of panic, I wondered what I was doing. Was I completely crazy after a year of widowhood?

Just then a woman wearing a bright silk scarf over her dark winter coat opened the courtyard door. *"Bonjour! Alors, entrez!"* she said pleasantly before setting off down the street toward the pealing bells of the church of Notre-Dame-de-Lorette.

I propped open the heavy green door with one bag, hauled the rest of my gear over the threshold, and entered the courtyard, feeling a bit like Alice entering Wonderland.

When I got off the minuscule cage elevator on the third floor, Madame de Chardon waited in her open doorway. Madame, small-boned and elegant, with a pink artificial flower pinned to her chignon, surveyed my abundant American belongings now filling up the small entry hall of her apartment.

"Bienvenue, Madame Magnus," she said. *"Je suis enchantée de faire votre connaissance."*

We shook hands firmly up and down exactly twice in the pre-scribed French way.

"Would you like a cup of tea?" she asked in French as she opened the curtained glass parlor doors. While she clanged pots in the kitchen, I perched on the drab flowered sofa and studied the portraits hanging from picture rails and the porcelain boxes balanced on lace doilies on Directoire marble tables. Madame brought in tea and packaged cookies on a tarnished silver tray.

To me the apartment was very French, and therefore charming. It was over two hundred years old with high ceilings and marble fireplaces in each room. Exposed pipes and conduits ran every which way, clotheslines draped with laundry ran under the ceilings, and dusty curtains hid God-knew-what in every niche and corner. I didn't care that a thin layer of grime covered everything. I was in Paris.

Madame indicated that I should not make myself at home in the rest of the apartment. I noticed the telephone in the dining room had a padlock on it, not that I had anyone to call.

The stale cookies had left a dusty taste in my mouth, so I went across the street to sit over a crème on the sidewalk of the Café de l'Espérance, now open and filling up with after-Mass and instead-of-Mass habitués. My ears ached from listening to them all speak French. I stirred my coffee and looked around with amazement. Here I was, at forty-three, suddenly on my own in Paris, transported as if by magic. There was no place on earth I would rather be, nothing else I would rather be doing. It had been three years since I had had a moment like this. Los Angeles was far away, and so was the despair and depression I had lived with for so long.

A year ago, at Christmas, Jack had been in a cancer clinic in Tijuana, the hospital of last resort. The Mexican doctors took him off morphine so that the organic herbal treatments they prescribed would be more effective. He suffered the agonies of withdrawal—sweats, hallucinations of snakes coming out of the walls, enormous pain. Even so, throughout his torment he had been uncomplaining and optimistic and brave.

My first Christmas as a widow I didn't feel like celebrating or doing anything. As soon as I would come home from work, I would go straight to bed. Adam and Jason, my sons, were still at home, and they didn't much feel like celebrating either. My medication for depression only caused my insides trouble and changed the taste of food, so that I had completely lost my appetite for food too. My appetite for living had left me long ago.

I tried to make a New Year's resolution, but I couldn't think of anything I wanted to do in my life, let alone in the coming year. I knew that each day was a mountain to climb. I had no wishes, or desires or hope, apart from freeing myself from the loneliness and pain.

Finally on New Year's Day as I lay in bed, too down to get up, I realized there was something I wanted: to learn French. My love affair with France and all things French had begun with my first ballet lessons as a child. I had been thrilled to travel to France with Jack several times and to communicate there, however ineptly.

Then I had utilized my three years of high school French. Maybe now was the time to do something serious about learning the language. Jack's premature death made me more conscious than ever of not waiting for "someday."

Linda and Steve, my Francophile neighbors next door, lent me a stack of brochures from language schools in France. I picked one in Paris. On January 2nd I phoned my travel agent, and then I requested time off from my job at the city library. Before I left for Paris, against the advice of my doctor, who was perhaps afraid I might drown myself in the Seine, I threw away the antidepressants that made food taste like rusty airplane parts. If I was going to France, I was going to taste the food and drink. The kids were glad that at last I wanted to do something besides cry in bed.

And now two weeks later, here I was, alone in this city of my dreams, getting ready to start school the next day. Sometimes magic can be performed with only a wish and a credit card.

After my coffee, I crossed the street again, and this time when I punched in the code the gate opened.

The next morning, euphoric to have someplace in Paris that expected me, I joined the Monday-morning throng hurrying down the steps of the Place Saint-Georges Métro station. The Parisians riding the train to Concorde in elegant suits looked vastly different from the T-shirt and jogging-clad public transport commuters of Los Angeles. I wore jeans and boots and a black leather jacket like the student I had suddenly become.

French school was the right prescription for what ailed me. No one knew me or my problems. All I had to worry about was my homework. I could be happy for a little while just being me, whoever that was. I hoped that in two weeks my French would be, if not perfect, more Parisian, more French!

Suddenly I had an appetite. For the first time in years, there were pleasurable things to do, learn, see, feel, taste. As I stepped on the train, I felt myself crave.

~Cherie Magnus

64

Finding Hope after Despair

There is no such cozy combination as man and wife.
~Menander

I was a lucky woman. I found the man, companion, friend, soul mate, nurturer and buddy whose mission in life was to make me happy. He pampered me, lavished me with affection, cheered me on, and tried to make the world a little brighter.

We were together twenty-two years. We thrived being together. We shopped, cooked, laughed, traveled, argued, embraced, loved, and planned for the future with our six-year-old son, a miracle child born after years of fertility issues.

After a near-fatal car accident and subsequent medical problems that tortured him for three years, Harry died in the hospital. He was fifty-seven.

These months since, I have felt more alone, more terrified and more devastated then I could ever have imagined. The sadness of our shattered dreams has been enough to make me double over in physical and emotional pain.

So where does the hope come in? I've tried to create a support system to help me through the darkest days and nights. While I do not have family members living nearby, and my husband was an only child whose parents died many years ago, I do have several amazing friends. They helped me plan the funeral and opened their hearts to my son and me.

When tragedy strikes, it is easy to see all of the ways that life doesn't make sense. I asked myself hard questions: Are my son and I really a family? Where do we fit in? How did I end up as a single mom? Will I ever be happy again and laugh aloud with that deep down belly laugh that comes out of you when life feels really great?

I honestly do not have the answers to all of these questions. But I do know that small kindnesses go a long way when life feels hopeless. There have been children and adults who have reached out to my son and me, invited us to join their families, made sure we were safe during the recent hurricane, and repeatedly told us they were there for us. They say that in times of crises, you find out who your true friends are. And I believe this is true.

I have discovered that there is no right or wrong way to grieve. I have spoken to rabbis, hospital chaplains and other clergy members, grief counselors and psychologists, as well as recent widows and widowers. The theme is the same — do what feels right for you.

Some people plaster the house with photos to remember their loved one. Others remove the photos. Some pack away the clothes, shoes and other personal items and give them to charity or to relatives or sell them on eBay. Others leave the rooms exactly the way they were.

Some people look for smells, sights, sounds, any traces of the ones they loved and lost, like sleeping in an old sweatshirt or smelling their cologne. Others try to keep themselves so busy that they don't have time to think.

I will never stop thinking about Harry and missing all the ways he cared for me. But I do seek out his traits — his kindness, his ability to help people he loved, his willingness to "fix" everything he could, his endless love for research and gadgets, the way he embraced fatherhood later in life, and many more. And I am beginning to see many of those traits in my young son, and I hope they will continue to develop as he becomes a man.

It has been nearly ten months since I lost the love of my life. I am strong some days, and weak others. Some days I can cry the moment

I hear one of our favorite love songs. Once in a while I am able to watch one of our favorite movies alone.

I know that my life will never be the same, and that I will never get over losing Harry. But I do know that in Harry's memory and for my own sake and the sake of my son, I have to find the rainbows and sunshine. Smile more, watch the autumn leaves fall from the trees, create new traditions, and explain the old traditions to my son. I have to find a new life for us. It is what Harry would have wanted. He even told me so, and my son and I deserve it.

~Debra Wallace Forman

65

The Joy I Choose to See

It took me a long time not to judge myself through someone else's eyes.
~Sally Field

"What happened, Mommy?" my six-year-old son asked. I was on my knees, at the bottom of the stairway, groping for the clean laundry I'd spilled on the floor.

"Nothing, honey. Don't worry, I just had an accident."

That wasn't the first time I'd misjudged and tripped on the steps while carrying a basket of folded laundry to the second floor. Unable to see my surroundings, tripping, falling, or running into objects had become the norm for me.

Retinitis pigmentosa, the incurable, hereditary retinal disease that had stolen my sight only two years prior, had invaded my life with no warning.

But what attacked my peace was my inability to perform simple tasks. Even the effort of matching socks needed more patience than I had. Burning my fingers while cooking on the stove increased my frustration. I lamented my fate. And how I wished that self-pity could be washed out like the ketchup stains on the boys' shirts.

"Let me help you with the chores," my husband asked over and over again.

But what would I do if he took over the care of the house too? I didn't want to feel useless.

Being blind erased my ability to perform so many needed tasks. Driving our four-, six-, and eight-year-old sons to soccer practice, to birthday parties. Shopping for them, checking their homework, even buying groceries had to be delegated to others.

What a helpful family I had. But no one could come to my aid when it came to fighting the feelings of worthlessness. Nor could anyone calm my desperation or help me climb out of my dark prison and feel worthwhile, or bring back meaning and let me live with significance.

A life of gloom was all I could see. Often while the house was silent, I sat on the sofa with a wrinkled tissue in hand.

One evening, while I dried dinner dishes beside the sink, my eight-year-old son Jason and his friend watched TV in the family room. "My Mom is blind," Jason said, "but she does everything like she can see."

"Like she can see?" I heard that comment loud and clear in my heart. My son believed in me, he trusted in my care, and he didn't feel deprived because his mom was sightless.

I was the one who had put limitations on myself. I was the one who saw my blindness as a disability.

Possibilities soon filled my head. What if I got a job? What if I changed my life? What if I tried something despite my blindness?

The secret desire to work outside the home stirred excitement. A job somewhere, anywhere would be a start.

But where would I begin? Before losing my sight, I had earned my bachelor's degree. But I had no skills or experience. Who would hire a blind person with no skills? I chided myself to stop that thinking. That was the first step, the crucial step—to hold any negative, destructive thoughts captive.

Since Spanish is my native language, I called an interpreting company asking if they needed interpreters. To my delight, they said yes. And they invited me to take a test—an oral test.

That very next day, the secretary called, "We're so impressed with the results that we want to send you to the Immigration and Naturalization Court tomorrow morning for your first assignment."

Wow! Those words nearly made me jump with joy. I'd actually passed the test. They trusted in my abilities to perform. Hearing that encouragement sparked a passion.

Using the white cane, a method of walking that had caused shame and embarrassment before, also changed. The cane became my best friend the next day. I exited the taxi, and swinging the cane back and forth, I made my way to the entrance of the court buildings. And to my relief, a kind person offered to help me find my way to a specific courtroom.

I interpreted basic levels of court proceedings. Maybe I wasn't worthless. I managed to do a good job in court. Maybe I wasn't useless. I was hired for more interpretations in other court proceedings. Maybe I wasn't unproductive. All the doubts about my inabilities melted away.

"Okay, guys," I called out to my sons. "You have homework and I have studying to do too. Let's get to work."

We all learned. I practiced, took courses to sharpen my skills, and using material in audio, I memorized lists of legal terminology. As my vocabulary increased, so did my confidence.

More determined than ever, I took the plunge and learned to operate a computer with software that reads the screen. As my fingers danced on the keyboard, I began to write. First I wrote short articles, devotionals, and then my story. I divided it into chapters, gave it a title, and it became my first book.

The inspiration it brought to readers answered the question I'd asked years prior. I was indeed contributing something to touch others, to inspire and encourage them.

More opportunities came my way. Folks asked me to share the details of my life. This prompted a career as an inspirational speaker. I was delighted to travel to speaking engagements across the U.S.

Blindness didn't have to define me, determine my future, or dictate my destiny. Lack of sight didn't mean lack of passion.

I still can't see what's in front of me, but I can see with my heart where I'm going.

~Janet Perez Eckles

66

Mirror, Mirror

To forgive is to set a prisoner free and discover that the prisoner was you.
~Lewis B. Smedes

I sat across from Dean Wilson—feeling alone and paralyzed in the seat as I patiently watched him read through my résumé and application. I distracted myself by focusing on the man in front of me. I noticed his wrinkled khaki trousers, ancient argyle sweater, classic professorial tweed jacket, and faded, worn-out sneakers—topped off with a straggly, unpretentious Einstein-esque hairstyle. Yet, despite his frumpy appearance, I heard compassion, kindness, and respect in his voice.

"Thank you for your interest in our counseling vacancy."

Then, he hesitated before completing his thought, "Although you have great credentials, honestly, I can't hire you at this time."

Unable to speak, I mustered an unenthusiastic but appreciative nod as I stood up, shook his hand, and headed for the door. Exasperated, I gained my composure, turned around, faced him, and said "Dean Wilson, I've been job hunting for over nine months—always with the same results. Would you mind sharing your reason for not hiring me?"

Sure," he graciously replied. "Your credentials are great but your level of obesity indicates that you have emotional issues that will diminish your effectiveness as a counselor."

Although his words felt like glass splinters in my heart, his empathetic candor left no lingering doubt—my obesity overshadowed my employability. When I returned home, I located the dusty scale that I had conveniently pushed into the back corner of my closet; I stepped on it thinking that I probably weighed about 200 pounds. As the dial on the scale teetered to its final resting number, the figure jumped up and slapped me in the face—298 pounds—two pounds short of 300!

Denial crept into my mind as I thought, "This scale is old. It must be wrong!"

Luckily, I fought the urge to buy a replacement scale and decided instead to take an honest look at myself in the mirror. I gasped for breath as I suddenly realized I had never actually acknowledged the obese woman who now stared back at me.

For several days I struggled to make sense of my situation. And then I had a shocking, life-changing realization: I was addicted to food! Sadly, I had given control of my life over to food, making it my emotional escape. As I swallowed a particular food, I literally swallowed and ignored healthy human emotions, stress, and even depression. The more I ate, the more I buried those emotions, creating my dependence on and obsession with food.

Despite my newfound awareness I felt confused, ashamed, and angry—mostly angry. Even though my training taught me that anger erroneously seeks to blame, I still wanted to blame someone—anyone—for my current dilemma. I quickly decided to blame my mother, for she too was obese and, therefore, responsible for teaching me poor eating habits and modeling inappropriate coping strategies that resulted in my emotional dependence on food.

Initially, blaming her felt good—a way of venting my anger, avoiding the truth, and sidestepping my own responsibility. Sometimes I shudder when I think of just how easily I could've continued victimizing myself in the never-ending blame-shifting game. However, my mother lived 2,000 miles from me.

So at some point I asked myself, "What can she do in the present to make my situation 'right'?"

Thankfully, I soon realized that blame shifting accomplished nothing but rendered me powerless to create the change I so passionately wanted.

So, I quickly turned my anger and shame onto myself until I realized that blaming myself without forgiving myself was just as futile and destructive as blaming my mother. In the beginning, though, I didn't realize just how powerful and crucial self-forgiveness was to winning my losing battle. Somehow, though, I instinctively knew that self-forgiveness meant loving myself enough to break my dependence on food.

Breaking this dependence also required diligence, for the process was slow, arduous, and painful, both physically and emotionally. I counted calories and walked—initially only for fifteen minutes at a time, for my arms and legs rubbed together, chaffed, bled, and then scabbed. In twenty-four months, I also learned to distinguish the difference between true physical hunger and emotional hunger as I grasped an important lesson: If I wasn't physically hungry, eating wasn't a solution. The solution was, however, embracing my fears and becoming vulnerable long enough to examine my emotional triggers—those catalysts that could easily put me back on the compulsive-addictive cycle of dependence.

During my two-year journey, I lost 165 pounds but gained a deeper, healthier appreciation of the value of forgiveness; forgiveness minimized my fears—relinquishing their control over me. In that sense, forgiveness eventually led to understanding; understanding led to freedom; freedom led to remedy; and remedy led to hope.

Hope keeps me strong as I look in the mirror and admit to myself, "I'm Sara and I'm a food addict."

Saying this statement is a gentle reminder of who I am, where I've been, and what I could easily revert back to if I didn't remain mindful of the many lessons I learned during my journey of self-discovery.

~Sara Etgen-Baker

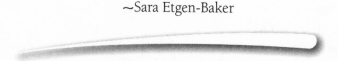

Life Reignited

When we lose one blessing, another is often most unexpectedly given in its place.
~C.S. Lewis

Ctober 19 started out like any other morning. A single mom, I rushed about the house getting my son and myself ready for work and daycare. I remember putting on my favorite pair of jeans even though I should have worn something a bit dressier for work. As we headed out the door that morning I tripped over some dinosaur toys strewn across the entryway. I told my son that when we got home that night we were going to have to really clean up the house so we didn't break a leg on all those toys. I dropped him off at daycare and headed to work.

I hadn't been at work ten minutes when the call came. My house was on fire. My boss rushed me to my home. As we turned onto my street, all I could see were fire trucks and police cars. We parked half a block away and I ran up the street. I reached my driveway to see the thick black smoke rolling out of my house. A fireman was chopping holes in my roof with an axe.

I remember officers talking with me, neighbors offering hugs, friends arriving, the fire chief explaining to me what would happen next, and the smell of the smoke.

Hours passed as I stood in the driveway and watched the firefighters work. They chopped holes in my home and threw burnt items out the windows.

As I watched I started to laugh. I didn't laugh because house fires are particularly funny. I laughed because I had told my son we had to clean the house tonight and now that seemed like an impossible task. I laughed because I was wearing my favorite jeans and we all know how hard it is to find a great pair of jeans. But most of all I laughed because I had to two options in that moment.

I could give in to the pain and cry, or I could choose to find the joy and laughter in the darkest of situations. I made the choice in that moment, in my driveway, surrounded by smoke, to laugh. I made the decision to find the positive and focus on that.

The fire allowed my son and me to rebuild our lives. Our lives were spared that day. We had the chance to start over fresh, to create the best life possible for us. The possessions that I thought meant so much were gone. But the things that really mattered in our lives stayed intact. Joy, gratitude, laughter—those things can't be burnt!

In the weeks after the fire, we were blessed by the generosity of friends and strangers alike. Our new apartment was bare, but our hearts were full and we were happy.

I learned that you really need very little to survive. Instead of eating at a kitchen table, we had lots of picnics on the living room floor. All the toys my son had before were barely missed.

Instead, we spent more time playing outside together, reading, and listening to music. All those knickknacks that I thought I had to have were replaced, but only with things I truly loved or that my son and I created together.

In our new life, we banned excess. When you each have only a few outfits, it makes laundry day much easier. Since I didn't have to spend so much time picking up the house, I actually had time to do some of the things I loved again. I sat and read a great book. I created art pieces to hang in our new place. I started getting a full night's sleep every night.

The fire simplified my life. The power that "stuff" had over me before was gone. My heart was more open and my mind was calmer.

Instead of just creating a new home I was able to create a new life. A life that I designed from scratch. This new life was filled with laughter, creativity, fun, gratitude, and very little stuff.

The fire lit a spark in me that had been out for a very long time. My passion for life was reignited and I was ready to live again. With my son beside me, and wearing my favorite jeans, I was able to laugh in the face of tragedy.

~Jessie Wagoner

A Long Hard Fight

Life is very interesting... in the end, some of your greatest pains
become your greatest strengths.
~Drew Barrymore

My friend died on April 13th. I remember sitting in that dirty bathroom stall with her, passing a pipe filled with the same evil that took her life. One day we were lost, struggling, and addicted, yet determined to change. Within hours, however, my friend, who I will call Serenity here, lost her chance.

It only took one hit for me to become addicted. Serenity took a little longer, but within months she was a full-blown addict. We wore the same clothes for days. Showers were a privilege, and food was revolting. Glass shards took the place of our meals, our mothers, our hearts and our souls.

We weren't forced into this life. We weren't born into poverty. We had families that would die for us. We had everything we wanted.

Our lives gave the impression of being picture-perfect, and we kept the tormenting thoughts and evil flashbacks well hidden. We believed nobody would understand, nobody except our pipe, and the thick white clouds of smoke that filled our lungs. Addiction pushed us out of our homes and into the back seat of the man with the powdered devil. School was replaced with drug binges and the temporary relief of the high. We lost contact with our families and with our true selves.

On April 13th, we were two very sick teenage girls. We had been up for days, and Serenity's demeanor was not normal. She passed up hitting the pipe, and talked about her family instead. I could tell she needed to go home. The drug was becoming less and less effective. The hateful thoughts grew and our self-respect died. We weren't meant for this life.

We brushed our knotted hair and put on our cleanest clothes. Serenity was the first to be dropped off. We said our usual goodbye and I love you.

Not much later I arrived at my parents' home. I knocked tentatively on the door. My mother's relief-stricken face appeared. No judgment. No anger. Her embrace was the most comforting I had ever felt. My father's eyes quickly filled with tears the moment he saw me, his broken, sickly-thin, addicted baby girl. His embrace told me, "I will protect you forever."

I spent the next few hours getting reacquainted with a home filled with love. I lay on my bed, staring into the familiar, innocent face of my childhood dog, the same innocence I had possessed before the drugs.

The telephone rang. The call was for me. It was Serenity's mother.

I expected a long speech. I expected hateful words. I wish that was what I heard. Instead, I heard cries of agony. "She's dead."

I was filled with a sorrow so deep it literally hurt. My best friend, the only person who ever understood me, was no longer here. My heart shattered. Hours later, there was another knock on the door.

I thought it was Serenity when I first saw her. She wasn't dead? Was she really right here? But it was her sister. She told me how her sister, my best friend, had lost her life. After arriving home, Serenity had smoked a stash of meth she had hidden months before. While under the influence of that poison, she pulled the trigger of a small pistol.

People often ask me why I think my friend killed herself. I always respond with the same answer. She didn't take her life. The drugs did.

People thought the loss of my best friend would end my drug

use immediately. But I thought giving up the crystal would mean giving up the only friend I had left. I don't remember much of the next few months, other than countless meetings with my drug dealer and sleepless nights spent weeping. I wasn't really living at all. The only thing keeping me on this planet was remembering the tears of Serenity's mother, tears I would never want my own mom to shed.

Then it happened. I felt myself being poked and prodded with needles. I could hear the sobs, so familiar, sobs of a mother losing her child. I heard an incessant ringing, and beeps so loud they hurt.

A male voice filled the room: "Toxicology report is back, ma'am. Your daughter has overdosed on crystal meth."

My mother screamed.

I left the hospital nine days later and immediately checked myself into a rehab center. I had been to one before, but I had never been willing to actually change. During my time there, there were dramatic ups and downs, but eventually I began to blossom again.

It's been over two years now since I lost my best friend. Her death was one of the biggest hardships of my life. She taught me so much during her time here on earth, but her death taught me even more. I've been sober for a year now, and I can honestly say I've never felt better.

My mother still worries, but her worry no longer consumes her. I've come to accept and love the person I am.

~Jeanette Rubin, age 17

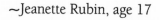

Two Sisters

Nothing in life is to be feared. It is only to be understood.
~Marie Curie

"Y ou may NOT put down your chalk; you may NOT return to your desk until you have correctly solved the math problem!" bellowed Sister. Once again I would be the reason my row of students lost the math relay.

This scenario played out again and again throughout my parochial school years in the 1950's. Math to me was a foreign language from another planet. No amount of study or tutoring could make me see its logic.

Being math-challenged caused me much verbal humiliation and shame. One Sister in particular was merciless in her attacks. After that exceptionally traumatic school year my parents transferred me to public school.

Unfortunately, those feelings of low self-esteem and inadequacy followed me through college and into adulthood. Trying new things and taking risks, even for fun, were still out of my grasp because of my fear of failure.

Marriage and motherhood were wonderful and gratifying additions to my life in the years to come, but I still lacked the self-confidence to fully enjoy life. Seeking therapy was the biggest step forward in my healing.

As I grew in confidence, I decided to find my parochial school principal. Finding her and beginning a correspondence with her was the beginning of a miracle. She not only remembered me, she apologized for the torment I had endured at the hands of the other Sister. She then asked if I could find it in my heart to pray for the other Sister, as she was terribly ill. I did. Time passed, and the notes from Sister became fewer and then stopped. Worried, I phoned the retirement center to learn she was very ill and had been moved to a nursing facility for retired nuns. Continuing to write to her even though I knew she couldn't respond became my gift to her.

Once again time passed and one day I received an e-mail from a nun visiting the same nursing home as my former principal. She introduced herself as a friend of Sister's and said she had noticed the cards and letters from me. She was interested in me because her own sister, also a retired nun, lived in the same facility. Her reason for writing was to ask if I knew her sister.

The letters of her name jumped from the computer screen into every cell of my body! There in black and white was the name of the abusive nun from my childhood.

Paralyzed, unable to speak, my brain could not take in what my eyes were seeing. This could not be!

It was three days before I was able to respond to this email. "Yes, I knew her, she was my fifth grade teacher," were the only words in my e-mail.

Several days later, mustering the courage to write more, I asked about her sister and her life as a teacher. It was interesting to learn she only taught grade school several years, was sent back to school, earned two PhD degrees, spoke five languages fluently, and taught at the college level in the U.S., Mexico and Peru. She was a brilliant woman who just could not teach children. These words were like balm on an open wound.

Beginning a correspondence with my former teacher was difficult at first, but got easier. She couldn't write back because of severe Parkinson's disease, but her sister was the go between for us. Now there were two nuns I was writing to in the same facility, my principal AND the abusive nun!

Here were two elderly, sick women, their careers over, nearing the end of their lives, and here was I, wanting so much to become a happier, healthier person, creating new ways of thinking and feeling, in addition to letting go of the past.

Crocheting two afghans, collecting class photos and mementos, booking a flight to the East Coast, I began the healing journey of a lifetime! To say I was not terrified would be a lie, but I was excited for the chance to try and heal my past.

Heading east with mixed feelings, there was no turning back. I would see this through to the end no matter what.

My principal was no longer the lively, intellectual, whirling dervish she had once been, but she had the same kind face and smile. Over lunch, we shared old times and enjoyed the books and mementos I brought along. Especially enjoyable were the memories of the operettas and plays she conducted. She was a wonderful musician.

The afghan I made for her was the perfect color for her room and she gratefully wrapped it around herself. Talking about both our lives became as easy as talking to a dear friend. Embracing her as I said goodbye, I marveled at the delicate, lovely woman I beheld even though her mind was beginning to fail.

Standing in the hallway outside my former fifth-grade teacher's room, saying a silent prayer that I would bear up through the anxiety, I stepped into the room. I wanted to see with my own eyes that she was just an old, sick woman who could no longer hurt me. At first, her steely gaze nearly stopped my heart. But she recognized me and then she grinned from ear to ear and her outstretched arms bid me to come to her bedside. Approaching with her afghan (which turned out to be the perfect color for her room too), I sat down and began showing her photos and mementos from school. She had a fabulous memory for details in the photos. She also told me about her years of teaching college and how much she loved her students.

Suddenly she stopped talking, and rested her hands in her lap with her head down. There were tears streaming down her cheeks as her eyes pleaded for my forgiveness. She opened her arms to me as I leaned forward to be enfolded in love by the woman I had feared so long.

Sister then told me my class was her first after she became a nun. There were forty-five students in the class and her instructions from the Mother Superior at the convent were to maintain complete control over every student, all day, every day, no matter what. She revealed she had no idea how to help with my math block other than to (scare) it into me.

She also told me that she was more afraid of me and the other students than we could ever have been of her. With this new revelation, I sank deeper into her arms and we laughed and cried together as both our hearts began to mend.

Both sisters are gone now, but my miracle journey of healing continues to this day. To be set free from the bonds of fear and to receive love from someone who I thought was incapable of love has been one of the greatest blessings of my life.

I can now smile when I think of the two Sisters, and I know they are smiling at me too.

~Ann Michener Winter

Reboot Your Life

Listen to Your Friends

70

The Year of Exploration

You can't be brave if you've only had wonderful things happen to you.
~Mary Tyler Moore

Touretta Lynn's School of Hard Knocks was no joke. My hands trembled as I double-knotted the laces on my white roller skates and tightened the throatlatch on my helmet. I raised my eyes to the dozen or so heavily-inked women gliding around the cement track. Though no two women were dressed exactly the same, there was a semblance of a uniform—ripped T-shirts, black fishnet stockings, and spandex shorts so tiny they'd make marathon runners blush. The women's expressions were also uniformly grim as they deftly crossed their skates on the turns, then pumped their arms to speed down the straightaways.

A heavy metal door slammed behind me, and Naptown Roller Girls Coach Sin Lizzie entered the Warehouse Lair. She wore blue nursing scrubs, and the blood-stain resistant fabric wasn't lost on me. At least she probably knew CPR and how to stitch up an open head wound. In a sport where the athletes adopt pseudonyms like Sandra Day O'Clobber and Nancy Drewblood, her medical training would be in high demand.

I peeled myself off the bench and took a moment to get my balance. Then I wobbled across the cavernous warehouse to join the check-in line. Stapled to the plywood wall to my right was a poster from the movie *Whip It*. Actress Ellen Page leapt over a fallen skater with a look of fierce determination on her face. My stomach flip-flopped, and I gulped.

The girl in front of me in line pivoted on fluorescent wheels that matched the hot pink streaks in her hair.

"Last week was brutal," she said, and I forced my gaze from the full sleeve tattoo on her arm to her freckled face. "I heard three girls puked."

"It's my first day," I admitted, fidgeting with my elbow pads.

The girl studied my 105-pound beanpole frame, gaunt arms, and sunken cheeks. She wished me luck and turned away.

I didn't tell her I used to be a kickboxer. I didn't tell her I used to have another fifteen pounds of pure muscle from jumping rope, working the heavy bag, shadow boxing, and cranking out pushups, sit-ups, and squats by the hundreds. I didn't tell her how I used to relish pushing my body to the brink of exhaustion, high on the thrill of hitting and getting hit. I didn't tell her, but I wanted to. Not like she'd have believed me anyway. I barely believed it myself anymore.

When I reached the front of the line, Sin Lizzie peered at me over her clipboard.

"Name?" she said.

Dogs can smell fear. Dogs and this woman. I forced myself to meet her gaze.

"Brass Nicoles," I said. "Reporting for duty." I was tempted to salute.

She handed me a waiver, which I signed without reading. Then I joined the rest of the trainees on the track and braced myself for the unknown, ready to conquer my fear.

It'd been four years since I'd graduated from a top-ten business school and landed a marketing job with "upward mobility." By twenty-five, I was my company's go-to creative powerhouse and had been accepted to a prestigious evening master's degree program. In whatever time remained, I laced up my gloves and transformed into a 120-pound, hard-ass Muay Thai kickboxer. For a while, I'd been able to do it all. I was promoted, got straight A's, and excelled at the gym. The more I juggled, the prouder I was.

Then, one morning, I walked into a coffee shop and was blindsided by my first panic attack. The experience was terrifying and left me profoundly shaken. The attacks grew more frequent, overtaking me anywhere, anytime, with no warning. It would be months before I received a definitive diagnosis: Acute Anxiety Disorder.

With the news came shame and self-loathing more debilitating than the attacks themselves. From the moment I rolled out of bed in the morning to the time I curled back under my covers at night, my only goal was to keep the panic attacks at bay. I lost my appetite and survived on protein shakes and dried fruit. I almost dropped out of grad school and nearly resigned my job. After months of steady decline, I made the heartbreaking decision to quit kickboxing. Emotionally and physically exhausted, I was in self-preservation mode.

I spent the next year getting back to basics. No more skipped meals, appetite or not. No more late nights at the office or doubling my grad school course load. No more skimping on sleep. But as the year drew to a close, I couldn't think of a single adventure or accomplishment that made me proud. Granted, I was slightly healthier and more functional. But I didn't recognize this girl either. She wasn't the least bit interesting. And if my own life didn't interest me, what progress had I really made?

So the next day, I did something drastic. I formed a steering committee of five close friends to help me confront my anxiety and rebuild my shattered psyche. I tasked them with issuing me monthly challenges that would test me in every way—challenges entirely outside my control that I vowed to complete no matter what. I called my experiment The Year of Exploration and started a blog so friends could follow along.

During the twelve months that followed, I tackled more than twenty committee-mandated challenges, as well as several of my own. I endured the Naptown Roller Girl's brutal training camp and learned the art of curling, sailing, and fantasy football. I visited new churches and begrudgingly took up running. I closed down my first bar and created a piece of abstract art with Tombi, a 10,000-pound African elephant. I even agreed to a series of committee-mandated blind dates (and nearly broke up with my steering committee in the process). I learned to redefine success and unearthed my will to live in the strangest of places.

It wasn't easy. I considered quitting every day, but I didn't. I still suffered brutal panic attacks, but I lived. I got frustrated, tired, and overwhelmed. But I persevered. No matter what my committee—and my life—threw at me, I didn't break. Maybe I wasn't a weak, worthless failure after all. Maybe I was a survivor.

When the year came to a close, I stood in front of sixty friends and family to complete my final challenge—a live reading from the memoir I'd been writing about my experiences. I've never been prouder of myself than I was that night.

Shortly thereafter, my friend Sarah invited me to a yoga retreat in Costa Rica. I felt a familiar pang of panic. What if I had an anxiety attack on the plane or in a foreign country? What if my disorder ruined my vacation and hers? Not to mention, I didn't know anyone else going on the trip, and I'd never done yoga. Then I thought about how far I'd come. I thought about all the times I'd been nearly paralyzed with fear, but pushed through it. I'd survived The Year of Exploration and emerged a stronger woman. I could do this. I took a deep breath.

"I'd love to," I said. "When do we leave?"

~Nicole K. Ross

71

Chicken Soup for the Soul

How Running Helped Me Heal

I've learned that finishing a marathon isn't just an athletic achievement.
It's a state of mind; a state of mind that says anything is possible.
~John Hanc

I t was a week after my mom had died, and I didn't know how to go on with life. Instead of going to work or the grocery store, I covered myself with blankets, wishing that I, too, could disappear. I was twenty-eight years old, and my mom had been fifty-four. It felt like I had been robbed.

So when I received an email from a friend about a 5K benefiting pancreatic cancer research, I ignored it. It seemed too close to the heart, as pancreatic cancer was the disease that had taken my mother away from me. But something about my friend's words—"I can help organize the whole thing"—stuck with me. I felt obliged to agree, if only to accept her support.

Together, my friends and I walked in honor of my mom. I tried to ignore the shirts of other participants, many bearing pictures of the loved ones they had lost. They were a painful reminder that my mom was no longer there for me to vent about life's everyday annoyances, or to see me get married or have kids.

My friends and I grabbed lunch after, and I actually enjoyed myself. But I immediately felt guilty.

In the weeks to come, I managed to reenter the world of the living.

I knew my mom would have wanted it that way. She was the type who never got defeated. In fact, when she was pregnant with me, the doctors had warned her that as a diabetic, she'd be risking her life to have me. "But I was going to have you, no matter what," Mom told me. It was this very spirit that helped me get by.

Besides, keeping myself busy was preferable to driving myself crazy with things like wondering what would have happened if I had had the chance to say goodbye. It haunted me that I had gone to work on her last day instead of taking time off to see her, although I knew she wasn't feeling well. But Mom had instilled a serious work ethic in me, discouraging me from ever taking a day off.

A year later, to my surprise, I signed up for the same 5K. It seemed like the right thing to do. I checked our team's website daily, feeling a twinge of pride each time a donation ticked up our total.

The majority of our team walked the 5K, but several members ran the 10K. When the race ended, I noticed the runners all had one thing in common: They were beaming. They made it look so rewarding—and effortless. I wanted in.

So I enrolled in a 10K two months later. Considering I could barely run a mile, it was ambitious. But my boyfriend and I devised a training plan so I wouldn't come in last. I followed it religiously and didn't let anything get in my way—not even a trip to San Francisco.

Running up and down the city's hills, I was flooded with memories. I had lived there after college and my mother had visited often. I passed Bloomingdale's, recalling the time she and I had gotten into a screaming brawl there, much to other shoppers' dismay. It had all started because my sister and I had a spat over the fact that I had been thirty minutes late meeting her somewhere. "Why can't you guys just get along?" Mom had asked. I turned on her, too.

I was about to beat myself up when I remembered what Mom had once said after her diagnosis. "I don't want you to feel guilty about anything." Her paper-thin hands had held me tightly. She knew I could be my own worst enemy, always eager to blame myself. A weight lifted from my shoulders. I ran with a surge of energy.

In the following months, I found myself laughing with friends again without feeling the remnants of guilt. And I was able to sleep without having nightmares about my mom's final moments. Life felt lighter.

When race day arrived, I gave it my all—not for myself, but for my mom—and for all she had taught me and continued to teach me. As I ran, whenever I felt like slowing down, I pictured her cheering me on, as she had done at all of my soccer games and recitals as a kid.

Crossing the finish line, I was filled with her love and a sense of peace. So much so that shortly thereafter I signed up for a half marathon.

~Kristin Julie Viola

72

A Journey of a Lifetime

Reduce the complexity of life by eliminating the needless wants of life,
and the labors of life reduce themselves.
~Edwin Way Teale

When Debbie turned forty she invited a bunch of us over to her house to celebrate. "Join me for Yoga and Chair Massages" read the invitation. I got the chair massages piece, and was really looking forward to it. At thirty-seven, I was developing chronic neck and back pain. For several months I sounded suspiciously like my grandfather as I groaned when I rose out of bed.

It was the yoga piece I did not get. Why yoga? It was a party after all and from what I knew, yoga meant we would be sitting still and breathing. As an avid runner and mother of three, living on the Main Line of Philadelphia, I didn't sit still much and couldn't see the purpose in it.

But Debbie was a dear friend and the first of my friends turning forty, so I went. I saw the yoga class as something to get through before I could move on to the massage and birthday cake.

As we gathered in Debbie's basement, the instructor, Julie, lowered the lights and asked each of us to sit on one of the mats that she had laid out side by side all over the floor. The room was warm from the heater. Candles on the casement window ledges surrounded the mats. The effect made me feel like I was stepping into a cocoon—would I emerge changed?

Still cynical, and convinced that my current fitness regimen of running four to five times a week would make this barely a workout, I sat on my mat. Though the guest next to me was only five inches away, it felt like we were miles apart.

Julie sat cross-legged at the front of the room and began guiding us through the warm-up. I closed my eyes and listened to her voice as she told us what body part to place where. I began to feel a peaceful warmth take over my body. I lost all awareness of those around me. Strangely, I began to experience a heightened sense of myself.

After the warm-up, we stood. As Julie continued, my breath moved in sync with my body. "Breathe in as you lift your leg up and breathe out as you place it behind you."

We picked up the pace. We moved seamlessly from pose to pose. I felt graceful and in tune with Julie's voice and my responses—nothing else. Though I was unaware of it at the time, the practice became quite strenuous. I began dripping with sweat and gladly accepted a towel from Julie.

In what seemed like a single breath, we settled into Sivasana, lying on our backs for final relaxation. On the mat, in my dark and peaceful space, I smiled. It was quite a different smile from the cynical one I had entered with.

I couldn't believe an hour had passed.

In that single hour, many things changed for me. I understood the power of taking time for myself, being present, and finding peace. I was left with the yearning to feel this way again and again. Before this moment, I wasn't even aware my life was out of balance. I should have seen the signs. My physical and mental exhaustion, my short temper with my children, the feeling of always rushing from activity to activity. I began to search for ways to find the peacefulness I felt in Debbie's basement again and again.

I started a regular yoga practice with Julie and I became hooked. I noticed physical changes first. I didn't sound quite like my grandfather when I rose out of bed each morning, and my runs no longer ended with me holding my lower back. I felt as if I were standing up taller.

I became more aware of when I could push a little harder, as well as when my tired body needed a rest.

Subtle but noticeable emotional changes began in my daily life. I felt gentler, and seemed to approach tense situations calmly. By slowing down, I found myself fully noticing and enjoying each activity. Without my constant focus on the goal, I began to see the beauty in the journey of each day.

As my personal yoga practice deepened, so did its effect on the rest of my family. I stopped trying to pack three to four activities into a single day, and instead tried to really enjoy one. We started to walk to the park instead of driving, telling stories as the path slowly wound towards our destination.

Perhaps the most profound impact was a decision my husband and I made about two years after I began practicing yoga. While I was undergoing tremendous personal change, Howard was stuck in a stressful and relentless surgical career at the University of Pennsylvania. The academic world was no longer insulated from the troubles emerging in healthcare, and the impact on my husband came in the form of increased operating schedules in multiple hospitals that translated into late nights, weekends, and the phone ringing twenty-four hours a day. He was a man who cherished being with his family and exercising, as well as working, yet it seemed he barely saw the former two for the latter.

Looking for a balanced life, he accepted a job offer and we moved our family to a beach community on the Jersey Shore. It was a bold, brave move, and we've never looked back.

Howard began his job and the kids settled into their new schools. I had embraced the yogic lifestyle and shared it with my family. I wanted to take it to the next level. As a teacher I could share what I'd gained from yoga—body, mind, and spirit—each and every day. I realized it was time to make formal what had been brewing for almost three years. I called up the local yoga studio and inquired about teacher training.

I became a yoga instructor and opened my own studio in the town we have now called home for seven years. I have been practicing yoga for almost ten years. (I know because Debbie called yesterday to make plans for her fiftieth!) When I think back on life before yoga, I do not chastise myself that I was so blind to the imbalances in my life at that time. I understand that yoga came to me when I needed it. I merely opened my eyes and accepted it.

Whether on or off my mat, I try to practice yoga each day. I've learned there is a reason it is called a practice. It is never perfected, and neither are we. Today, I simply try to accept the gifts my practice has allowed me to enjoy and look at each day as a new opportunity.

~Stacy Ross

73

What Would You Do?

Every day, take some time for yourself. Love yourself. Honor yourself.
Give priority to your physical, mental, and emotional wellness.
~Author Unknown

My preschooler began to chatter about starting kindergarten in the coming year. I sighed as we scouted for gym shoes with non-scuffing soles. She was growing up so fast.

I loved being a mom. It was all I had ever wanted to do my entire life. But now that I'd had my two little ones, I realized that being a full-time mom was only an option for a limited time. Eventually, they would be off to college and then my purpose would be fulfilled. That was the end. Until then my job was to sign permission slips and pass out lunches.

Was that really all I had to contribute to the world? What would I do with myself when I was no longer useful to my children? Would the next thirteen-plus years of my life revolve around me waiting for school to let out so I would have something to do?

These depressing thoughts whirled around in my brain throughout the next several days. I moped about the house doing my chores and chasing the children. Either as an effort to cheer me up or because he was afraid my sullen face might stay that way, my husband finally pushed me out the door to meet friends for coffee.

We mulled over the same topics as always. We chatted about all the typical young mom things—diapers, tantrums, how to sneak veggies into meatloaf, and mom groups. It was good banter, and I usually enjoyed it. But I couldn't shake the nagging feeling that one day our children would grow up and we'd be left without anything to say.

"If you could do anything, without cost, location, and education being factors, what would you do?" I asked.

The table went silent as everyone began to explore a question they had never dared ask themselves before. There was real enjoyment in examining our inner selves without limits. There was freedom in not having to subject our dreams to reality. The answers started pouring out—everything from being an accountant who loves working with numbers to a doctor who loves helping people heal. We learned so much about each other that evening. About who we really were and what we were really passionate about. We weren't being ungrateful or unrealistic about the lives we were living. We were acknowledging something that was deep inside us and igniting passions too long suppressed. Some of us even surprised ourselves at what we discovered.

We left that night with a challenge. Somehow, we needed to find a way to feed the passion inside us. Some of the ladies actually did find jobs locally that matched their interests and fit into their lives. Others found ways to volunteer with a similar purpose to their inner passion, leaving them feeling just as fulfilled.

The bottom line is that we became better mothers, wives, and friends when we talked about our passions. Our happiness comes from finding that purpose and meeting it in some way.

"What about you? What would you do, if you could do anything?" my husband asked later that night after I had shared the events of my evening.

"Write." I replied, "I want to be a writer."

Now pass me that thesaurus.

~Jaime Schreiner

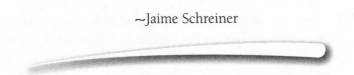

74

Starting All Over

It takes the same amount of energy to smile as to frown.
~Author Unknown

Ralph spoke first. "Jay, everyone is afraid to leave."

"Ralph, I'm not afraid, I'm terrified!" It was time for me to re-enter society. I'd graduated from a drug and alcohol rehabilitation program. My emotions overwhelmed me and I began to sob, feeling intense pain.

"Do you realize how much more honest you are than when you first walked through that door?" he said.

Dr. Ralph helped me regain my composure. "Thank you, Ralph. There is no way to repay you for all you've done for me," I said.

His response was immediate, "Do two things—no more dope, and make a contribution."

I'd completed something for the first time. Entering Concept House, my life had been an absolute disaster. Alcohol and drugs destroyed everything that was good, and it turned me into someone barely recognizable. I was a liar, a thief, and a person who was physically and verbally abusive. My words and actions destroyed every relationship. My behavior destroyed my career.

Rehab was not something I wanted to do. Addicts live in a fantasy world where everything is okay. But the family I'd abused and thrown away rescued me nonetheless. They insisted I enter a rehabilitation program. The choice was cleaning myself up, or returning to life on the street.

I spent the next six months relearning how to behave responsibly. At the age of thirty-seven, I felt a strange mixture of shame and wonder. It was like a new adventure, but guilt and regret accompanied me along the way. Rigorous intense therapy sessions, both individually and in groups took me to all the places I'd rather have forgotten. But this was time to face reality, and it was crucial if I was to change.

To say a metamorphosis took place isn't an exaggeration. People who kick the habit and stay clean know that's true. People who knew us before and after know it, too.

After leaving Concept House, I moved into a large home shared by addicts like me. We were trying to find a better way. All of us had to start over. Each day my old habits revisited my mind, and the cravings were sometimes intense. Staying off drugs and not drinking made me emotionally vulnerable. The chemicals I used to put in my body numbed the pain of daily life. Stress was washed away as troubles vanished in a fog of mindlessness. Now without those escape mechanisms, I felt all the things I'd spent most of my life avoiding.

March 31 marked the day I got clean and sober twenty-one years ago. My sister said, "We're all proud of you and love having you back in our lives." My ex-wife, who I'd subjected to terrible abuse, told me, "Jay, I see the change in you. It's good that you're a part of [our son's] life."

Nearly all aspects of my life have changed. When I left rehab I didn't believe any of this could be possible. My confidence had been lacking, and I'd been unsure of where to go and what to do. I was afraid of people, never trusting anyone or anything. Somehow I persevered. Making a career change was one of the most challenging aspects of this entire process.

The change came slowly and continues every day. Not a day goes by that I don't think about having a drink or taking a drug. That's the way it is for me.

Twenty-one years later, I still feel uncomfortable in unfamiliar surroundings. Fear has not left me completely. I make mistakes. I have symptoms of depression. The difference now is that none of these things have led to relapse. Another difference is that I try my best to face reality with as positive an attitude as I can muster.

My neighbors say, "It's nice to be around you, you smile a lot and make me laugh."

"Thank you." I say. I look into their eyes and tell them, "It's nice to see you, too." My words are sincere.

The old Jay rarely had a kind word for anyone. The truth is that I was a pretty nasty guy. These days, doing volunteer work and making charitable donations fills me with joy I'd never known. Before I embarked on this journey, not only was I selfish, I resented the fact that there were bills to pay. Now, being responsible is a source of pride.

A simple thing like taking a walk makes me happy. Even greeting my neighbors has taken on significance. Possibly this is because I used to walk with my head down, averting my eyes from human contact. The guy around the corner from me sits in his yard when the weather allows. We enjoy a little chat.

"Hey Jay," John calls the moment I'm in sight. It makes me feel good.

My reply is always, "I'm glad to be alive, my friend. How are you today?"

He gets up from a lawn chair, walks over to his fence and extends his large hand. "All is well, no complaints." Even though this has become routine, it remains a source of uplifted spirits.

The littlest everyday occurrences aren't little anymore. I've learned to appreciate small things. I tell many people "simplicity is sublime." Something inside me wants to share that perception with the world. I truly love being able to put a smile on someone's face. Helping other people is my purpose.

I'm not a nasty guy today.

~Jay H. Berman

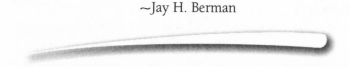

Gratitude, Schmatitude

If a fellow isn't thankful for what he's got,
he isn't likely to be thankful for what he's going to get.
~Frank A. Clark

I'd never been the bubbliest person, but lately nothing made me happy. In fact, since my fiftieth birthday, each day held some new woe to grumble about, taking me quickly from discouraged to depressed. Desperate to find a way out of the mucky-muck, I called my friend, Pam, who always seemed cheerful no matter what life handed her.

Gratitude, she claimed, was the answer. Wallowing only makes things worse. "Instead, start each day with five things you're grateful for. We can e-mail our lists every morning to encourage each other."

With her sunny disposition, it didn't seem that Pam needed encouragement, but I certainly did and so I agreed to give it a try. After a fitful night of tossing and turning, wrapped in my old flannel robe, I shuffled to the kitchen.

I heard an e-mail land in my mailbox. "Gratitude list." I read through bleary eyes. It wasn't even 7:00 A.M. How was I supposed to make a list when I was tired, irritable, and just plain miserable? The coffeemaker gurgled away as I tried to come up with something, but before a single thing came to mind in came another e-mail from Pam: "Let's go. Where is it?"

With a sigh, I rubbed my throbbing temples, poured a steaming mug and inhaled the deep, rich aroma. Aaahh. The computer keys click-clacked against the silent morning as I pecked out the letters: "First cup of morning coffee."

I yawned at the sun peeking from behind fluffy white clouds in a sky of cornflower blue. Wait, sun? Blue skies? The weeklong downpour had finally ended! Click-clack. "Not raining."

Only two and I was ready to quit. Gratitude, schmatitude! This was ridiculous. How was gratitude going to change anything anyway? I had real issues to deal with—insomnia, a bad back, and the latest and by far the worst—hearing loss. I was way too young for that! It was humiliating to wear ugly, uncomfortable hearing aids. Still, I thought, my fingers poised over the computer keyboard, they did help. I grudgingly typed, "I can hear." That was it. She'd have to settle for three.

"Only three?" she replied. "Scroll down."

I dragged my mouse down the screen. She'd added comments next to my gratitude!

"First cup of morning coffee"—Nothing like it!"

"Not raining"—Sun... like God smiling."

"At least I can hear"—Good, I have plenty to say. Now, send two more!" She'd added a smiley face.

"Can't think of anymore!" I fired back. "Hardly slept, head's pounding, and there's nothing in the house for breakfast."

Another e-mail: "Then let's have breakfast out."

Forget it! That would mean getting showered and dressed. I'd planned on staying in pajamas all day. Maybe even go back to bed. My fingers moved over the keys. "Thanks, not today." I hit Send, swigged down the last of my coffee and refilled my cup.

"Suit yourself, but you still owe me two more to complete your gratitude list."

Instead, I sent her an e-mail whining about sleepless nights, hot flashes, and sluggishness. This was the season of life I swore I'd handle gracefully. Instead, I was a cranky mess, peeling off layers of clothing and chugging ice water to keep from melting. I hit Send and fanned myself with a magazine.

Another e-mail! "So what? We're all getting older. Everyone has problems. Look at me, a single mom with a limited income, an elderly parent to care for, and a car on the fritz more often than not. Still, I'm grateful for: God in my life. My children. Family. A roof over my head. A day filled with possibilities."

She was so upbeat! My fingers flew over the keys. "How do you do it, Pam? How can you feel so thankful when life is so hard? Don't you ever get overwhelmed?"

She wrote back. "Sometimes, but what good does it do? If I turn it around I'm happy for what I have and hopeful for what I want."

I had to admit, it seemed like a good philosophy.

Pam continued: "My knees hurt from arthritis, but at least I can walk. I have to juggle bills, but I'm blessed to have a house. Wrinkles are just another word for smile lines. It's simply a matter of outlook, Sue. That's why I'm pushing you to see the positive side of things and develop an attitude of gratitude."

"Take your hearing aids, for example. You think they're so horrible, but I never noticed them. Before you got them I thought you weren't interested in what I had to say. Remember our phone calls? I was ready to find someone else who wanted to listen to me. Turned out you didn't hear half of what I said."

And I thought I'd pretended so well.

"But now you do," she typed. "Those ugly little things saved our friendship."

I pictured her dazzling smile as I read the e-mail. Everything she said made sense. Not only had she put a positive spin on my complaints, she never once griped about her aching knees, clunking car, or mounting stack of bills. No, despite her challenges, she was thankful for all she did have, even happy. Maybe there was something to this gratitude stuff?

I thought about everything she struggled with. Suddenly, my stuff didn't seem as monumental. I sat down at my computer, and in the subject line typed a single word: "Gratitude."

My fingers flew over the keys, 1. With age come aches and pains, but the gym could help with that. 2. Sleepless nights? I could catch up on my reading. 3. Hot flashes? I could wear lighter fabrics in layers. 4. Today will be a brighter day. And, 5. I'm grateful to have such a wise friend.

I hit "Send", ready to share a wonderful dose of thankfulness.

~Susan A. Karas

76

I Think I Can

The greatest discovery of all time is that a person can change his future by merely changing his attitude.
~Oprah Winfrey

Purpose and meaning were what I was searching for. After graduating high school, I ventured into the workforce, uncertain of what I wanted to do with my life. I couldn't even figure out why I was here. After trying about half a dozen careers, I had a life full of disappointments. I had hit rock bottom. Nothing seemed to work out. Flat broke and without a college degree, I became depressed and my future seemed anything but promising. I felt my faith dwindling. I needed solace. So, I felt like church would be a good place to start.

I began attending a local church. Little did I know that this church would be the very place where my life was changed forever. It was Easter time and the pastor talked about how Easter is a season of new birth, a time of growing, a time for solace. Well, I seemed to be in the right place. While attending the church, I met a special woman named Martha, who not only helped me find faith, but would reveal to me something that I had never known before.

At the time, I also went back to college because I wanted an opportunity to explore my talents. While going to school, I wrote a letter to the editor. Writing had always seemed interesting to me. What prompted me to write was my disagreement with the opinions expressed by others in my local newspaper. I wanted to put in my two cents. Little did I know that of all the letters the paper receives, mine would make the cut.

The next weekend, it was back to church. "I saw your letter to the editor," Martha said. "Great job. Are you a writer?"

"Not even," I replied.

"Well, I think you are, and you really need to do more. I am on the board of a publishing company and have years of experience in the writing business. I am a published author myself."

Somehow I managed to maintain my composure. I couldn't believe this. A woman from a publishing company thinks I can write. During all my years in school, I had been told the exact opposite.

Then reality set in. Not only had I been told all my life that I could not write, but even if I attempted this it would be extremely challenging. Would it be worth it?

I drifted back in time and remembered a line from a children's story: "I think I can, I think I can." The words of that little engine that could were inspiring. "I know I can, I know I can" became my enduring words of faith.

I needed that simplicity. I was a broken spirit. My Asperger syndrome had always made things more difficult for me. I had been wounded in battle but I wasn't dead. I picked myself up, bandaged my wounds, and began to prepare for the journey. No looking back now. I think I can, I think I can. I know I can, I know I can.

The next time I went to church, Martha asked me, "Do you have any other pieces that you've written?"

"Well, yeah, actually I do." I said.

"E-mail them to me," Martha said. "I'd love to read them."

I e-mailed Martha poetry, essays, and letters to the editor that I had written. A few days later a new e-mail message from Martha appeared. "You are a writer, Tyler, a very talented writer. Have you ever considered making a career out of it, perhaps journalism? You seem to enjoy talking about the news and you articulate messages so well."

The next week, Martha and I went out for coffee. She told me she would help me develop my writing. As time went on, Martha and I began to meet regularly during the week to discuss my writing. Her patience and commitment to seeing me succeed as a writer made it all worth it.

The key for me was having someone believe in me. The more I failed, the more I asked for help and tried to improve as writer.

Today I am an accomplished writer and was a student at Beaufort County Community College before pursuing journalism at East Carolina University. I have been published in CNN iReport, *USA Today*, *The New York Times*, *The News & Observer*, *The Daily Reflector* and *The Fayetteville Observer*.

The message I heard at Easter came alive for me. I experienced a new birth, and courage. Like a bird leaving its mother's nest, I developed a strong will to fly, began to spread my wings. As I did, I said over and over again, "I know I can, I know I can."

~Tyler Stocks

77

Dear Daddy

The trouble with learning to parent on the job
is that your child is the teacher.
~Robert Brault, rbrault.blogspot.com

"Dear Daddy,

I really don't have a lot to say. You really never yell at me or anything. I am mad that you are always gone on the weekends. When you would go out on the weekends, it would make me sad and mad because you and mommy would leave me home alone and have me take care of the dogs. Sometimes I would stay up till like one in the morning when you guys were out because I didn't want you guys mad if Lady or Jax peed or pooped in the house."

This is part of a letter my daughter wrote to me after the worst weekend of my life. I was in a motorcycle club and spent all of my extra time riding, drinking and partying. On this particular weekend, my wife and I had come home still fighting from a drunken argument we had the night before. It was bad. We even told the kids we would be getting a divorce.

I had let something other than my family consume who I was.

I can't lie. I had fun riding with the club. I would ride hundreds of miles in a day. One week I put over 3,000 miles on my bike. I was living the dream. I had the wind in my face, and cold beer and a wild party waiting at every stop for the night. I would come home on Sunday afternoons or evenings and be greeted by my kids. They would ask what I did. I couldn't tell them because it was not child-appropriate.

When I was a soldier, the kids would brag to their friends that their daddy was a soldier and fought in Afghanistan. They would brag that I jumped out of airplanes and helicopters. Sometimes they even came and watched me do it. Now all they could say was that their daddy was in a motorcycle club and they didn't know what I did. They used to be proud of me but now I was a ghost. My hero status had faded.

I needed a total makeover mentally, and my internal GPS needed to do some recalculating. My kids were losing faith in me, my wife had decided I wasn't the man she married. I had lost track of who I was. I know I could never get those times back but I could, with time, be the man I was supposed to be.

On the following Tuesday, while my wife was at work, I had asked the kids to write letters to me. I told them I didn't want them to hold back. I wanted them to tell me all the things they didn't like that I had done. I wanted them to tell me how it made them feel. I wanted the hard truth.

Any human can listen to a religious leader, a friend, or their parents. I'm here to tell you that a child's words written on a piece of paper is the loudest voice you can hear. I hadn't lost my children to the club. They still cared enough to tell me all the things I had done wrong. They loved me the way I loved them. They loved me enough to help my GPS recalculate.

"It also made me really upset when you guys stopped playing games with us or even taking me and my brother to the mall or somewhere. But that goes back to the fact you guys were always gone on the weekends. It also makes me upset when you sit on the phone all the time. It makes me feel like you have better stuff to do than talk to me or my brother."

Today my children are counting down the days till Christmas and wondering what is under the tree. I have asked them not to buy me a single gift, because they have given me the greatest gift anyone could receive. They gave me a second chance at being a real father. My wife gave me a second chance at being a real husband.

I'm still in the motorcycle club, but I'm once again the president of my family, my original club. We all make mistakes, but it's not about the mistakes you make, it's about the way you fix the problem.

I keep these letters on my nightstand for those days when I think a beer is the answer, or when I want to try to find a way out of watching yet another version of "Jingle Bells" at the school play. I read the letters often, sometimes just to remind myself how wonderful my children are.

Your kids will grow up with or without you. You can be a memory in their past or you can be a part of their future. I want to be both.

~Paul Bowling II

78

Nose to the Wall

The first step toward creating an improved future
is developing the ability to envision it.
~Author Unknown

I hesitated at the door to the physical therapy building. Why bother? I'd just gotten over an elbow injury. Before that, four retinal detachment eye operations had left me with badly impaired vision. Now I'd torn a tendon in my calf and foot. The good periods between injuries seemed shorter each time. The golden years—ha! They ought to be called the broken years. Why was I wasting my time? After three weeks of therapy, I still couldn't walk without sharp pain.

The exercises the therapist assigned were embarrassing. Not only did I have to walk on a line across the room as if I were being tested for drunk driving, I also teetered like someone failing the test. I couldn't balance on one foot for even fifteen seconds. Knowing what I'd lost was bad enough. Why display my feebleness publicly? Other exercises were simply wimpy or silly. Bend over and touch my knees. Stretch my foot with a loose elastic band. What good would they do?

Worst of all was nose to the wall. I had to stand a foot from a wall and, back straight, lean forward to touch my nose to the wall. And then repeat fifteen times. It seemed like something a cruel guard would do to humiliate a POW.

That's what I felt like—a prisoner in the war against aging. Maybe it was time to accept that the war was over. I should give up strenuous yard work, carpentry, and the few sports activities I had left. I should buy a condo, watch TV, and eat ice cream. Nobody but my wife would see what I'd become.

"Excuse me," a voice said behind me. A woman about my age, using a walker, panted from the exertion of navigating from her car to the building. I opened the door for her and stepped aside.

She smiled and thanked me. She passed into the foyer and hobbled to the second door. Feeling foolish standing there, I limped along and opened that door.

She grinned. "Ah, the lame leading the lame. Enjoy your pain today!"

My therapist had me warm up on a stationary bike. Four or five other senior citizens were on treadmills. We were all working hard and going nowhere. Most of them looked as vacant as I felt, going through the motions. Even if we fixed whatever plagued us this month, something else would be sure to zap us next month.

The woman with the walker struggled to mount the bike beside mine. She worked her way inch-by-inch to climb onto the seat.

"Want to race?" she asked once she'd made it.

I laughed.

"I'm serious," she said. "First one to three miles wins. But you have to set your resistance level higher, because you don't need a walker. If you were on crutches, I'd set mine higher."

"But we're not going anywhere," I said.

"I am. Today when I close my eyes, I will be biking down a quiet country lane on a spring morning. The doves and cardinals are singing. You can smell the locust blossoms, so sweet they make the bees drunk. The bees roll around on the ground and we must avoid running them over. There's a curve ahead that'll take us to the stream. Be careful going across the narrow board that's used for a bridge—you don't want to hurt yourself."

"It sounds like you've been there. Is it a real place?"

She grinned. "To me it is. More real than here."

"Sounds nice."

The man next to me was plodding along on a treadmill with

glazed eyes. She whispered loud enough him to hear. "A lot of people find this place depressing."

"No kidding."

"So I'd rather spend these twelve minutes riding down my lane, wouldn't you? You look like someone who's competitive, which is why I suggested racing."

"Let's do it." I set my dials and we started.

At first I pushed hard. She was right. I am competitive. But I soon shut my eyes to the workout room and pictured the lane—sunlight streaming in through the big oaks overhead. I visualized a dry, sandy lane, and after a while the swish-swish of the machine did sound a bit like tires on sand. I slowed down to take in the sights and sounds.

At first it was her lane, just as she described it, but after I crossed the plank bridge—confidently and without a wobble like I would have done five years ago—I changed the scene. I pictured my favorite bike trail along a river, the water rippling and sparkling and a fish jumping.

I was no longer on a machine going nowhere. I was enjoying an outing. I had not biked that trail in years. Why not? Even if I couldn't play tennis, I could still bicycle. Tomorrow, instead of brooding at home, I'd strap the bike to the car and drive to the river.

I faced the fact that it was my attitude, not my injuries, making me miserable. I had created my own prison of loss and embarrassment. Why not energize this moment—right now in boring physical therapy. Wasn't this very moment as valuable as any other moment in life? If my body didn't respond to therapy, I'd still enjoy today's fantasy. By fighting physical therapy, I was the one killing those hours of my life.

When I put my nose to the wall later, maybe I'd pretend I was leaning forward for my first shy kiss. Or leaning to an open window to sniff freshly-baked chocolate chip cookies. Or just enjoying the silliness of leaning my nose to the wall.

As I was conjuring up other nose-to-the-wall possibilities, my racing companion interrupted.

"You'd better step on it. I'm a tenth of a mile ahead. Are you going to let an old woman beat you?"

"Not on your life." I pushed hard to get to the peak of the next hill, where a field of golden hay waved in the sun.

~Garrett Bauman

Chapter 9

Reboot Your Life

Take Time for You

79

Doing Nothing Perfectly

I like the physical part, but I'm also drawn to the spiritual.
For me, yoga is not just a workout — it's about working on yourself.
~Mary Glover

One of the most useful things I have learned in life is how to do nothing. It didn't come easily. In my family, being still wasn't valued. My father was a workaholic who held down three jobs that took up most of his days, nights, and weekends. On top of that, he was a perfectionist. Everything he did had to be done just right. There was no room for error in anything, a philosophy that applied to his daughters as well. I had absorbed the message early on that doing nothing wasn't allowed, and that whatever I did, it had to be perfect if I wanted approval from my dad.

And that became my approach to most things in life — look busy and never let anyone know I wasn't perfect.

When I married, I tried to be the perfect wife, housekeeper, and cook. When I became pregnant, I vowed to be the best mother ever. But life has its own agenda, I discovered, and doing my best didn't necessarily mean being the best. I had to put myself aside to care for my busy husband and newborn daughter. Eventually, I felt overwhelmed and needed help.

That's when I discovered yoga. It quickly became part of my life.

It was a way to remain active and in shape, and I could fit it in and around my other obligations during the day.

With the help of books and videos, I taught myself the poses. I learned how to breathe intentionally, the mainstay of all yogic practice.

And then the stillness came. It was not what I had expected. In the beginning, I had to push away my guilt that I was doing nothing. I soon found out that courting stillness was the most active nothing I had ever encountered. I had to relearn the three Rs: release judgment, relax the internal critic, and reconnect with the inner source.

My internal critic was not happy. I could hear my father accuse me of being idle. I could imagine him telling me to get busy and do something useful. Yet somehow I knew that I *was* doing something useful, perhaps not something he would have approved of, but something that was extremely valuable for me.

This feeling was so strong that it kept me balanced when the world was shoving me in contradictory directions. It became a pool of peace from which I was able to draw nourishment. My whole body would relax and my mind would become clear so that I could make decisions from a broader perspective. I had tapped into an inner space that I didn't know existed until I started doing nothing.

Many years have passed since I began my breathing practice. My daughter is an adult now, with children of her own. Each morning I still find time to sit quietly and watch my breath. Doing nothing continues to be a powerful, peaceful tool with which to start my day. And I am learning to do it perfectly.

~Ferida Wolff

80

Annual Reboot

A person needs at intervals to separate from family and companions
and go to new places. One must go without familiars in order to be
open to influences, to change.
~Katharine Butler Hathaway

"Who's going with you to Sedona?" Mama asked.

I hesitated, thinking of how to frame my answer. "I'll be with my co-workers at the Phoenix meeting, but then they're flying back to North Carolina. I have to go to a conference in San Francisco right after that."

"I don't like it," Mama said, her blue eyes looking straight into mine. "It's not safe for a woman to travel alone."

"Mama, if I can go through cancer treatment, I'm certainly not afraid to get in a rental car and drive across the state of Arizona."

"I still don't like it, you going by yourself."

I hoped my tone had not hurt her. She'd been through enough. She was just a mother looking out for her young, even if her young was forty-five years old. It was time to pull out my trump card. "I won't be alone. God will be with me," I said.

She took in the words of her determined, "headstrong" middle daughter. "Well, you'll be in the best of hands, but be careful."

And that's how my first solo journey started—a serendipitous trip to Sedona that was wedged between business in Phoenix and San Francisco. Before that I'd been settled into my middle-aged life, working as a research nurse, married to a busy psychologist, raising two teenage sons. Life seemed like a predictable chain of events. The one creative outlet I had was writing, which had taken the form of a first novel about women who were also in midlife. My characters were in group therapy trying to become what they'd once dreamed of before they were weighed down by routines and responsibilities.

When I was diagnosed with breast cancer, my predictable chain of events suddenly became a scary journey into the unknown of surgeries, chemotherapy and radiation. I took each step with the help of my faith, family and friends. Over time, I learned that I could survive, and even thrive, when I faced my fear and kept going, choosing to live instead of cower.

Finally, I finished my treatment and was allowed to travel. I felt myself coming to life as I made plans for the trip. There were moments of fear when I wondered what I was getting myself into and how I would handle it if my rental car broke down or I suddenly became ill. I trusted that along my path there would be people to help me, just as there had been through my cancer journey.

Traveling alone gave me the freedom to interact with strangers, instead of limiting my conversations to companions, whether family or friends. On this trek, I enjoyed chatting with a shop owner (a fellow North Carolinian) and with a couple hiking in Oak Creek Canyon. In the past when I talked with strangers during a family vacation, my older son, embarrassed by my spontaneity, would remark, "Mom acts like she's just run into her best friend."

Unencumbered, I could be in the moment. I lingered at the sight of wildflowers next to the red rocks and watched the drama of nightfall with strangers, sitting atop our cars, not worrying I'd be late for any obligation.

I left Sedona renewed.

Back at home, I resumed my pre-cancer pace with work and family responsibilities—something I said I'd never do. Over the next few years, I piled on layers of stress. My life was out of balance. Then, with my fiftieth birthday approaching, I decided to give myself the gift I really wanted, another trip alone.

I chose Jekyll Island, Georgia, where I'd previously been on a family vacation, a place with natural beauty that pulled me like the tide. Each morning I laid out my goal for the day: to move as the spirit led me, freely living in the moment. I read Psalm 103:5 that spoke about youth being "renewed like the eagle's," which seemed appropriate with me turning fifty and needing to unplug from a busy life. I rode my bike on the half-mile loop through the marsh, stopping to watch morning unfold, freely breaking into song without any other person in earshot.

I rode to the historic village, shaded by huge, moss-draped oaks that reminded me of the trees I played under as a girl. Sitting in the grass, I felt as if it were a childhood summer day when I spent hours with pretend friends. At night I swam in the old-fashioned hotel pool with lights that added to its turquoise allure. Moving freely about the island, I discovered I'd been drawn to a place that took me back to my childhood—a time when I was free and lived in the moment.

When I crossed over the Palmetto-lined causeway, heading home from Jekyll, I felt as rested and renewed as I had when I left Sedona. I decided I would go on a trip alone every year from then on.

Over the years, I've kept that promise. I've traveled to Martha's Vineyard, where I had delicious conversations while staying in my first hostel. I've ridden my bike at sunset at Assateague Island. I've watched hydroplanes land on Mann's Harbor in the San Juan Islands of Washington State. I've ridden a horse through a Teton meadow.

It was something that started by chance and now happens by choice. I've opted to live my life fully.

~Connie Rosser Riddle

81

Awakened by the Creator Within

*Don't die with your music still inside. Listen to your intuitive
inner voice and find what passion stirs your soul.*
~Wayne Dyer

I t was almost midnight on a cold winter night. I had just finished
nursing my newborn son. I swaddled him in his blue and white
blanket and placed him, protected from the world, in his bas-
sinette near my bed.

I headed to the laundry room and put my son's tiny clothes in the
dryer. How could one little baby create so much laundry? I finished
the dinner dishes. On the way back to my bedroom, I checked on my
two-and-a-half-year-old daughter, who was sleeping peacefully in her
new big girl bed. Exhausted, I kissed her on the cheek and headed
back to my room.

When I peeked at my son, his eyelids were fluttering. A smile
flashed across his face. As I watched him dreaming, I thought about
my life and my own dreams that seemed so long ago.

I kissed my sleeping husband good night and snuggled under the
covers. Staying home with my children, nurturing them, and watching
them grow was something I had always longed for. But during these
pensive moments, I felt something deep stirring inside me. I could
hear my creative soul whispering to me: "Remember your dreams. You

promised yourself you would paint and write when you took time off from teaching to stay home with your children."

My saboteur within quickly chimed in: "You are too busy to do this. After all, you have two children and a husband who need you. You have laundry, cleaning, food shopping and an endless list of things to do. You don't have time to create and besides there is no money in art. Don't be selfish."

The seed for my dream of painting and writing was planted at a very young age. My mom was an avid reader who took my siblings and me to the library on a weekly basis. I fell in love with picture books from the very start. Sketching every character and making up stories in my imagination, I secretly dreamed of writing and illustrating a children's book. Now, my saboteur was trying to talk me out of it.

I listened to her and let her put an end to my foolish dream. I threw myself wholeheartedly into motherhood. I loved nurturing my children's minds and hearts, exploring nature with them and teaching them about their five senses. I also taught them to listen to the promptings of their most important sense of all—their intuition. Like my mom did, I took them to the library on a weekly basis. Once there, I got lost in the world of books again. I think I read every children's book in the library to my daughter. I also started a journal for each child and recorded our memories and their exciting milestones.

I was having fun, but still there were times when I felt my dream stirring deep inside me. I could hear my soul whispering to me in a powerful yet faint voice: "You must paint and write."

One day I was dusting my bookshelf. *The Artist's Way* by Julia Cameron, a book I had read several years earlier, caught my eye. I opened it and the first thing my eyes saw was a quote by Carl Jung: "Nothing has a stronger influence psychologically on their environment and especially on their children than the unlived life of a parent."

"Aha," I thought. Following my dream wasn't just for me. It was not selfish. I needed to listen to my dream so that my children would be able to listen to their own dreams. I realized I couldn't live my life through them. It wasn't good for anyone.

Still I tried to ignore my creative soul by keeping busy. The war inside me grew bigger, so big that I felt like I was going to explode. One morning, as I was in my walk-in closet getting dressed, it felt like my closet was closing in on me. I heard a faint yet powerful voice, which I later learned was my courageous inner warrior, state, "You must paint or drink heavily." I knew I had to make a choice. That day I called a local art center and signed up for an art class. I have been painting and writing ever since.

I am living my dream and modeling for my children that they must listen to their own. That is my gift to them.

~Christine Burke

82

My Writing Roller Coaster

Life is like a roller coaster—scream Whee... on the way down,
and let the momentum carry you back up the next hill.
~Jonathan Lockwood Huie

I always knew creative writing was my thing, but I didn't actively pursue it until I was thirty years old. I started writing slice-of-life essays and I had dreams of one day being published. The Internet wasn't what it is today, so I relied on writing reference books and a writing group to guide me along.

While juggling two little kids and working full-time outside the home, I wrote sporadically during my lunch hours and when the kids were in bed. After a year of stolen minutes scribbling here and there, one of my stories was accepted for publication in a local parenting magazine. To say I was excited and elated was an understatement. That first published story ignited a fire and deepened my passion to keep writing and to keep submitting to other publications.

Life was busy, but I found time to write. Sometimes those lunch hours were compromised by errands, and sometimes the kids' bed-times were not exactly on time. But I kept at it when I could and was fortunate to get another story published.

Over time, frustration crept in. I wasn't writing as often or as much as I would have liked. When you have kids, plans are often sidetracked and disrupted. My family would always come first, but writing was my escape, and my lack of time to write was bringing me down. My big dreams and the passion fueled by my few published stories were starting to fade. I began to complain about not having time to write.

Then various life challenges intervened. My job situation changed. I battled depression. Due to family demands, I eventually had to leave my writing group. My kids were getting older, which meant my household lifestyle was changing. My inspiration, fire, and passion withered away. The writing life I was once so excited about stalled. Then it stopped.

I just couldn't get back into it. Many of my reasons for not writing were valid, but I would later figure out some were just excuses. I blamed everything and everyone but myself for my stalled writing career. I stopped writing for almost two years.

As my life got better again, my heart told me it was time to resume writing. I wrote when I found a scrap of time here or a flicker of inspiration there. I felt shaky and uncertain, but I submitted an article to a local magazine and they accepted it. My kids got older and busier, but I kept writing when I could.

Then my kids approached their tweens. I started feeling sorry for myself and moaning, yet again, about having no time to write. It was as though I was on a writing roller coaster. As soon as I would hit a high, a huge low with a sharp turn would follow, threatening to derail me. Again.

I had read that writers—successful "published" writers—have writing routines. They write something every day, at the same time, without fail, no matter what.

I listed my excuses: Those writers probably don't have kids. They don't work outside the home. They probably have a housecleaner and can write all day, whenever they want. I slouched and pouted, moaning about my lack of writing time.

By then the Internet was in full swing, nothing like it was when I'd first started writing. Through researching and connecting with other writers online, I soon learned how many of them were, just like me, moms who worked outside the home. And yet they still managed to have a writing career. While tripping over baby bottles and toys on the way to their jobs, they found ways to engage in their passion, including a better attitude and a writing routine. They didn't make excuses.

Some wrote early in the mornings, seven days a week, while everyone slept. Some were weekend-only writers. Some wrote three nights a week after everyone else had gone to bed.

No matter when or how often they wrote, they set a schedule and stuck with it. They were determined, productive, happy, and proud of what they were doing.

I broke down my day and realized my usual morning routine of watching the news with a cup of tea before work while everyone was still asleep was the perfect time. I'm a morning person and I was willing to sacrifice a bit of sleep to do what I loved — and my household wouldn't suffer for it.

At 4:30 A.M., the house would be quiet and there would be no distractions. Prepping my writing area (the kitchen table) with my work-in-progress the night before would save time. I would have an hour, sometimes more, to dedicate to my writing. And if I wrote Monday through Friday, like my regular workweek, it might help maintain a working/writing/family balance.

It worked!

Some mornings are harder than others; either I'm tired or I can't get my writing gears to work. But I show up every day in front of my computer and write something. And then I show up again the next day. And the next.

Five years have gone by, and I have kept to my routine. Sure, the roller coaster picks up speed sometimes, threatening to derail me. But I keep facing forward, holding on tight and knowing that with the right attitude I will always stay on track.

~Lisa McManus Lange

83

Clean Start

If you don't go, ten years from now you won't even remember what you were doing that week. But if you go, you'll remember exactly where you were!
~Author Unknown

Thirty-five years into what I thought was a happy marriage, my husband dumped me for a younger model. I couldn't seem to get over it. My life was an ongoing pity party with me as the guest of honor.

Then one day I accidentally caught my reflection in the hall mirror. The sad sack reflected there was someone I'd try to avoid sitting next to on an airplane. I suddenly realized I was sick of this misery. I wanted the joy back in my life. I wanted to wake up with a smile on my face.

As if the Fates were applauding my return to sanity, an old friend called. "Would you be interested in going on a cruise of the Greek Islands?"

Even though it would strain my budget, it might be just what I needed. "If you can stand my company, I think I can squeeze it in."

That trip lived up to all my expectations and ripped holes in the black cloud that had been hanging over me. My friend and I clambered through ancient ruins, ate delicious Greek salads, ogled sexy Greek men, and spent a fascinating day in the central market in Istanbul.

But the absolute pearl of the trip was our visit to the Turkish baths.

We almost didn't go. On our last morning in Istanbul, I put the question to my friend Cammy. "Well, are we going to the baths, or not?"

"I don't know. The idea feels a little scary."

"Yep," I agreed, "but when will we have a chance like this again?"

She considered, reaching for another pastry to buy time. Then nodded her head decisively. "You're right. We shouldn't miss it!"

I gave a mental fist pump.

A cab dropped us off. Minutes after entering, we knew the experience would be memorable. In the babble of voices surrounding us, not one word of English could be heard. We paid, though what we had paid for remained deliciously uncertain.

We were led to a tiny box of a dressing room. Sign language from our escort made it clear we were to disrobe.

When she left, I whispered to Cammy. "Are we supposed to leave our passports, credit cards, and clothes in here? Did you see that lock? A two-year-old could break in."

"I guess we should have left our stuff back in the room. Well, we're here now. Let's just say a prayer and cross our fingers," Cammy whispered back.

I stared at her. When did Cammy get so brave?

We wrapped our scanty towels around our goose-pimpled bodies and stepped out of our cubicle. We were led into a bath area resembling something out of the Arabian Nights. It was a circular room of white marble, the ceiling towering twenty or thirty feet above us. Light poured in through windows circling the wall high above our heads, and basins mounted at intervals overflowed, the water making a soothing sound as it cascaded to the floor.

Our guide gestured toward the basins and departed. Nervously we each sat down next to one, hugging our knees to our chests and clutching our tiny towels tightly. The wait was probably no more than ten minutes, but it seemed an eternity as second thoughts about the wisdom of coming here chased each other through my head.

I was about to suggest to Cammy that we forget the whole thing and leave, when two giant thong-clad women walked through the door.

I murmured softly, "Should we make a run for it? They don't look very fast."

The women reached us and took our arms, drawing us gently but firmly toward the raised altar-like section in the middle of the room. Its similarity to the sacrificial stone atop the pyramid at Chichen Itza flashed into my mind, as gentle pressure forced me into a prone position. Before fear had time to blossom into full-blown panic, I found myself being rubbed all over with what appeared to be a small mop. The mopping was a delight once I relaxed, and after that I was pummeled and prodded until I was mellower than I thought possible. When the magic fingers finally stopped their ministrations, my body felt like a wet noodle. A sigh of pure happiness slipped out before my arm was again taken in a firm grip.

At the basin, water was poured over my head as the precursor to a good head scrubbing. I realized I'd leave here looking not like a sophisticated woman of the world, but like a drowned rat.

I relaxed. What did I care? Our trip to the Turkish baths would be kept sparkling and alive by frequent retelling. I'd be smiling when I woke up tomorrow.

~Pam Bailes

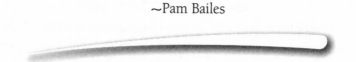

One Year of Celibacy

You are important, valuable and unique.
Don't let any one tell you otherwise. Live your truth and be amazing.
~Ricardo Housham

After walking away from a secure corporate job, leaving depression, drug addiction and eating disorders behind, I was ready to step into my new life. And yet, I found my romantic relationships were still chaotic and loaded with insecurity and pain. No matter how hard I tried, my love life was still a battlefield.

For the majority of my life, I had been dependent on the attention of men. My relationships were transitory, and my self-esteem was based on the person I was with.

In past relationships, I was desperate to feel loved and therefore ignored every red flag. I was the girl who sacrificed everything in an effort to please my man.

No matter which man I was involved with, the patterns were always the same — a roller coaster of drama fueled by misunderstandings, anger and regretful words.

Every once in a while, a loving moment would peek through, but those moments were fleeting and always followed by defensive accusations. I wanted love so much that I convinced myself this was how relationships were supposed to work.

Finally, I saw the pattern and realized I would need to quit bad relationships for good. What I wanted was a healthy relationship. What I needed was inner peace. What I tried was celibacy.

My intention for starting a one-year romance detox was to be able to feel beautiful without a man having to prove it to me. My rules: No dating, no kissing, and no sex!

The first few months of singlehood were excruciatingly painful. A euphoric high was quickly followed by a sad loneliness. At times the loneliness took over and hindered my ability to function.

Even though I was doing the work and showing up for myself, I still held onto resentment. On some level I felt like a failure that I couldn't even keep a relationship working right.

But now, almost a year into my dating sabbatical, I've gained tremendous insight into who I am and what I really need in life.

Before my experiment, I would fill my world with inappropriate relationships in an effort to feel loved and worthwhile. I would stay in relationships way past their expiration dates, and I would fall in love with men who were really unhealthy for me.

Taking a year off from the distraction of looking for love has allowed me to find true unconditional love, the kind of love that I could only find within myself. Self-love is the greatest gift my celibacy has given me.

Maya Angelou said, "You alone are enough. You have nothing to prove to anybody." When I was in a relationship, I worked so hard to prove my love. I would overextend myself because I feared losing the love of the person I was with.

Through my love sabbatical, I have recognized that I am enough just as I am. I don't have to try to be someone else to get people to like me, or to keep someone in love with me.

A year ago, this girl was angry, afraid, insecure and stuck. Today my life is fueled with compassion, purpose, love and joy. I am in the best relationship of my life, and I am single. Just me, my heart, and my higher power.

~Shannon Kaiser

85

Back to School

The whole purpose of education is to turn mirrors into windows.
~Sydney J. Harris

As I prepared for bed that night, my mirror showed a middle-aged, slightly overweight woman, graying at the temples, skin yet unlined. Everyone said I looked younger than my forty-five years, but I knew my age. And sometimes, like tonight, I felt every year of it.

I had always aspired to get a degree, but raising a family had taken priority. Now with my last child in middle school, I thought, why not try to achieve something while I still had the opportunity—and the mental capacity. When Bob returned that weekend from a business trip, I showed him the flyer.

He frowned as he studied it. "Is it time for John to apply to college?" He was referring to our second son, who was in high school.

I shook my head. "It's not for John. It's for me."

"For you?" A broad smile lit up his face and his arm came around me. "I'm proud of you."

"Are you sure? I mean, you're away so much..."

He placed a finger on my lips. "If that's what you want, we'll make it work."

The kids had mixed reactions. Our daughter, already in cosmetology school, thought it a great idea. Our John was horrified that we might be in college at the same time. James, our youngest, wanted to know who would take him to football practice. I explained that things would be a little different, but if everyone chipped in, it wouldn't be difficult. Then Bob surprised me by saying he would make some adjustments so he could be home more.

The next day we drove to the community college and picked up a course catalog. I confided in my friends, and they all advised me to go into the medical field, where jobs are always available. I had no interest in the medical field, so after careful research and talking to several people, I chose to major in occupational therapy.

Days passed in a flurry of excitement, enrolling in classes, shopping for supplies and attending orientation. I felt like a kid again, but as the first day of classes drew near, I became petrified. I was simply too old. I really didn't want to study any more. My home would fall apart. People would laugh at me. Finally, after much prayer and with encouragement from my family and friends, I stuck with my decision.

As I walked into the building that first morning, I saw groups of students looking no older than my son John sitting on the floor in the hallways. I had not sat on the floor in years. I entered my classroom and scanned it anxiously for people my age. I saw a few. I chose a seat way in the back, hoping to avoid attention.

The professor came in, introduced himself, and began writing on the board. During a pause in his lecture, he looked directly at me and said, "It's been a long time, hasn't it?" I could have died, but no one seemed to notice. For the rest of that day, I did what I saw the other students do, and gradually, my self-consciousness faded. I found the classes and assignments interesting, and I left that day feeling I might survive. By the end of the first week, I had made a few friends — some older, some younger.

I knew that studying and keeping up with my duties at home would be challenging, but I wasn't prepared for how much. When Bob was away, I had to chauffeur the kids to their various activities. No sooner would I begin to study than it was time to put down my books and grab my car keys. Math and science were never my strong subjects, so I devoted more time to those, and with the help of small study groups, I was able to make A's. When the first semester ended, I had a 4.0 GPA and I was placed on the Dean's List, the President's

List and the Honor Roll. I was elated. I had managed to hold my own with people half my age.

By the second year, Bob and the kids were all doing their share, and I had learned how to comfortably balance my school and home life. One of my professors encouraged me to join the Phi Theta Kappa honor society. That meant being involved in extracurricular activities, which would take away from my studying as well as my family time. But the benefits included scholarship funds, so I decided to join and I began to take honors classes.

I also enjoyed participating in as many activities as I could. I entered a writing contest and had my story published in the college magazine and even taught a class at a local elementary school. In English 102, we acted out the Oscar-nominated films for that year, and I drew some applause as Morgan Freeman in *The Shawshank Redemption*. My hard work paid off. I was awarded a scholarship to study for a bachelor's degree.

As I drove away on the last day of school, I thought about what a difference returning to school had made in my life. That night I studied myself in the mirror. How different I looked! I had cut my hair, colored it, and shed the excess weight. I had more energy and enthusiasm for life than I could ever remember having. Even Bob commented on how much younger I looked. He spent more time at home, too.

Helping people do simple things, like bathing and dressing, which I took for granted, now seemed like my calling. I was hired by the hospital where I had done my internship. Fourteen years later, I'm still employed. It's never too late to try again.

~Angela Joseph

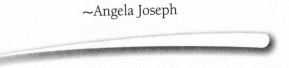

86

A Happy Heart

One of the symptoms of an approaching nervous breakdown
is the belief that one's work is terribly important.
~Bertrand Russell

"**S**o what do you do?" Back in the 1970s when strangers at parties asked me this, I probably should have fudged. I could have said I worked for the county, and left it at that. Instead I felt compelled to provide a flat-out conversation stopper.

"I'm the psychiatric social worker for the nursery at MacLaren Hall," I'd answer. "That's where the police and children's protective services workers bring neglected and abused kids to wait for court disposition. I do play therapy with the toddlers and try to get help for the abusing parents."

I'd smile and wait. People usually inched away, as if I might be slightly contagious. I'd watch as eyes glazed and jaws dropped.

Or they'd say, "I couldn't do that," and sidle off in search of someone who had a more socially palatable occupation.

Burnout rates are astronomical for those who work in my profession. Social workers, like police, rarely get thanked for what they do. Often they're criticized by the very people they strive to aid, or vilified by the press and the general public for not doing enough.

So I didn't expect accolades, or parades, or even sympathetic ears from strangers at parties. Nobody wants to hear horror stories about babies who've been abandoned in garbage bins or children who'd been mistreated. I understood that, and I generally didn't tell them.

I did have sunny tales to relate. Several addicted parents I'd counseled had successfully completed rehab, found jobs, and regularly visited their children, who were in foster care. Maybe I'd mention the unresponsive four-year-old who started speaking again as we sat on the playroom floor manipulating finger puppets. It wasn't all doom and gloom.

When I'd first become a caseworker for the county, my husband Bob, a police officer, listened patiently when I vented. His job was equally stress-filled, and so he empathized. Over the years though, he'd sought relief in vodka. Eventually he sought treatment for alcoholism. He'd been in several outpatient programs, and on and off the wagon, but nothing really took. I'd occasionally thought of divorce, but I shoved that troubling notion aside. He needed me.

Not long before I started at MacLaren, Bob entered an in-patient program. This one worked. He made a commitment to sobriety, but no longer was around to give me much emotional support. He spent every free minute in twelve step meetings and hospital aftercare programs.

I needed to find other support systems for myself. I recognized that some of my colleagues already suffered from compassion fatigue, burnout, and depression. Some coped by eating compulsively or relying on tranquilizers. I wanted to continue with my job, but I certainly didn't want to pack on unneeded pounds, or float through my days like a zombie, or eventually be diagnosed with post-traumatic stress disorder.

I started to frequent an art gallery that published a magazine. I wrote articles for it, and made new friends who were artists, photographers and poets. I enrolled in an aerobic dance class and lost myself in choreographed routines where I'd imagine I was a Broadway dancer.

My marriage continued to unravel. Then one day, toweling off after a particularly invigorating aerobics session, I noticed my heartbeat seemed to stutter. By the time I got dressed, it beat normally again. I forgot about it until a few days later at work, when I broke out in a cold sweat. The stutter had returned.

I made an appointment to see my doctor, who gave me an electro-cardiogram. "You're experiencing premature ventricular contractions, commonly called PVCs," she explained. "It's not dangerous yet, but it could be. What's going on in your life?"

"I think my husband and I are headed for divorce," I confessed. "I worry about that, and about the little children I work with. I try to take care of myself. I go to aerobics three times a week. But I probably drink too much coffee."

"Caffeine, too much exercise, a high stress job, plus anxiety over your marriage, all could be contributing factors," she said. "The sooner you make a decision about your marriage, the better you'll be. Not knowing one way or another how it's going to work out just adds to your stress. Don't remain immersed in uncertainty. Don't be afraid to take the first step."

She suggested I substitute tea for coffee and try to get more sleep.

Bob resented the evenings I spent with my art gallery friends and would have preferred that I devoted my free time to going to recovery meetings with him. As thrilled as I was that he was doing so well, I honestly didn't want my life to revolve around his sobriety, as it had around his drinking. I wanted to write and dance.

The problem soon resolved itself after Bob confessed he'd fallen in love with one of his outpatient counselors. We agreed to separate.

I continued working at the county facility for a few more years, through one administrative upheaval after another. A few times I thought about leaving for a job with more regular hours, one that wouldn't require me to work on Sundays. But each time, I'd think of the children in the nursery and would decide to stay on. They needed me.

Then one afternoon, after I learned that the play therapy room was scheduled to be converted into an additional dormitory, I felt my heart skip a beat once again.

The arrhythmia was back, but this time I knew what I had to do. I might not be burned out yet, but I could smell the smoke. Even though I'd invested fifteen years in county employment, a future retirement pension wouldn't keep my heart healthy today. I didn't need to be a martyr.

I updated my résumé, sent out some job applications and within months landed a new job in the private sector with an HMO. It wasn't perfect, but it was a change. And my happier heart calmed down.

It's been over twenty-five years now since I've experienced any irregular heartbeats. It's not that I lead a stress-free life. I've worked overseas with Peace Corps and held other demanding jobs. I remarried and saw my second husband through a long series of illnesses and eventual hospice care.

I continue to do the important routines—I keep caffeine to a minimum, exercise reasonably, and get enough sleep. I owe myself good health. I need my heart to live. Now when people ask me what I do, I have a favorite response. "I keep a happy heart," I say.

But the real secret is that I don't remain immersed in uncertainty. I don't allow myself to feel trapped by the perceived needs of others. I take that first step.

~Terri Elders

87

Second Chance

For those who are willing to make an effort, great miracles
and wonderful treasures are in store.
~Isaac Bashevis Singer

When my marriage of twenty-eight years ended, I moved from Ohio to Taos, New Mexico. It was an opportunity not only to start a new life but to finally design one that fit me. At fifty I'd realized that the first half of my life had belonged to everyone else. I decided the second fifty years would be mine.

Our two children had graduated from college and were on their own. The Taos house was in my name. When our home in Ohio sold, my husband and I split the money. My share was enough to allow me build a studio addition onto my New Mexico retreat.

I was a professional artist and planned to continue my artistic pursuits. But I determined my future life would be different from my past. I would have a new attitude. I used to say, "I do this kind of art. I don't do that kind." In my new life I would dispense with previous definitions of who and what I was, ignore all presuppositions about myself and simply stand back and see how I developed.

The decision was incredibly freeing—and frightening. What would I do if there were no better person in me trying to emerge? What if I were really as empty as I often felt? Years ago I'd begun to ask myself, "Who am I? Where am I going?" Now was the time to find out.

The separation from my husband had so unnerved me that for the first few weeks I found it difficult to walk in the house without losing my balance and bumping into furniture. I was dazed, a stranger in a strange place. It felt odd that no one was waiting for me to come home to cook a meal, no one cared about what I did, or would be upset, worried, or inconvenienced if I were late or didn't come home at all.

In the past I'd done my best to be a loving and supportive wife and mother, but in doing so I'd restricted my own life. As a child I was frequently told that what I did or believed made my mother and grandparents unhappy. Because of those messages, I'd come to feel responsible for the wellbeing of everyone around me. That carried over into my married life and resulted in my putting my life on hold whenever someone indicated even a possible need for me. It took very little to make me turn my back on myself. Divorce had finally lifted that constraint from my shoulders.

Many evenings after my move I stood in my yard out on the Taos mesa, a cool breeze on my cheek, contemplating the mountains, sky, and vast space around me. The magnitude of the setting made me feel comfortably insignificant. It was as if I were nothing in the world, unable to hurt or disappoint others. It was refreshing. I had no power over, or responsibility to, anyone or anything other than my dog.

However, freedom brings its own demands. How was I going to use my new life? I began by designing the two-story studio space to add to the house. I contacted the home's original builder. He agreed to take on the project.

Soon I realized I was spending an unhealthy amount of time watching TV while waiting for the studio to be completed, so I built a three-by-five foot Navajo loom, bought yarn from the local weaving supply store, and began the first of several rugs. This was another step into the unknown.

I joined an adult woodworking class at the local high school and learned to build and carve furniture. Before the class was over, I'd made a cabinet for an awkward space in the house. I began carving animals into the post at the bottom of my new studio stairway. I'd never done that before.

I'd been painting and drawing all my life. Now I was attracted by the idea of three-dimensional work. The Taos house was under construction when I bought it. At that time I was taking ceramic classes in Ohio and had the resources to make tiles for the kitchen backsplash and to paint and fire others for the bathrooms. Once in New Mexico, that equipment was no longer available to me, so I bought a kiln and clay. Since each floor of the new studio had a sink, I proceeded to make tiles for their backsplashes, then larger ones for the walls being built around the front yard.

In a class with a local potter I learned to construct modified tubular bodies for the clay figures I hoped to make and sell. After a few months, my work found acceptance in local galleries. I also produced and sold tiles with petroglyph designs. This was yet another path for me.

One summer I drove to Loveland, Colorado for classes in making bronze figures. My life expanded once more.

There were a few families on the mesa where my house was located. I was fortunate to be welcomed by an unpretentious couple. In Ohio, we'd had a neighbor who would gush about having given a perfect party with perfect food. I had kept my family healthily fed but was far from being a chef. After listening to that woman talk, I was paralyzed by the thought of inviting anyone to my house.

My new neighbor came as a blessing to me. She didn't feel she had to put on a fancy meal. She just served dinner, whatever she had been planning to prepare. Company was welcome to join if they wished. She believed people and friendships were more important than the menu. She helped free me from my fear of social failure.

She and her husband also kept an eye on me in an unobtrusive way. I had never lived alone before and was afraid I'd die and no one would notice or feed the dog. We arranged a signal. If I hadn't opened the bedroom curtains by noon, she would call to be sure I was okay. This simple arrangement added to my growing confidence.

Those years in Taos were filled with tremendous personal growth and exciting new experiences. I stopped limiting myself to fit the expectations of others. I ceased using phrases like "I should have" and "Why didn't you?"

I grew naturally, fully, my spirit expanding with joy. I began to know who I was and came to accept and like myself as a person of value. I didn't change the outside world very much, but the one inside me became filled with sunlight and confidence. Those years remain the most satisfying time of my life.

~J.C. Andrew

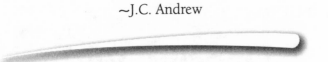

88

Dancing with a Cane on My Head

To dance is to be out of yourself. Larger, more beautiful, more powerful.
~Agnes de Mille

I was in the Middle East in a room full of mirrors, dressed in a belly dancing outfit, surrounded by similarly dressed women. We were all carefully balancing a cane on our heads as we performed the camel, the shimmy, arm waves, and the duck.

I was forty-two years old. And I wasn't even a dancer. One of my sisters is the dancer of the family. I'm the uncoordinated sister. Yet there I was hip lifting. Twirling. Stomach rolling. Figure eighting. We dropped the canes and executed elaborate moves with scarves of peacock blue and brilliant red, the fabric flying in the air and twisting around our bodies. Finally we danced in a circle with pleated Isis wings of gold and silver.

My family had spent three years in the Middle East for my husband's work. Now the time had come for the first of my three children to leave the nest and return to Sydney, Australia for university. I was devastated and wasn't sure how I would cope without her. Even though I was busy with my own job and our two boys, the house would seem so quiet without her.

Suddenly, I left my job and decided to look for something different to do. I saw an advertisement for belly dancing nearby. I thought it would be cool to do something with a Middle Eastern flavor, so I attended. With a simple scarf tied around my hips and sneakers on my feet, which I was quickly told to remove, I stood nervously in a roomful of women of all shapes, sizes and ages. They were all wearing sparkly belts around their hips that jangled with coins.

I was hooked from the first hip drop. After that very first class, I noticed a few women waiting. I asked them what they were doing and they told me they were taking part in teacher training for belly dance.

"Join us," they said.

I laughed. "I have no dance background at all and this is my very first class."

"So what?" they said.

I stayed and commenced teacher training for a dance I knew nothing about.

It wasn't easy. My body wasn't flexible. I wasn't very good at first. In truth, I wasn't very good for years. But I knew I wouldn't be, and it was that acceptance that kept me going back week after week. That and the trust I placed in the women I danced with, a trust they, in turn, gave back to me along with encouragement.

I danced with that group of women for the remaining four years I stayed in the Middle East. I attended two of their weddings—one in Dubai and one in Sweden. I supported many of them in dance competitions, including one memorable competition held in the desert. With their encouragement, I danced in a competition myself. My dance teacher employed me as an instructor and a manager. I travelled to Istanbul and bought entire belly dance outfits from the Grand Bazaar.

My participation in belly dance started as a hobby with the side benefit of fitness. It became a passion. I believe it always was. How else could I fall in love with a dance with one hip drop?

More important than the actual dancing were the friendships I made that continued even when we eventually moved from the Middle East. These women were and are so inspirational to me that I cannot imagine my time in the United Arab Emirates without imagining their faces too.

When I left, my women friends gifted me with a beautiful necklace of gold, with my name in Arabic calligraphy. I treasure it always and I also treasure what else these friends gave me—a way to cope when the first of my children left home. I danced my way through it.

~Sue Mannering

Chapter 10

Reboot Your Life

Adjust Your Attitude

Eight Thousand Miles

You cannot tailor-make the situations in life but you can tailor-make
the attitudes to fit those situations.
~Zig Ziglar

Desert winds blew sand devils around us as we trudged behind a donkey cart loaded with our backpacks. We had arrived in Mali, West Africa, to visit our youngest child, Mary, who was serving in the Peace Corps. Since Mali was a Muslim country, I'd followed Mary's advice and left my cross necklace at home, but now I felt vulnerable without it. What if my husband's fears came true? What if we were kidnapped by terrorists and held for ransom, like those tourists we'd heard about on the news? Or what if we were lost forever in the Sahel's barren landscape? There wasn't even a road to follow. We were putting all of our faith in Mary, who had only been in the country for two years.

Suddenly, a dark slender man in army fatigues appeared. He shouldered his ancient rifle and discharged a mighty blast. Mary quickly explained. "He is just alerting everyone that you've arrived. You're the first volunteer's parents to visit."

Soon, we were surrounded by some four hundred singing and dancing villagers. They insisted that we lead what had become a parade into their village. When we arrived, the generous Malians gave us small, handmade gifts. Tears rolled down my cheeks. I felt honored and appreciated—the opposite of what I'd felt nine months earlier when I'd felt pressured to resign from my job.

For twelve years I'd worked at the hospital. One day they told me I was no longer needed. I understood that it was a cost-cutting move to replace me with someone with less experience and a lower salary. But my understanding didn't excise the wretched pain of feeling discarded and useless.

At sixty-two, what opportunities existed for someone my age? In the past, during similar budget cuts, I'd watched as other employees left, awash in bitterness. I refused to behave that way, no matter how scared I felt.

My mother often said, "Act like a lady." Despite my concerns, that is what I did. For a month, I cleaned my files and wrote detailed notes. I made it easy for my replacement to do my job. The program would continue, but I wouldn't. The most painful part of all was that no one would even notice my absence.

"Dear Lord," I prayed, "show me the way." As He so often does, He answered through someone else, a fellow health educator at another hospital. When I shared my worries about my future, she told me about a conference she had attended recently.

"I've just learned the most helpful tool," she said. "No matter what the situation is, there is an opposite, a benefit. Our typical response is to focus on the losses of job, marriage, home, or even health. Instead, the speaker told us to concentrate on finding what we gained with our loss."

At first, I resisted her advice as I grieved. I didn't care about "opposites." I wanted my job back. I missed my office, my co-workers, the routine. I missed the meaningful challenges of organizing health education classes for sick people. But as time passed, I grew tired of my dreary sorrow. Maybe I should try my friend's advice and seek some opposites.

The reverse of loneliness would be friendship. I called a neighbor and asked if she would like to take an exercise class with me. Soon, we became good friends. Although I missed my busy hours at work, I now had more personal time. I had choices. I tackled cleaning projects I'd delayed due to my long work hours. I volunteered at a mental health program.

Yet it wasn't until our trip to Africa that I understood the power of opposite thinking. We had cashed in our frequent flyer mileage and flown eight thousand miles to that village. We brought many presents—deflated soccer balls, Frisbees, pens, scarves, and inexpensive watches—believing that somehow we could improve the villagers' lives. Instead, they taught us the opposite. Our lives were the ones that needed improving.

Despite living in mud huts without modern conveniences, running water, or sanitation, the villagers appeared content. Frequently laughing and greeting each other, the beautiful Malians truly cared for their neighbors. Although we slept on the ground in our daughter's tiny courtyard, I felt a peace I hadn't known since I left my job. I admired the Southern Hemisphere's brilliant stars and thanked God for bringing us here. I had expected we would spend our time helping the poor villagers. Instead, they were teaching us that having less meant less to worry about and more time and energy for each other. These wonderful people of a different faith taught us an important lesson.

When we returned home, we decided we didn't need a large house. We sold our house, gave away or stored most of our belongings, and left town in our twenty-two-foot trailer. It felt so freeing to have less to care for and so good to have more time for family who needed us. We traveled to Illinois to attend to my mother-in-law, who suffered from dementia. After we arrived, the nursing home staff decreased the numerous medications they'd administered to control her behavior. Family and friends once again enjoyed visiting her.

After she died, we traveled. For a year we lived happily in our tiny trailer, as we looked for a new home with fewer expenses and lower state taxes. Eventually, we found a small mountain cabin in Colorado, near our grandchildren.

After my job loss, I thought my life work had been stolen from me. In seeking opposites, I discovered new opportunities that enriched my life. As I age, I still mourn when a new loss occurs, but soon, I seek its opposite. I am always rewarded.

~Carol Strazer

Forgiveness
and Freedom

Forgiveness does not change the past, but it does enlarge the future.
~Paul Boese

The dream startled me so much that I woke up gasping, my hand clutching the comforter. My husband's gentle snore and the familiar shapes in our darkened bedroom reassured me that what I'd seen wasn't real.

Even so, the image of my father wearing a red shirt, lying on his back on my living room sofa, would not go away. Nor would the words he'd said—one short sentence that I could not forget.

The clock on the nightstand told me I needed to go back to sleep but I hesitated to close my eyes. I feared the dream might continue, that Dad would once again say, "You haven't forgiven me yet." Five words that made my stomach churn.

The next day, I told myself it was ridiculous to allow a dream to unsettle me so. And it was only a dream. Dad had died in 1995, so suddenly that there had been no time to say anything to him. We'd had no final moments together. In life, my father would never have worn a red shirt or a red tie, not a red anything. He would also never have asked for forgiveness.

My father had been a complicated man, and during all of my adult years, I had a love/hate relationship with him. He provided the necessities of life in my growing-up years. He was fun to be with some of the time. My three brothers and I knew he loved us, but we also knew that he could turn from loving father to a man who belittled and verbally abused us if we moved outside the lines he'd drawn. We were to believe only what he believed, there was no discussion, no difference of opinion, no respect for our thoughts. It was a love so conditional that we lived with a tiny thread of fear every day.

He verbally and emotionally abused my mother even while loving her deeply. Having to watch silently hurt me. None of us suffered physical abuse from him, but we bore the scars of the cutting words hurled at us during his flares of temper.

He raged like a bull in a Spanish bullring when I wanted to leave the Midwest and teach in California. He disowned my youngest brother because the young college student had the nerve to fall in love with someone of a different race. The bitterness I harbored against my father sat inside me like a weighty rock for many years.

When he died, I had conflicting emotions—sadness that I'd lost my father, the man who loved me, sang songs to me when I was a little girl, who made special foods to cajole me to eat. Another part of me felt only relief that I would never again have to listen to him rant and rave, nor would I have to stand by and watch as he verbally abused my mother. Along with the relief came shame that I would feel this way. I never spoke about it to my mother or my husband. Instead, I carried it with me for the next fifteen years.

The dream brought it all to the surface. All that day, whenever I passed through my living room, I saw my father in the red shirt lying on the sofa and I shivered inwardly. Why now? What made this pop up so many years later? My sensible self knew he wasn't really there. I only imagined it.

Days, and then weeks, passed and I still had trouble looking at my sofa. No way would I sit on it! I churned inside. Why the dream? Why the red shirt? Why was he asking for my forgiveness? I couldn't put it together, didn't know what I should do, and it felt like a wound that refused to heal.

One afternoon, I needed a break while cleaning house, so I fixed a cup of steaming hot tea, grabbed a freshly-baked sugar cookie and sank into my favorite chair. Suddenly, Dad appeared on the sofa, and, yes, he had on that same red shirt. "You still haven't forgiven me," he said so softly I had to strain to hear the words.

Then began an epiphany. Instead of all the negative memories about my father that I'd harbored for so many years, I thought about the positives. My Girl Scout troop sponsored a Father-Daughter Dance and Dad escorted me, beaming with pride. He taught me to be loyal, to love my country and to believe in God. He encouraged me to go to college when our family really could not afford it.

As I sipped my tea, I remember the wonderful support Dad gave me when my first child was born with severe birth defects. I had a vision of the secondhand bike he'd fixed up like new as a birthday gift for me. I thought about my wedding day when he'd walked me down the aisle while I held on to his strong, steady arm.

I set my cup of tea on the end table and silently forgave him for all the hurt he'd inflicted over the years. It was time to bring some balance to my memories. Besides that, I finally realized that my forgiving him would afford both of us peace of mind. What good, I asked myself, did holding a grudge all these years do? It didn't help anyone, most of all, me. Once it was done, Dad disappeared from the sofa. I never saw him or his red shirt again.

What significance the red shirt had, I still do not know. But now, the good times about my life with Dad are remembered more than the dark ones. He came to ask my forgiveness, but the one who felt cleansed and free of bitterness turned out to be me.

~Nancy Julien Kopp

91

Steady the Course

Some people believe that holding on and hanging there are signs of strength,
but there are times in life when it takes much more strength just to let go.
~Ann Landers

can't get past this," I sobbed. "I don't even know how to live on my own. I've been married my entire adult life! What will I do?" After twenty years of marriage, my husband and the father of my children, the only man I'd ever been with, had left me.

All I could do was cry. It took everything I had in me just to get up each morning. There were decisions that I knew I had to make, issues I had to address. But how could I? I couldn't find the part of my brain where rational behavior lived.

My whole being was overwhelmed by my emotions, the raw throbbing hurt that attended my every moment and choked my sense of survival. I questioned my self-worth, my sense of who I was so tied up in who he was. I'd heard about the dark hole that swallows up the depressed. Looking down into such an abyss myself, I contemplated suicide. I was afraid, but I didn't know how to stop what was happening to me.

I prayed for a miracle. At first, my prayers were for the marriage to be restored. But as time passed, I realized that I couldn't lay my husband's actions on God—he hadn't made the choice to leave, my husband had. I still prayed for a miracle, but my new prayer was for strength to go on.

One Saturday morning, a friend called and suggested a boat ride. I am afraid of water, so I argued that this was absolutely the worst idea possible. I really, really, really didn't want to go!

But she persisted. "Oh, come on now. It will be good for you," she said.

"Good for me?" I retorted. "You know I hate the water. I don't swim all that well. What if I fall overboard?"

"Then I will pull you out," she said. "I'll pick you up in an hour."

At first, the boat skipping over the water was a great feeling, and I enjoyed the wind hitting my face and blowing my hair. I imagined that the boat would take me far away, far from my problems.

Suddenly, we hit a choppy spot in the middle of the lake where the waves pitched us back and forth. I clung to the sides of the boat while my friend clenched the wheel, determined to steer us to calmer waters. At that point, all other concerns paled. The most present need was to steady the boat. The realization hit that perhaps all I needed to do with my life — for right then, anyway — was to steady my course and hang on.

It was a turning point for me. Over the next year, I planted flowers, sewed curtains, and cleaned the house from top to bottom. I gave in to creativity, cooking up new recipes and painting a stained glass effect on a window. I went to counseling. I read books. I prayed. But most of all, I just hung on.

At last, healing came. I even reached a point where I was content to be alone and just to be me. My children said, "Mom, what's happened to you? You seem to be so together." I laughed. I was trying to appreciate the good things: my children, my friends, each new day, dreams for the future.

Then the unexpected happened. A wonderful man came into my life — a kind man, full of love and patience, a man whose first thought was for me rather than for himself. I had never known that kind of love before.

I wish I could say that I handled this well. But I can't. I cried yet again. I was so frightened by my past marriage experience that I couldn't commit or trust. A vision of that boat ride brought me back to my senses as I remembered that I needed only to steady the course. With time came trust, a wedding, and the most meaningful love that I have ever known.

So often we believe that miracles must be grandiose. We watch for the lightning to flash and wait to hear the thunder. But sometimes, miracles can be found in everyday lessons. An epiphany can happen on a boat ride.

~Eloise Elaine Ernst Schneider

92

The Bedtime Ritual that Changed My Life

Gratitude is an opener of locked-up blessings.
~Marianne Williamson

My first semester of graduate school was the busiest, most stressful time of my life. In addition to moving across the country, finding an apartment, learning to navigate a new city, trying to meet people and make new friends, and taking literature and fiction-writing courses, I was also thrown into teaching an undergraduate writing class five days a week.

Other than leading occasional creative writing workshops for middle school and high school students, this was my first time teaching. I was overwhelmed, to put it mildly. I cobbled together a syllabus and class rules from what I remembered of courses I took in college. Still, I had problems with students texting and talking during class. Up in front of the class, I felt overdressed and stiff. I was terrified my students would call me out as a fraud, sensing I had never done this before. I imagined them thinking "What right do you have to be teaching us? You're not a real professor—you're just a grad student."

One of the courses I was taking was a fiction-writing seminar. We each took turns sharing our work with the class, receiving feedback from fellow grad students. The night before my first story went up for critique, I had a panic attack. I could not fall asleep. My heart raced, and it felt like a 400-pound grizzly bear was sitting on my chest. I made it through the critique, but my anxiety remained.

That first semester, living on my own in a one-bedroom apartment, I often felt lonely. Anxiety, however, was my near-constant companion. I worried about not being a good teacher. I stressed out over my ever-growing pile of books to read and schoolwork to complete. I felt nervous in social situations—awkward, not myself. I wondered when it had become so hard for me to make friends. All of this caused my anxiety to fester and grow, its weight pressing down heavier and heavier on my chest.

In October, my dad came to visit. Having him around was like a fresh breeze sweeping into my life and airing out everything. He helped me see the beauty and fun in my new surroundings, things I had been missing when my vision was blurred by an anxious haze. We discovered an amazing hole-in-the-wall restaurant a few blocks from my apartment. We took walks on a trail beside the river. We even wandered through Indiana's largest corn maze. My dad took pictures of the autumn foliage and exclaimed over the fresh produce at the farmer's market. "If your mom and I lived here, we'd come here every week!" he said, hefting a large pumpkin into the trunk of my car. "What a neat place to live, Dal. You are so lucky!"

Lucky. It was a word I hadn't used to describe myself in a while. But, deep down, I knew my dad was right. I was lucky be in a graduate program, pursuing my dreams. I was lucky to be getting experience teaching. I was lucky to spend every day reading and writing and growing and learning, lucky I got to explore a new part of the country that I had never lived in before.

At the end of the week, I dropped my dad off at the airport. Walking back to my car, I wiped away my tears and resolved to take charge of my life and my health, to conquer the ache of loneliness and stress that had cast a shadow over the first half of the semester.

"Lucky." The word ran through my mind the entire drive home. I was indeed lucky. My dad had helped me see it. But how could I make sure I remembered it?

I thought back to a piece of advice my grandma once gave me:

fall asleep counting your blessings. So that's what I did. I climbed into bed that night feeling an all-too-familiar tightness in my chest—a signal of anxiety brewing for the busy week ahead. But I focused my thoughts on all that I had to be grateful for in my life: a comfy bed, a roof over my head, enough food to eat, warm clothes. I thought about my friends and family back home and all the love I had in my life. Even if I felt far from home at times, I knew I was always loved. I was never truly alone.

Rather than tossing and turning for hours, I fell asleep quickly. I woke up feeling more optimistic than I had felt in a long time. It was a start.

From then on, counting my blessings became my nighttime ritual. It was amazing how many things I found to be grateful for once I took the time to look. Gradually, my list of blessings included specific events and details from my new life: the nice e-mail from a student thanking me for the comments on her paper, the smile from a fellow grad student in the school hallway, the cozy hum of the radiator heating my apartment in the morning, a seat saved for me on the bus to campus, the smell of my first attempt at pumpkin pie baking in the oven, the comfort of a mug of chai tea on a snowy day.

As I became more grateful for my life, my anxiety loosened its grip. I grew more comfortable in my new surroundings, more able to be myself around new people, and I found it easier to make friends. Before long, I was looking forward to dinner every Friday evening with a nice group of friends I'd made in the English department.

I was less anxious teaching, too. As I became more confident in myself, I felt more empowered in my role as a teacher. I focused on what I could bring to the classroom as a young, enthusiastic new teacher, rather than worrying about the reasons I should feel daunted or overwhelmed. I channeled my energy into being the best teacher I could be—inspiring my students and helping them succeed. When the semester drew to a close, I was honored with an award for teaching excellence based on student evaluations of my course.

As the winter chill and shorter days set in, and final exams and grading loomed ahead, my anxiety sometimes reared its ugly head again.

Even today, more than a year later, it still does. But I now have a tool to combat my anxiety: gratitude. By focusing on the many blessings in my life, I remind myself what is truly important. No longer am I worried about surviving the stresses of daily life. I know I can thrive no matter what circumstances arise.

~Dallas Woodburn

Best Day Ever

The world always looks brighter from behind a smile.
~Author Unknown

The rain fell gently. I stared out my kitchen window as my morning coffee got cold. Pretty soon my quiet house would be bursting with activity, as it was every day. My husband would rush out the door to his twelve-hour shift. I would be in charge of the children, all five of them.

Soon my three daughters would wake up to get ready for school. I would make sure they brushed their teeth, combed their hair, got dressed, and ate breakfast all in time to rush out the door to make the school bus. My son was in the afternoon kindergarten class, so I would have to repeat all of the above with him, while holding my infant son on my hip.

My mind drifted back to the years before I got married and had children. I had fantasized what my life would be like. I would marry my Prince Charming, live in a beautiful house that was spotless. My children would all be well behaved, neat as a pin. I loved my children and husband, but I never imagined it would be so hard.

The girl's alarm clock rang and startled me back to reality. I dragged myself away from the window, not ready for the day's marathon. This particular morning I was more somber than most.

My oldest daughter picked up on my mood. "Mom, why are you sad?" she asked.

I asked her why she thought I was sad.

"I just said you look pretty, Mom."

I was so absorbed in my own self-pity that I didn't even hear my daughter tell me I looked pretty. I forced myself to smile and said I was sorry I didn't hear her.

"See Mom, when you smile, you look even prettier!" she chirped.

This time, I didn't have to force myself to smile.

When I woke my son up for kindergarten that day, I did so with a big smile. At first I had to force the smile, because I didn't want him to pick up on my sadness as my daughter did. But that forced smile felt so good that before I realized it I was truly smiling.

That afternoon the clouds gave way to the sunshine. I decided to break our normal routine. Instead of putting my son on the school bus, I bundled him and his baby brother up and decided we should walk the ten blocks to school. The walk was invigorating, and my son gleefully chatted all the way too school. As we approached the school he asked excitedly, "Can we do this again tomorrow? Please?"

"Of course we can," I said, and I meant it.

As I walked back home, I practically grinned all the way. Wait, was that a skip in my step? I picked up the speed and sang a silly song along the way. My baby boy started giggling as be bounced in the carriage. Soon I was giggling right along with him.

When I approached my house, my neighbor waved to me and invited me in for a cup of tea. "I'm so happy to see you — it's been a long time," she said.

It had been. I couldn't even remember the last time I'd seen her, and we lived right next door from each other. As we sipped our tea, we caught up and had many laughs. We promised to get together more often.

Back at home, as my youngest child slept, I did some self-evaluating. So far, this day was one of the happiest I'd had in a long time. Not much was different, just the fact that I allowed myself to see things through a different perspective. And I allowed myself to smile.

My children would be home from school soon, and my baby would be awake. Instead of just watching TV and feeling sorry for myself, I took out my camera and photographed my baby boy as he slept. He was beautiful, a true gift, as all my children were. I was so clouded by the day's chores and obligations that I had been missing out on what was truly important in life, my family.

That evening I gathered my children in the kitchen and smiled at them. "Who wants to bake a cake?" I asked.

In unison, they shouted, "I do, I do!"

As we started our cake, I looked at my children and felt so truly blessed that I could practically hear violins playing in the background. Years ago, before I had my children, this was my fantasy of how it would be.

Then right on cue, plop, my youngest daughter dropped the whole bag of flour onto the floor right next to where her baby brother was sitting. The flour was everywhere and my baby boy was covered from head to toe with it. He looked up at us with his toothless grin and giggled contagiously. We all started to laugh until our sides hurt. I ran for my camera and took photos of my flour-covered baby and my children and our delightfully messy kitchen.

Later that night, after I read my children a bedtime story, my middle daughter said, "This was the best day ever!"

I couldn't have agreed more.

~Dorann Weber

94

Picture This

Beauty is how you feel inside, and it reflects in your eyes.
It is not something physical.
~Sophia Loren

My seventh grade yearbook picture boasts a handwritten caption: "Always remember, this picture isn't nearly as nice as the person." Somewhere out in the world, another yearbook from 1975 bears the same caption—under the photo of my friend, Trudy. We both endured the humiliation of having a bad picture that year, and we each wrote the phrase under the other's photo.

The year of the bad yearbook picture marked a sea change in the way I thought about myself. Before age twelve, I was self-confident, with high self-esteem, a flair for the dramatic, and an interest in many and varied subjects. I dreamed of being a writer, and had already submitted a manuscript to a publisher.

I knew I had the right to be in the world. I belonged. And it had nothing to do with how I looked.

But at age twelve, I started to care more about my appearance than my intelligence, my hobbies, my sense of humor, or my kind disposition. With that decision came the doubts. My stomach wasn't as flat as my friend Laura's. My smile was crooked. My hair was blah. Maybe I wasn't as wonderful as I'd believed myself to be. Maybe I didn't have the right to be walking around, looking the way I did.

As I moved on to eighth grade and then on to high school and college, the doubts only multiplied. The pretty girls got everything—the boys, the attention, the school glory. They dressed up in lovely gowns to go to the junior prom and the senior ball while I stayed home. They were the cheerleaders and popular girls, the ones everyone else looked up to. They were the desired. What was I? Yes, I got good grades, and yes, everyone said I was "nice." But the rewards for those things weren't as obvious as what the pretty girls received, and thus didn't seem as worthy. If the rewards weren't as worthy, didn't that mean I wasn't as worthy?

At one level, I knew appearance shouldn't be so important, and I didn't try all that hard to improve mine. But the pressure and desire were there. Every time I saw a picture of myself, I felt the same way I had in seventh grade—disgusted, ashamed, mad at myself. Why wasn't I prettier? Why was I a failure at looking attractive? If a picture is worth a thousand words, each photo of myself was an essay about how worthless I was.

Almost every experience I had was colored by my perception of how I looked. I couldn't look at a single picture I was in without berating myself. I envied my friends who were prettier, with better figures, who were wonderfully photogenic. Sometimes I was downright jealous. They seemed to have no trouble attracting attention while I struggled to be noticed. One friend said to me, "I know I'm pretty." This wasn't braggadocio; she was simply stating a fact. All my attractive friends seemed to take it for granted that their appearance wasn't something they had to worry about. They constantly received positive reinforcement. I longed for the compliments they so readily received. I yearned for the adoration and admiration.

At the same time, I knew I was being ridiculous. Why did I care so much? By adulthood, I'd accepted any number of things about myself. I would never swim in the Olympics. I would never pitch in the major leagues. So why couldn't I accept I would never be beautiful?

Besides, I didn't particularly value beauty in others. Sure, I admired my pretty friends and envied them, but what I liked most about them wasn't their pleasing appearances. I loved Danielle's sense of humor, Jackie's expert cooking, and Hannah's enthusiasm for life. And in everyone else? What sent shivers down my spine was kindness to others. News stories depicting strangers helping each other in need always brought tears to my eyes.

But I couldn't seem to apply the same standards to myself. If pictures were taken of an event I attended, what became most important was how I looked. How washed out and plump I was at my brother's wedding. My hair was a mess at the county fair. I never could truly enjoy an experience that involved picture taking because I worried ahead of time that I would later have confirmation that I'd looked unattractive.

I often felt ashamed for feeling the way I did. I was perfectly healthy, with no disfigurements. I might not attract positive attention, but I didn't attract negative attention, either. In every other way, my life was extremely pleasant. Why did I care so much about such a superficial aspect of my life?

The low point came when I refused to watch the DVD of my stepfather's memorial service. Not because I would be sad—though that was part of it—but because I didn't want to see how I looked, especially when I took to the podium to talk about Dan and ended up in tears. My face would surely have scrunched up unattractively. This was a man I had loved and looked up to for thirty-five years. Was I really taking away from his memorial service solely the fact that I might not have looked my best? Especially at the moment when I was being my most authentic self, when I was showing my true emotions?

That low point became the turning point. I had lived for almost fifty years and had spent most of them worrying about my appearance. I vowed from then on to live my life without caring so much about how I looked. I would enjoy experiences rather than analyze how I looked doing them, and channel my energy into more valuable pursuits—whether for my career or my relationships. Sure, I would attempt to look my best. But that would be a far cry from what I'd been doing—hoping to look like someone other than myself, and caring about that above all else.

These days, I admit I have setbacks. I can't seem to completely turn off my displeasure when I see a picture of myself with more than one chin. I still think I look heavy in almost every photo. I search for, and find, gray hairs and wrinkles. But it is better. I am learning to value who I am on the inside. I started thinking of it this way—at my own memorial service, what do I want people to say about me? That I was beautiful? What an empty and lonely sentiment. No. I want to be known as a kind person, most of all. Generous, wise, creative, and intelligent, too. When I think about it, appearance doesn't even make the list. So why worry about it when I'm alive?

I believe that life really is different for attractive people—maybe easier; perhaps, in certain circumstances, better. But in the end, does it really matter? I don't think so. Maybe Trudy and I were on to something when we said the picture wasn't nearly as nice as the person. Maybe we suspected being nice was better.

And now I am convinced it is.

~Carol Ayer

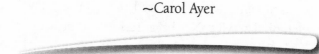

95

All Things New

They must often change, who would be constant in happiness or wisdom.
~Confucius

"Mom, you don't need to call all the time to check on me," our twenty-year-old son, Joe, said. "I've got to go. And Mom, you need to get a life."

Before I could say goodbye, he hung up. His words echoed in my head. "Get a life." I felt like I'd arrived to work at the best job in the world and been handed a pink slip. Being a mom meant everything to me.

It seemed one day our house bustled with activity, and then the next day it was quiet. There were no teenagers bursting through the front door asking, "What's for dinner?" There were no more late-night chats about school, crushes, or jobs.

In an effort to lift our spirits, one weekend my husband Loren said, "Let's go for a drive." We caught the ferry and drove up Whidbey Island. Standing on the bluff at Fort Casey, Loren and I watched tugboats drag barges through the Straits of Juan de Fuca. We'd visited the favorite Washington state park dozens of times with our kids.

Tears dripped down my cheeks as a chilly March wind whipped off the water. "It feels strange to be here without them. I can hear their laughter in the air and see Ben chasing Joe down the beach, whacking him with kelp."

"I know." Loren pulled me close under his arm while we strolled to our car. "I wonder what they're doing today."

Scenes from their childhood played in our minds as we drove from the park. The emptiness we felt with half our family missing ruined our outing. A few miles from the ferry I interrupted the silence. "Well, we can't just mope around the rest of our lives. I think we need to go to new places, places we never took the kids, places not already filled with memories. We need to build new memories of our own."

"Hmm... " Loren nodded. "You might be right."

While my idea simmered, Loren and I talked of dreams long left dormant. We considered changes we needed to make to move forward. Plans took shape as we envisioned our future together.

In May we traded our family car for a sporty SUV. In June Loren took a two-week vacation. We packed our clothes, loaded an ice chest filled with fruit and sandwiches into our new car, and hit the road. Instead of heading north or east like we'd always done as a family, we drove south.

Traveling down Highway 101, we explored the Oregon and Northern California coastlines. Whenever we needed a rest, we pulled off the highway at the nearest beach. Seated on the tailgate of our vehicle, we ate meals from the ice chest. We held hands, strode miles of oceanfront beaches, and sat on driftwood logs to watch the sunset.

We booked a room at a B&B, something we'd never done. The innkeeper operated a side business making fused glass and offered classes to guests. We marveled over glass vases and platters, swirled with color, displayed in the dining room. "Do you want to sign up for a class?" I said to Loren.

He gave me a skeptical grin. "I don't know. We've never done anything like that before."

Smiling, I shrugged my shoulders. "That's the point. Come on, it'll be fun."

We paid our forty dollars and signed up for an afternoon class. Huddled over a workbench in the innkeeper's studio, we spent several hours learning the process of fused glass. I watched Loren select colored glass chips from numerous supply bins and arrange them in unique patterns. We each made two coasters, had hours of fun, shared a new experience, and learned a new craft.

We had so much fun on our trip we started a list of other places we wanted to visit.

However, when we returned home once again, we faced a quiet empty house. After twenty-two years of raising kids, we felt lost until we realized we finally had time to focus on our own interests. We cleared out the kids' bedrooms and turned one into a study. Loren registered for college and earned a degree. We repainted our daughter's old room and transformed it into an art studio. Loren built me a painting table and I signed up for watercolor classes with a local artist.

We skated along fine until that first holiday season approached. Without the flurry and excitement of our kids it was miserable. Alone, we slogged through the field of the Christmas tree farm our family visited each year. From a dark corner of our closet Loren retrieved cardboard boxes labeled "Christmas." I loved the sights, sounds, and smells of the season, but when we unwrapped the first decorations, I held up a calico cat fashioned from wallpaper with buttons sewn on to attach the legs. "Bethany made this," I sniffed. "And here's the rabbit Joe made, but he's not here to hang it on the tree."

Loren wrapped his arms around me and pulled me onto the couch. "Hey, I've got an idea. Why don't we buy new ornaments?"

His suggestion seemed a wild extravagance. I gazed into the box of homemade decorations. Each one came with years of memories. "Okay." I jumped up from the couch. We rewrapped the ornaments in tissue. Loren carried the boxes back to the closet.

On Saturday we went to the store. "I feel like newlyweds on our first Christmas together," I said.

Loren laughed. "We're a long way from those days." Eyes wide with delight we strolled each aisle. A string of twinkly lights for the tree and several packages of shiny ornaments lifted our spirits and helped us glide through the season.

One evening early in the new year Loren said, "Hey, let's catch a movie."

"What, right now?" I glanced at my watch. "It's nine o'clock."

After a moment's thought I raced to grab my coat. "You're on."

Near midnight, stars twinkled in the sky as we strolled from the theater. "I don't remember the last time we went to the late show."

Loren gave my hand a gentle squeeze. "Not since we were dating."

When we arrived home we spotted the answering machine blinking. Loren pressed the button and we heard Joe's voice, "Hello... Hello... Pick up the phone... Hey, it's ten o'clock. Where are you guys?"

I laughed as Loren and I snuggled into bed. "He told me to get a life."

~Kathleen Kohler

96

The Relationship Dance

The truest expression of a people is in its dance and in its music.
Bodies never lie.
~Agnes de Mille

L isa and I arrived at the fundraiser for a local non-profit and dutifully wove our way through the lines of people placing bids on vacation packages, sports tickets, gift certificates to hotels and restaurants, jewelry, and kitchen makeovers. Every sheet seemed to be filling up with people eagerly trying to outbid one another. It was great for the charity but well outside of what I could afford.

I started looking for a way to slip through the crowd and locate our table for dinner when I spotted Lisa looking down at a bid sheet. When I walked over to join her, I saw was that the bid sheet was empty. Not one person had bid on the item. What could be that unappreciated, so awful that not one person would bid on it? A complimentary colonoscopy? A Brazilian wax for men? Fruitcake for life?

My eyes widened in horror when I read the description. It was worse than I imagined—three ballroom dance lessons.

Lisa looked at me with her soft puppy-dog eyes and lips that were a breath away from a pout.

"Really?" I asked.

"It sounds exciting!" she said.

I squeezed my eyes shut. Why couldn't it have been a colonoscopy?

Lisa handed me a pen. I sighed. "I love you," I said as I wrote down a bid.

"I know you do," she said.

I've heard that people who face near-death experiences have images from their life flash quickly through their minds. Every former emotionally draining, ego-sucking, fear-inspiring dance experience I had ever had careened through my thoughts. In third grade I played Frosty the Snowman. My mother volunteered to make the costume. Somehow she fashioned a bed sheet over a frame she made from coat hangers. I couldn't see anything, but was told that all I had to do was dance. I still remember the sound of hundreds of children laughing.

I began practicing dance at home with a broom and later with my Great Dane, Luke, who was large enough to put his paws on my shoulders when I stood in front of him. I moved from slowly rocking from side to side to occasionally putting one foot forward or back and rocking in one awkward movement that resembled someone tentatively trying to step on an escalator. Luke must have lost patience with me as he disappeared a short time later.

One ballroom dance lesson turned into almost five years of them. I realized that as I'd struggled with dance over the years, I had also struggled with failed relationships and even a failed marriage. My prior relationships resembled my earlier clumsy attempts to dance. I either held the person too close and stepped on their toes or held them too far away and they drifted off. I wasn't a very good dance partner. I didn't pick up on the rhythm of relationships and thought more about my own dance steps than those of my partners. I had a picture in my mind of how the dance should be done and held rigidly to that even when the music changed.

In ballroom dance I learned a new sense of partnership from our dance instructor Francesca. To dance well in ballroom you have to believe that the whole is larger than the sum of the parts. There's no room for selfishness. Nearly all communication is non-verbal. To become adept at the fiery passionate intimacy of tango, the amorous and sensual foxtrot, or the deeply romantic and graceful waltz, partners have to connect with one another and cooperate.

As Lisa's and my partnership on the dance floor grew so did our relationship off the floor. Learning to dance changed my understanding of how to love and that has made all the difference.

~Chris Jahrman

97

Just Drive Warrior

Always do what you are afraid to do.
~Ralph Waldo Emerson

At forty-one, I was in my first auto accident. I looked in my rearview mirror just in time to see a young man looking at his phone slam into the back of my car. I had nowhere to go. I braced, closed my eyes, and hugged the steering wheel. He hit me going about 35 miles per hour.

Filled with adrenaline, I jumped out of the car and walked around aimlessly. I remember people asking, "Are you okay?"

I heard myself say, "I don't know." I was so dizzy and nauseated I just wanted to go home.

When that adrenaline wore off, I felt everything. My entire body hurt. I went to the doctor. I was told I had a concussion, my back was out of alignment, and my right leg had been jammed up into my hip by the impact.

After some physical therapy and down time, my head healed. Then my leg healed and finally my back healed.

But every time I got into the car, fear came over me. Would someone hit me again? I would drive down the freeway thinking, "He's too close. He's going to hit me." At each stoplight I would spend the whole time looking in the rearview mirror, thinking, "She's coming in fast. Will she stop in time?" I would find myself bracing for impact. I'd slam my own brakes, afraid I was too close to another car. I'd close my eyes and wait for the hit. My fear grew with each day.

I knew I was doing it. But I just couldn't make the fear go away. I'd ask myself, "How long are you going to be scared? Get over it already."

But I couldn't.

One day I was driving to an appointment. The roads were wet and there was a threat of snow. Fear filled my entire body. It's bad enough driving on dry pavement. But in wet, snow or ice, my paralyzing fear becomes almost unbearable.

"This is it," I decided. "Enough is enough! I will face my fear. This year I will become a warrior. I will drive without fear! I will."

It took everything I had. I had conversation after conversation with myself as I was driving down the road. I'd stare at the sparkling street covered with the frost. I'd glance at the outside temperature gauge in my car that read twenty-five degrees.

"Don't look at that!" I'd tell myself. "Just drive, warrior!"

I heard myself say out loud, "Don't focus on the fear. Focus on your path."

Don't focus on the fear. Focus on your path.

I felt my grip start to lighten up on the steering wheel. For the first time I heard the radio playing my favorite 80's hits. Had that been on the entire time?

What I focus on is what will be. If I focus on the fear, then I will live in fear. If I focus on my path, my destination, and possibly a little 80's music, I'll reach my destination.

I am a warrior and no fear is going to stop me.

~Diana Lynn

98

Pickles

You yourself, as much as anybody in the entire universe,
deserve your love and affection.
~Gautama Buddha

work in a pickle shop. Okay, we sell things other than pickles—sauces, salsas, and marinades—all packaged in large glass mason jars with matching shiny gold lids. But pickles are what we are known for. When you envision an old-fashioned pickle shop, the stereotypical ideas you might have—food sold in barrels, employees wearing button-downs and jeans and dirty aprons, and a plethora of America-the-great themed décor—are all true. So I just say I work in a pickle shop.

When I was hired, I was told that part of my job was to keep the conversation going with customers. This made me nervous. I had never been a very talkative person. But I fudged the truth on my application, and said that I was totally comfortable with talking with strangers.

Fake it till you make it. That's what I did. I sucked it up, put on my button-down, my jeans, my dirty apron, and I entered that pickle shop with a smile on my face. And I decided to just let my real self shine through.

A year and a half later, I am the most tenured employee and have no problem easing into conversations with new customers. I smile, ask them about their day, comment on the great sale. Then I convince them to buy three jars of our pickled garlic.

It is in this pickle store that I learned what self-esteem truly was.

Previously, I had always pictured it to be a quality solely possessed by the skinny blond cheerleaders in high school. I am neither skinny, nor blond, and I'm certainly not a cheerleader. While working my way up the ladder at the pickle shop, I worked my way to a broader definition of self-esteem as well.

Self-esteem is knowing who you are and not being afraid to let it shine. My big smile and loud laugh, once a source of embarrassment, has become a sort of trademark for me. It helps me with my sales because customers feel like I am a real person, not just a robotic saleswoman.

Self-esteem is not being completely shut down by a mistake. I once had a customer tell me I was annoying. Pre-pickle shop, I might have crumbled and refused to talk to another customer. Instead, with my new self-confidence, I smiled, apologized, and moved on to the next person, knowing that this woman was the exception, not the rule.

Because of my pickle-shop self-esteem, I applied myself at college. Freshman year I was elected to the boards of two large clubs while maintaining a 4.0 GPA.

It took eighteen years and a store full of pickles to teach me to be happy with myself.

~Fallon Kane

My Perfect Imperfect Life

Most folks are about as happy as they make up their minds to be.
~Abraham Lincoln

A few years ago, I was standing at the barre waiting for my adult ballet class to begin when I heard a voice behind me. "So, do you have this perfect life?"

My first reaction was to wonder who was being asked what I thought was an odd question. Then I remembered there were only two of us in the room. When I turned around, the other woman was looking straight at me.

I had no idea what prompted her question or how to answer. Was she serious? Who has a perfect life? Sure, on occasion I may have said I found the perfect dress or the perfect pair of shoes, but never would I use that word to describe anything about me or my life. I felt a twinge of guilt for somehow giving her that impression.

She watched me. I finally managed to mutter a quick, "No."

By then the teacher had entered the room and turned on the music to start class. With a sigh of relief, I moved my feet into the best fifth position my untrained body was capable of. But as soon as my knees bent for our first plié I realized my concentration had been hijacked. This woman's words wouldn't stop echoing in my thoughts.

I wanted to know how she came up with her very flawed perception. If she knew anything about my life, she never would have had the nerve to ask me that question.

I did my best to continue through the motions until it was time to do our floor exercises in front of the mirror. For a few moments I didn't see the usual reflection of my older self attempting to use a beautiful art form to improve my balance, posture, and gracefulness. I only saw the little girl whose father died when she was two, the child who walked home from elementary school every day to an empty house, who learned to sew her own clothes to save money, who became scarred from a painful hospital stay.

Perfect. My life had been far from it.

When those memories faded, I was left with a vision of the woman I had become, the woman molded by all those things I considered imperfect. I now saw the woman who had learned to be self-reliant and resourceful, who valued her family and her friends, who didn't take life for granted. Was that the perfect this woman had detected?

I still don't know, but I no longer feel guilty or feel like I must keep a running tab of all the difficult times to prove my life isn't perfect. Though I might still squirm a bit if ever again asked if my life is perfect, I would have a different answer. Because now I see that, despite all its imperfection, it is.

~Marilyn Boone

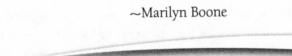

The Stay-at-Home Mom

Fear is only as deep as the mind allows.
~Japanese Proverb

I often drive long distances to visit my family members who are spread out all across the country. "You are so brave," a friend said. " I could never drive that far by myself." If only she knew.

Back when I was a young mother, I gathered my son and daughters, strapped the baby in the stroller, and hiked the long trek to the supermarket. As we carefully walked along the shoulder of the road, I held tight to my daughter's hand. Soccer moms whizzed by in their new minivans, while I sulked in self-pity. I resented my husband's demanding job, and his long commutes. He could never get home early enough to take us shopping. Today there was no milk left and the baby was out of diapers, so we had to get to the supermarket.

At one time, I owned a car. I was driving on the highway, and my car started shuddering. It stalled out, right in the middle of a busy intersection. The car behind us screeched to a halt, almost hitting us. My heart was hammering, as I tried to start the car again. Horns were honking around me as I prayed.

I kept cranking the ignition, concerned for the safety of my children in the back seat. Just as I melted down into tears, the car started up again. After that, I became convinced that if I drove that car, our lives would be in danger.

I started avoiding car trips. A simple drive around the corner would send me plummeting into extreme anxiety. My heart would race. I'd get lightheaded and panic. Soon I was terrified to drive at all. We sold the car.

Our decision to sell it hindered our lives in a major way. As anyone who has lived in suburbia knows, it is impossible to function without an automobile. Friends volunteered to drive my son to tee-ball practices. They drove the girls to friends' birthday parties. My husband ran most of our errands after working ten-hour days. I felt isolated at home, staring at the walls all day.

"I would get you a car, but you would never drive it," my husband said. The words made a deep impression on me. How could I admit that I had a huge problem? If I kept giving in to fear, soon I would be afraid to leave the house at all.

I went for a medical checkup. There was nothing physically wrong with me, but there was a name for what I had: panic disorder. I suffered from attacks while driving. The intense feelings of doom, perspiration, lightheadedness, trembling, and sheer terror were all symptoms.

If I stayed on this path, I would miss so many wonderful things that life had to offer. My four children would too.

As time went on, our lives got busier, and my friends could only help so much. One beautiful summer day, my six-year-old stood outside watching her friends get in their parents' cars with their beach towels and sandpails.

"How come we never go to the beach, Mom?"

"We don't need the beach," I said. "We have a pool in the back yard."

The pool was actually an inflatable baby pool, and deep down inside I knew that the older kids were too big for it. How long could I keep making excuses for my problem? It was hurting everyone around me.

We bought a used minivan. It was in good condition and it was the only vehicle I felt safe driving the children in. Going around the corner was a major ordeal at first. I kept a paper bag in the car in case I started hyperventilating. I soon learned that if I chewed gum, it would keep me from breathing too fast. Sipping water helped too.

When symptoms started coming on, I talked myself through them by saying positive affirmations until I calmed down.

Gradually, I increased the distance I traveled in small increments. But despite my progress, I refused to drive on highways. Just the thought of driving on a highway again terrified me. The beach was still a distant dream.

Then fortune intervened. A friend had driven us to *The Sound of Music* auditions at a college. Her daughter and my children, Bill and Michelle, were offered parts in it. We were the only people from our area in the play, and practices were three times a week in the early evenings. My friend couldn't always drive us to rehearsals. My husband had to work. It was up to me. If I didn't drive on the highway, our children couldn't perform in the play. I couldn't let them down.

The first time I drove on the highway to rehearsal, I was frantic. Every time a truck whizzed by, I gripped the steering wheel in panic, clutching it so hard my hands grew numb. I stayed in the right lane, knowing that if my anxiety became too bad, I could pull over. I was afraid I would faint.

My children tried to calm me down by talking to me. Michelle and her friend practiced their songs, distracting me from the fear. I prayed and chewed gum. My desire to see my children succeed was more powerful than this overwhelming, paralyzing fear that had wreaked havoc upon my life.

Fortunately for all of us, the children kept getting cast in productions all over New Jersey. Soon I was traveling everywhere for dance classes, play rehearsals, band and vocal concerts, as well as Cub Scouts, Brownies and soccer games.

It was amazing. The more I drove, the more comfortable I became with it. My panic attacks happened less frequently, until one day I realized that I couldn't remember the last time I had had one.

A year later, on a brilliant July day, I braved the highway and drove us all to the beach. As I watched my children running along the shoreline, laughing and splashing each other and building magnificent sand castles, I realized this beautiful family moment would have never happened if I hadn't faced my fear.

Now I drive all over the place. Some people think I'm a brave person. If only they knew that at one time I couldn't even drive around the corner to the grocery store.

~L.A. Strucke

Thriving

Your greatest responsibility is to live a life that nourishes your highest truth.
~Mollie Marti

I was diagnosed with breast cancer in 2001. For the next two years I battled that awful disease with the help of my strong faith in God, a loving family, a caring church family, and the amazing staff at the Tom Baker Cancer Centre in Calgary, Alberta. When my hair was just starting to grow back and my strength was starting to return, I looked in the mirror and said, "Now what?"

When I was in the throes of battle, I didn't look ahead more than a day or week at a time. My entire focus was getting through each treatment and praying every single day that God would just give me a little more time to spend with my family and friends. I didn't look toward a future because I honestly did not know if I would have a future. I was in a life or death battle.

When the doctors told me that I was clear of cancer and that I could now consider myself a survivor, of course I was ecstatic, but I was also a little confused. What did surviving really mean? I now had years ahead of me and I had no idea what to do with those years.

For several weeks I was in what I would call a holding pattern. I spent a lot of time praying and thinking about what I wanted out of life after cancer.

I was a mom with a growing family before cancer, so I naturally plugged myself into their daily lives again and felt recharged about having the energy to attend their school events and help them with homework again. There was a new attitude to the way I approached daily life. I no longer took for granted the blessings in each day, but lived in the moment and thoroughly enjoyed the daily surprises that come with raising children.

I started to volunteer again at my church. When the position of Children's Minister was offered to me, I accepted. Only months after taking on that job, I felt a calling to take a few classes at seminary. That led to a four-year program to get my Master of Religious Education degree. Two years into that degree program, I was helping my daughter plan her wedding! Truly, I was as much surprised by these turn of events as my family was at my willingness to try something new and be as engaged in life as I was now. Instead of asking "Now what?" I was asking, "What's next?"

One day, as I was purging some old and mostly forgotten files from my computer, I came across a story I had written long before I had cancer. It was an untitled manuscript, an unfinished work that I had written and then forgotten about. I was just ready to press the delete button when my husband looked over my shoulder and said, "You should finish that story and publish it."

I think I laughed out loud at his foolhardy suggestion. I had a part-time job. I was just finishing up my degree. I was a very busy mom, and the thought of writing a book had never occurred to me. Still, the idea took root and within a few short weeks I had completed the manuscript and submitted it to a publisher.

That first book led to writing two more, and ten years after my cancer diagnosis I won a Canadian Christian Writing Award for my blog. I continue to be humbled by the literary awards I have accepted over the past few years.

I now have two thoroughly adorable grandchildren, and when I am not cuddling with them, I continue to write. We're empty nesters now, my husband and I, so we like to camp and travel and spend quality time with each other and with our family. I teach creative writing and language arts to junior high school students and I am still active in my church teaching Sunday school. For the most part, that two-year battle with breast cancer seems like just a tiny season of my life that I look back on once in a while to acknowledge that I lived through it and survived.

But I did way more than just survive. I thrived.

~Lynn Dove

Afterword

Reboot. Reinvent. Revitalize. Revise. It's amazing how many empowering life-changing words start with "Re" but involve real work too! The 101 stories that you've read in this volume have surely refreshed your attitude and reenergized you, whether you have already rebooted your life or are just thinking about it. And if you've read the stories, you know it's worth doing the work, because our writers report such positive changes in their lives once they follow their dreams, pursue their passions, and find new purpose and meaning in what they do.

I was thrilled when I discovered my coauthor Claire Cook a few months ago. Our meeting was fortuitous. Claire re-tweeted an interview I did on Forbes.com about tips for inspirational writing. I don't know why, but for some reason I decided to look up this friendly looking person who had tweeted about me, and I discovered that Claire had not only reinvented herself and become a super successful novelist, but that reinvention and rebooting are particular specialties of Claire's! She was even working on her own book on the topic.

We talked and I realized I couldn't find a better writing and editing partner than Claire for this book. Claire totally gets what we're all about—stories from ordinary people having extraordinary experiences, the power of storytelling to change lives, the value of real-life examples as motivational tools. And I know that Claire uses real stories in her own book. When you read about real people, the lessons become more memorable, and your own ability to improve your life seems more realistic.

Claire's new book is out now. It's called *Never Too Late: Your Roadmap* to Reinvention (*without getting lost along the way*). Claire shares everything she's learned on her own journey—from writing her first book in her minivan at forty-five, to walking the red carpet at the Hollywood premiere of *Must Love Dogs* at fifty, to becoming the *USA Today* bestselling author of eleven novels and a sought after reinvention speaker. It's a great companion piece to this Chicken Soup for the Soul volume.

Thanks for being one of our readers. Maybe we'll even get to meet on Twitter!

~Amy Newmark
@amynewmark

Meet Our Contributors

J.C. Andrew lives in Sedona, AZ and is a professional artist and writer. She produces fiction, short stories, and poetry. Her most recent project is the mystery *Painted Death*, a book based on her experiences in Alaska. E-mail her at Andrew_arts@esedona.net.

Carol Ayer's personal essays have been published by *The Christian Science Monitor*, and in previous editions of Chicken Soup for the Soul. Her other credits include *Woman's World*, *True Story*, and *The Washington Pastime*. Learn more at www.carolayer.com.

Pam Bailes, having reached the age where such things are possible, divides her time between her two passions. Half is spent banging out stories on the computer, the other half shanking golf balls into the desert. She is abetted in these endeavors by her Jack Russell, four horses, and her daughter who lives nearby.

Garrett Bauman successfully finished his course in physical therapy and now rides a real bicycle on the sandy trails of South Carolina's islands and wooded trails in rural New York. His work has been in a dozen Chicken Soup for the Soul books and in many other publications. E-mail him at garrettbauman@frontiernet.net.

Jay H. Berman is disabled but remains as active as possible. He spends most of his time reading and writing. Occasionally, his political commentary appears on blogs like dailykos.com. Jay's primary interests are politics, literature, history and baseball.

Jan Bono's specialty is humorous personal experience. She has published five collections, two poetry chapbooks, nine one-act plays, a dinner theater play, and written for magazines ranging from *Guideposts* to *Woman's World*. Jan is currently writing a mystery series set on the southwest Washington coast. Learn more at www.JanBonoBooks.com.

Marilyn Boone is a former elementary school teacher, having received her Bachelor of Science degree in Education from the University of Tulsa. She is an active member of Oklahoma Writers' Federation, Inc. and her local writers' group. When not writing, Marilyn enjoys traveling, gardening and baking.

Paul Bowling is the father of two children, husband to his wife of fourteen years and a veteran of Operation Enduring Freedom in Afghanistan. He is still a member of a motorcycle club and continues to ride and write when he has the opportunity. Paul has never taken any formal writing classes; it's just simply something he enjoys doing.

Dr. Robert J. Brake is a resident of Ocean Park, WA, and a retired college teacher. He earned his Ph.D. at Michigan State University and has published several hundred essays and three books. Since his Eden Express adventure, Brake has served on numerous nonprofit boards and has dedicated his life to serving others.

Christine Burke is an artist, writer and educator. She studied art under Karl Kuerner, who was mentored by Andrew Wyeth. Look for her upcoming children's book titled *A Dream Inside* (Cedar Tree Books). Christine taught in the public schools and now teaches art lessons and workshops to children and adults.

P. Avice Carr calls herself a tumbleweed. She uses the tumbleweed to explain moving and writing stories, gathered along the way. She stayed in Ontario long enough to graduate from Western University. Learn more at www.pavicecarr.wix.com/tumbleweed.

Sharron Carrns' roles in life, work and writing draw upon her years as a wife, mother, God mom, mentor, small groups director and corporate training specialist. She lives in Spring Lake, MI with her husband and two of her children.

Jennifer Chauhan is the Executive Director of Project Write Now (www.projectwritenow.org), an organization dedicated to fostering a love of writing in young people. She has an M.A. degree in English Education from Teacher's College, Columbia University. She lives on the Jersey Shore with her three children.

Born and raised in England, **Christopher Clark** moved to Cape Town in 2009 after travelling to more than fifty countries worldwide. He received a Bachelor of Arts degree in Media and Writing from the University of Cape Town, and now writes about travel and international affairs for a number of local and international publications.

Esther Clark lives in Southern California with her husband of forty years. They spend summers with their children and grandchildren in their lakefront home in Michigan, near where Esther grew up. Esther enjoys public speaking, leading Bible studies, entertaining, international travel, bike riding, hiking, and snow skiing.

David Cranmer is the editor and publisher of BEAT to a PULP webzine and books. Under the pen name Edward A. Grainger, he writes the Cash Laramie and Gideon Miles short stories and is a regular contributor to Macmillan's website Criminal Element. He lives in New York with his wife and daughter.

Lynn Dove is "thriving" by teaching, writing, blogging and cuddling her grandchildren every chance she gets! Lynn loves to connect with readers through her award-winning blog: Journey Thoughts (lynndove. com).

MaryLou Driedger is a retired educator who taught in Hong Kong, on the Hopi Indian Reservation in Arizona, and in Manitoba, Canada where she received the Teacher of the Year award. She is currently a newspaper columnist, art gallery tour guide and university faculty advisor. Her favorite role in life is being a grandmother.

Neither blindness at thirty-one, unthinkable tragedy nor painful injustice defeated **Janet Perez Eckles**. In spite of adversity, she has become an international keynote speaker for Spanish and English-speaking audiences. She is a #1 bestselling author, radio host, life coach, Master Interpreter, columnist and Christian leader.

Terri Elders lives near Colville, WA, with three cats and a dog. A lifelong writer and editor, Terri's stories have appeared in multiple editions of Chicken Soup for the Soul. She co-edited *Not Your Mother's Book... On Travel*. She blogs at http://atouchoftarragon.blogspot.com and can be contacted at telders@hotmail.com.

Shawnelle Eliasen and her husband Lonny raise their brood of five boys near the Illinois banks of the Mississippi River. She's thrilled to have contributed to many Chicken Soup for the Soul titles, and currently contributes to several inspirational publications and blogs twice weekly for Guideposts.org.

Sara Etgen-Baker's love for words began when, as a young girl, her mother read the dictionary to her every night. A teacher's unexpected whisper, "You've got writing talent," ignited her writing desire. Although she ignored that whisper, she never forgot those words. So, after retirement, she began writing memoirs and narratives.

Melissa Face teaches high school English and devotes her free time to writing. Melissa's stories and essays have appeared in numerous magazines and anthologies. She lives in Virginia with her husband, son, and daughter. E-mail Melissa at writermsface@yahoo.com.

Tanya Feke, MD is a board certified family physician and patient advocate. Her book *Medicare Essentials: A Physician Insider Explains the Fine Print* is a bestseller on Amazon. She is also a film critic for *Record Journal* and runs a health and entertainment website at www. diagnosislife.com. She enjoys time with her family.

Liz Maxwell Forbes is published in a number of anthologies. Recently a story from her "back to the land" days appeared in *Chicken Soup for the Soul: O Canada The Wonders of Winter*. When not writing, she enjoys time with her life partner, her dog and her garden in seaside Crofton, BC, Canada.

Debra Wallace Forman is an award-winning journalist, motivational speaker and editor, with more than thirty years of writing experience. She achieved her dream of using her writing to improve the world. She is the proud mom of an eight-year-old son, Adam, who has shown her what true love is all about. E-mail her at debrawallace@verizon.net.

Dr. Shari Hall, a Yale and Columbia graduate, formerly worked with wounded warriors at Walter Reed in D.C. An international recording artist, she recently released her second album, *Faith*. She enjoys being a mother of two and inspiring others to live a healthy, passionate life. Email her at sharihallinfo@gmail.com or visit http://sharihall.com.

Marijo Herndon currently lives in New York with her husband, Dave, and two rescue cats, Lucy and Ethel. Marijo's stories, ranging from humor to inspiration, appear in several books and publications.

Katherine Higgs-Coulthard writes from her home in Michigan where she lives with her husband, their four children, and one spoiled rotten Border Collie mix named Hershey.

Jennie Ivey lives in Tennessee. She is the author of numerous works of fiction and nonfiction, including several stories in the Chicken Soup for the Soul series. Learn more at www.jennieivey.com.

Chris Jahrman grew up in sleepy towns in Indiana and Oklahoma that were so small that drivers rarely used turn signals—because everyone knew where everyone else was going. He now lives, works, and writes in the Pacific Northwest where the people are colorful and the skies are gray. You'll find his books on Amazon.

Val Jones, a professional freelance writer, has taught English for twenty years. A breast cancer survivor, she founded the Facebook community, Victorious Val & the Breast Cancer Crusaders, to encourage survivors, co-survivors and supporters. When she's not writing, Val volunteers in the breast cancer community.

Angela Joseph is an occupational therapist by day and a writer at all other times. In addition to freelance writing, Angela has authored *Women for All Seasons*, a Christian nonfiction book, as well as the Egypt series of Christian women's fiction. Angela also enjoys reading, photography, travel and glass etching.

Shannon Kaiser left her successful career in advertising to follow her heart and be a writer, life coach, inspirational speaker, travel writer and author. She is a six-time contributing author to the Chicken Soup for the Soul series. Visit her award-winning website playwiththeworld. com.

Fallon Kane is a twenty-year-old student currently studying psychology and criminal justice at Adelphi University. This is her fourth Chicken Soup for the Soul story published. Other than writing, Fallon enjoys food, running, and research. She would like to thank the Murwins at Awesome Country for inspiring this story!

Susan Karas is a contributing writer for *Guideposts* magazine and various anthologies, including Chicken Soup for the Soul. Susan is a praise dancer, appearing at many venues to honor the Lord. A dedicated mother of two, Susan resides on Long Island with her teacup Maltese, Bentley. E-mail her at SueZFoofer@aol.com.

Uber athlete and *The New York Times* bestselling author, **Dean Karnazes** was named by *TIME* magazine as one of the "Top 100 Most Influential People in the World." Among his many accomplishments, he once ran fifty marathons, in all fifty U.S. states, in fifty consecutive days. Dean lives with his wife and family in the San Francisco Bay Area.

Andrew E. Kaufman is an international bestselling author, who lives in Southern California with his Labrador Retrievers, horses, and a very bossy Jack Russell Terrier who thinks she owns the place. He began his career as a writer/producer at the CBS affiliate in San Diego, then moved to the Los Angeles market, where he decided that writing about real life wasn't nearly as fun as making it up. Learn more at www.andrewkaufman.com.

Lynn Kinnaman is a writer, web designer, marketing coach and tech-savvy woman. She's published books and magazine articles for decades. Owner of Works by Design, she builds websites and also coaches/advises small businesses and individuals. She continues to write and publish fiction and nonfiction in her spare time.

Kathleen Kohler writes stories about the ups and downs of family life for numerous magazines and anthologies. She and her husband live in the Pacific Northwest, and have three children and seven grandchildren. Visit www.kathleenkohler.com to read more of her articles or enter her latest drawing.

Nancy Julien Kopp draws from her growing-up years in Chicago and many more in the Flint Hills of Kansas for essays, stories, poems, and articles. She is in fourteen Chicken Soup for the Soul books, other anthologies, magazines, newspapers, and e-zines. A former teacher, she still enjoys teaching through the written word.

Lisa McManus Lange is a writer in Victoria, BC. She is multi-published with many anthologies including Chicken Soup for the Soul. Her first young adult novel, *Newbie Nick*, has been published by Lycaon Press as an eBook. Find her at www.lisamcmanuslange.blogspot.com, www.lisamcmanus.com or e-mail her at lisamc2010@yahoo.ca.

Lori Lara is a writer, blogger, black belt martial artist, and trauma survivor. She passionately shares the hope and healing of Jesus with people struggling with depression, PTSD, grief, and addiction. She lives in Northern California with her husband Robert and two sons. E-mail her at lori@lorilaraphotography.com.

Erin Latimer is a writer, blogger and tea connoisseur who resides in the city of Vancouver, BC. When she isn't writing she enjoys blogging and making silly videos about writing for her YouTube channel. E-mail her at erinRlatimer@gmail.com.

Arlene Ledbetter holds a Bachelor of Arts degree from Dalton College. She has written adult Sunday school curriculum, been published in a number of magazines and has stories in *Chicken Soup for the Soul: Think Positive for Kids* and *Chicken Soup for the Soul: The Multitasking Mom's Survival Guide*. Learn more at www.arleneledbetter.com.

Jane Lonnqvist is a retired special needs teacher who became a program coordinator and columnist. She has been married to her husband Jeff for forty-two years. They have two married sons and two grandsons, Dylan and Jacob. She plans to continue writing and fundraising with craft projects.

Patricia Lorenz is the author of thirteen books and hundreds of stories in many publications, including over sixty Chicken Soup for the Soul books. She has rebooted her life many times and is currently following her dreams while she's still awake in Largo, FL. To contact her as a possible speaker, visit www.PatriciaLorenz.com.

Diana Lynn is a freelance writer and small business owner in Washington State. This is her sixth story in a Chicken Soup for the Soul book. Her goal is double digits! E-mail her at Diana@recoveringdysfunctional. com.

Cherie Magnus, a California native, was a dance research librarian in the Los Angeles Public Library and a dance critic for local newspapers before moving to France, Mexico, and finally to Argentina in 2003. She returned to Los Angeles in 2014. E-mail her at tangocherie@ gmail.com.

James C. Magruder has been published in *Writer's Digest*, *Writer's Journal*, *HomeLife*, *Christian Communicator* and several Chicken Soup for the Soul books. He blogs about the writing life at www.thewritersrefuge. wordpress.com. His son, David, mentioned in his story, is also a professional writer today.

Sue Mannering, an Australian, moved to the Middle East in 2005 with her family of five. She now lives in Southeast Asia with her husband. While moving children into and out of college, she blogs about travel, food and life, writes articles and teaches English. She is always working on her latest novel. E-mail her at s_mannering@hotmail.com.

Dawn A. Marcus, M.D. of Franklin Park, PA passed away in October of 2013. She was the beloved wife of twenty-eight years to Richard J. Marcus, M.D.; mother of Steven and Brian. Dawn was a professor at the University of Pittsburgh, where she visited patients with two therapy dogs.

Sean Marshall currently lives in Cozumel, Mexico with his wife and three daughters. When he's not scuba diving, he's an active proponent of lifestyle design and helping others take the steps necessary to create their ideal lifestyle.

Karen Martin loves traveling, sunshine and good stories. She'll interview anyone who will let her and writes copy for small businesses, film companies and fundraisers. At print time, she was shopping for plane tickets to Peru to pick up her four kids. You can read her stories or contact her at www.karenthewriter.com.

Lisa Morris currently teaches fourth grade ELA in Niceville, FL. She has been teaching for twenty-three years and recently added adjunct professor of education to her résumé. Lisa has published five educational books to date and many memoirs and articles. E-mail her at lovealab@aol.com.

Giulietta Nardone lives in Massachusetts with her husband and two cats. Her stories have been published in books, newspapers and broadcast on the radio. In addition to writing, Giulietta paints, sings, acts, hikes, bikes, travels and saves historic buildings. E-mail her at giuliettan@gmail.com.

Sylvia Ney is a freelance writer, publishing newspaper and magazine articles, photography, poetry, and short stories. She serves as President of Texas Gulf Coast Writers, and is a member of Bayou Writers Group in Louisiana. To learn more about her, visit her blog at www.writinginwonderland.blogspot.com.

Maggi Normile may enjoy sparring, leaping over obstacles, and running in mud, but she also enjoys low-key activities like writing, reading, and watching classic movies. When she isn't finding new adventures to try, the Pittsburgh, PA native is active in her church and missions. Visit her blog at faithandsole.blogspot.com.

Angela M. Ogburn attended Georgia Southern University and is currently an instructor at Elgin Community College in northern Illinois. She has been previously published in academic journals and in fiction anthologies. When not working, she enjoys traveling, writing, and spending time with her husband and their dog, Henry.

Rebecca Olker earned her Bachelor of Arts degree at UC Riverside and her Master of Science degree in Taxation at Golden Gate University.

She works as an accountant in Santa Cruz. When she is not writing, Rebecca enjoys knitting, going to the beach with her dogs and spending time with family and friends.

Alli Page is a special needs tutor and founder of exhilaratedliving.org, an inspirational website designed to help readers lead fulfilled, healthy lives daily. When she is not writing or tutoring, you can find Alli playing her cello or ukulele and dreaming of further travel adventures.

Kristi Paxton lives life in Iowa woods and eastern rivers. Her happiest moments include family, friends, coffee, and the great outdoors. Kristi writes, teaches, walks, reads, and loves to kayak. The Paxtons and pup embark on their Great Loop adventure September 2014. E-mail her at kristi.a.paxton@gmail.com.

Marsha Porter has reviewed thousands of films, written hundreds of articles and dozens of short stories. She fell in love with writing when the 500-word essay was the punishment du jour at her Catholic grade school.

Heather Ray grew up in Maine and now lives in Daytona Beach, FL with her two children. She attended the University of Maine and has since taken a career in training others. She enjoys long walks, snorkeling, swimming, good friends, and spending quality time with the kids. This is her first publication.

Denise Reich is an Italian-born, New York City-raised freelance writer. She has contributed to numerous Chicken Soup for the Soul books and currently writes for the Canadian magazine *Shameless*. Denise can usually be found dancing in media events, drawing, reading, or cheering at rock concerts and baseball games.

Connie Rosser Riddle is a middle school nurse and writer who lives in Durham, NC with her husband, David. She continues to take yearly solo journeys and has recently completed a memoir that describes these adventures. E-mail her at ConnieRosserRiddle@gmail.com.

Sioux Roslawski is a third grade teacher in St. Louis. She rescues dogs, dotes on her granddaughter, is a teacher consultant for the Gateway Writing Project and is a three-time skydiver. (Someday she'll solo dive.) In her spare time, Sioux writes. More of her writing can be found at http://siouxspage.blogspot.com.

Nicole Ross is a corporate marketer, freelance copywriter, aspiring novelist, recovering blogger, and chronic hobbyist who is equally at home on the back of a horse, inside the boxing ring, pounding away at her keyboard, or perched in downward dog atop her yoga mat. Learn more at nicolekristineross.com.

Stacy Ross has a B.S. degree from Cornell University and an MBA degree from the University of Rochester. She currently writes part-time and teaches yoga in New Jersey. You can read more about Stacy's family experiences on her blog, Eggshells and Laughter, at eggshellsandlaughter.com.

Jeanette Rubin has maintained her sobriety, and continues to speak against drug use. Jeanette plans to study child development and juvenile delinquency. She has dreams of traveling the world and sharing her story.

Tanya Rusheon is a happily married mother of one little boy and two very hairy Himalayans. Her new career as a stay-at-home mom is progressing well. What little free time she manages between caring for the new baby and grooming the cats is devoted to writing. Tanya hopes to finish her first novel later this year.

Theresa Sanders is honored to be a frequent Chicken Soup for the Soul contributor. She lives with her husband near St. Louis, where she is completing her third novel, set (coincidentally!) at the Jersey

Shore. Connect with Theresa on Facebook at www.facebook.com/pages/Theresa-Sanders/208490939276032.

Eloise Elaine Schneider is a writer and artist. She often combines her two loves by illustrating her own books. Eloise Elaine's profile website can be found at http://fineartamerica.com/profiles/eloise-elaine-schneider.html.

Jaime Schreiner is a freelance writer and speaker from the Canadian Prairies, where she lives with her husband and two daughters. She has been published in Chicken Soup for the Soul, Hallmark, and Focus on the Family's *Thriving Family* magazine. Learn more at jaimeschreinerwrites.wordpress.com or e-mail her at jaimeschreiner@yahoo.ca.

Jennifer Sky, a former model and actress, has written for *The New York Times*, *New York Magazine's* "The Cut," the *New York Observer*, and *Interview* magazine. Her e-book, *Queen of the Tokyo Ballroom*, published by *The Atavist*, is part of her memoir-in-progress about the true life of a teenage girl working in the fashion industry. She is a models' rights advocate and lives in Brooklyn.

Elizabeth Smayda has two stories published in Chicken Soup for the Soul books and one this year in the Alzheimer's Society of B.C.'s publication. She works in the field of social services and co-authored a study involving eating disorders published in 2005. She is so grateful for her family!

Tyler Stocks is a sophomore history and English major at East Carolina University in Greenville, NC. He's a freelance journalist and has been published in numerous newspapers and magazines. He lives in Greenville with his girlfriend, his dog, and his blind kitten. Learn more at www.tylerpaulstocks.com.

Amy L. Stout is a wife, mommy, and autism advocate who loves travel, coffee houses, books and especially Jesus! As a child of the

King, her tiara is often missing, dusty, bent, or crooked, but she will always and forever be "His Treasured Princess." Reach her through histreasuredprincess.blogspot.com or Brightencorner@hotmail.com.

Carol Strazer has had several of her essays appear in the Chicken Soup for the Soul series. She published her first novel, *Barbed Wire & Daisies*, a historical fiction based on a little known story from WWII. She and her husband help maintain their mountain community church. They enjoy their children and six grandchildren.

L.A. Strucke is a writer, songwriter and producer. She graduated from Rowan University in 2005. Her four children are her inspiration. This is her third contribution to the Chicken Soup for the Soul series. Contact her at lastrucke@gmail.com or www.lastrucke.com.

B.J. Taylor loves how she looks and feels, which helps her to choose wisely. She's an award-winning author whose work has appeared in *Guideposts*, Chicken Soup for the Soul books, and numerous magazines/ newspapers. You can reach B.J. through her website www.bjtayloronline. com. Check out her dog blog at www.bjtaylorblog.wordpress.com.

Kamia Taylor has been winning writing contests since sixth grade, and drafted legal documents for real estate companies for twenty years. She is now on disability and living on a small organic farm and wildlife sanctuary with five rescued dogs. She plans to write more and expand her dog rescue efforts. E-mail her at BigBlackDogRescue@gmail.com.

Brian Teason is an attorney. He was the 1997 and 1998 U.S. 50 Mile Road Champion, 1997 50 Mile Trail Champion and has represented the U.S. at two World Championships. Since his comeback, he has set the national age group road record for 100 miles.

Kay Thomann is a newlywed. She and her new husband enjoy summers in Alaska and winters in Iowa, with intermittent trips south. She continues to write stories to entertain and inspire her readers and is grateful to have been published in *Chicken Soup for the Soul: From Lemons to Lemonade*.

Kristin Viola is a Los Angeles-based writer who has contributed to the *Los Angeles Times*, Zagat, *Angeleno* and other publications. Aside from running, she loves traveling, reading and a good glass of wine. E-mail her at kjviola@gmail.com.

Jessie Wagoner is the laughing lady behind the www.thenilaughed.com. She is mom to one wonderful son and is a full-time reporter. In her little free time she enjoys traveling, reading and going on adventures with her son.

Pat Wahler is a grant writer by day and award-winning writer of essays and short stories by night. Her work can be found in both national and local publications. A lifelong animal lover, Pat ponders critters, writing, and life's little mysteries at www.critteralley.blogspot.com.

Roz Warren writes for *The New York Times*, *Funny Times*, *The Jewish Daily Forward* and *The Christian Science Monitor*, and has been featured on the *Today* show twice. Read more of her work at www.rosalindwarren.com.

Dorann Weber is a freelance photographer who lives in New Jersey with her husband and five children. Three dogs, a cat and chickens complete the Weber home. Dorann became interested in writing when she entered greeting card competitions where eight of her verses were published. Her works are also written in a short storybook.

Kathy Whirity is a syndicated newspaper columnist who shares her sentimental musings on family life. Kathy is the author of *Life is a Kaleidoscope*, a compilation of some of her most popular columns. Learn more at www.kathywhirity.com.

Ann Michener Winter has been writing creative nonfiction and poetry since age eleven. She is previously published in two Chicken Soup for the Soul books. Ann is from Pasadena, CA, and has lived in Santa Barbara for forty years.

Ferida Wolff is author of seventeen books for children and three essay books for adults. She writes a weekly blog, http://feridasbackyard. blogspot.com, which looks at the nature/human connection. She has a passion for traveling and observing the world's birds, plants, and animals. She can be reached at feridawolff@msn.com.

Deborah K. Wood is a writer, consultant, life coach, and adventurer on the journey of Life. She has been writing (and rewriting) forever, and believes in the healing power of telling one's story.

Peter Wood is the author of *Confessions of a Fighter: Battling Through the Golden Gloves* and *A Clenched Fist: The Making of a Golden Gloves Champion*. He teaches English at White Plains High School in New York. When not writing, he enjoys painting, running and yoga. E-mail him at peterwood05@aol.com.

Dallas Woodburn has written fiction and nonfiction for a variety of publications including the *Nashville Review*, *Los Angeles Times*, and *Louisiana Literature*. Her short story collection was a finalist for the Flannery O'Connor Award for Short Fiction. Connect with her at writeonbooks.org and daybydaymasterpiece.com.

Brenda Lazzaro Yoder is a speaker and writer on faith, life and parenting. She has degrees in mental health counseling and education. Brenda won the Powerful Connection award for teachers and is a school counselor with a private practice. Brenda lives on a farm with her husband and four children. E-mail her at yoderbl@gmail.com.

Sabrina Zackery now uses a new OS system in her personal and professional life. Her company, MZ3 Productions, focuses on family and children entertainment. Her award-winning screenplay, *The Horse* *of His Dreams*, is slated for production. Follow her on Facebook at www.facebook.com/MZ3Productions.

Heather Zuber-Harshman is a writer, speaker, and professor. She recently completed a mystery novel, and submits short stories for publication while posting stories about faith, cooking, and traveling on her blog. In between projects she enjoys bicycling, traveling, snowboarding, and camping with her husband Dale and son.

Meet Our Authors

Amy Newmark was a writer, speaker, Wall Street analyst and business executive in the worlds of finance and telecommunications for more than thirty years. Today she is publisher, editor-in-chief and coauthor of the Chicken Soup for the Soul book series. By curating and editing inspirational true stories from ordinary people who have had extraordinary experiences, Amy has kept the twenty-one-year-old Chicken Soup for the Soul brand fresh and relevant, and still part of the social zeitgeist.

Amy graduated *magna cum laude* from Harvard University where she majored in Portuguese and minored in French. She wrote her thesis about popular, spoken-word poetry in Brazil, which involved traveling throughout Brazil and meeting with poets and writers to collect their stories. She is delighted to have come full circle in her writing career — from collecting poetry "from the people" in Brazil as a twenty-year-old to, three decades later, collecting stories and poems "from the people" for Chicken Soup for the Soul.

Amy has a national syndicated newspaper column and is a frequent radio and TV guest, passing along the real-life lessons and useful tips she has picked up from reading and editing thousands of Chicken Soup for the Soul stories.

She and her husband are the proud parents of four grown children and in her limited spare time, Amy enjoys visiting them, hiking, and reading books that she did not have to edit.

Claire Cook wrote her first novel in her minivan outside her daughter's swim practice when she was forty-five. At fifty, she walked the red carpet at the Hollywood premiere of the adaptation of her second novel, *Must Love Dogs*, starring Diane Lane and John Cusack.

"The exuberant and charming Claire Cook is one of the sassiest and funniest creators of contemporary women's fiction," according to *The Times-Picayune*. *Good Housekeeping* called her writing "laugh-out-loud," *Redbook* "gleefully quirky" and the *Chicago Tribune* "funny and pitch perfect." The *Today* show featured Claire as a "*Today's* Woman."

Claire has been a finalist for the Thurber Prize for American Humor and the Beach Book Festival fiction and grand prize winner. She's spoken and given keynotes at conferences from New Orleans to Denmark, and her books have been translated into fourteen languages.

Claire was a teacher for sixteen years before writing her first book, working with children from preschool to middle school, and teaching everything from multicultural games and dances, to writing, to open ocean rowing.

After many years in Massachusetts, Claire and her husband have moved to Atlanta to be closer to their two adult children, who actually want to hang out with them again.

Claire is now the *USA Today* bestselling author of eleven novels and her first nonfiction book, *Never Too Late: Your Roadmap to Reinvention (without getting lost along the way)*. Find out more at ClaireCook.com.

Thank You

hank you, all of you life changers. We owe huge thanks to every one of you who shared your story about how you have rebooted your life. Your stories will inspire tens of thousands of people to follow their dreams, pursue their passions, and find purpose and meaning in their lives, even if that means starting over.

We know that you poured your hearts and souls into the thousands of stories and poems that you submitted, and we appreciate your willingness to share your lives with us. We could only publish a small percentage of the stories that were submitted, but our editorial team read every single submission—and there were thousands! Even the stories that do not appear in the book influenced us and affected the final manuscript.

We want to thank VP & Assistant Publisher D'ette Corona for making the first pass through the stories and putting together a list of contenders for us. She also worked with all the contributors to approve our edits and answer our questions as we perfected every story that appears in the book. Managing Editor and Production Coordinator Kristiana Pastir oversaw the long journey from Word document to finished manuscript to proofs to cartons of finished books and Senior Editor Barbara LoMonaco oversaw the story submissions and proofread the final layout.

Lastly, we owe a very special thanks to our creative director and book producer, Brian Taylor at Pneuma Books, for his brilliant vision for our cover and for the interior design.

~Amy Newmark and Claire Cook

Sharing Happiness, Inspiration, and Wellness

Real people sharing real stories, every day, all over the world. In 2007, *USA Today* named *Chicken Soup for the Soul* one of the five most memorable books in the last quarter-century. With over 100 million books sold to date in the U.S. and Canada alone, more than 200 titles in print, and translations into more than forty languages, "chicken soup for the soul" is one of the world's best-known phrases.

Today, twenty-one years after we first began sharing happiness, inspiration and wellness through our books, we continue to delight our readers with new titles, but have also evolved beyond the bookstore, with wholesome and balanced pet food, delicious nutritious comfort food, and a major motion picture in development. Whatever you're doing, wherever you are, Chicken Soup for the Soul is "always there for you™." Thanks for reading!

Share with Us

We all have had Chicken Soup for the Soul moments in our lives. If you would like to share your story or poem with millions of people around the world, go to chickensoup.com and click on "Submit Your Story." You may be able to help another reader, and become a published author at the same time. Some of our past contributors have launched writing and speaking careers from the publication of their stories in our books!

We only accept story submissions via our website. They are no longer accepted via mail or fax.

To contact us regarding other matters, please send us an e-mail through webmaster@chickensoupforthesoul.com, or fax or write us at:

Chicken Soup for the Soul
P.O. Box 700
Cos Cob, CT 06807-0700
Fax: 203-861-7194

One more note from your friends at Chicken Soup for the Soul: Occasionally, we receive an unsolicited book manuscript from one of our readers, and we would like to respectfully inform you that we do not accept unsolicited manuscripts and we must discard the ones that appear.

Chicken Soup for the Soul.
Find Your Happiness

101 Inspirational Stories
about Finding Your
**Purpose,
Passion, and Joy**

Jack Canfield,
Mark Victor Hansen & Amy Newmark
Foreword by Deborah Norville

Others share how they found their passion, purpose, and joy in life in these 101 personal and exciting stories that are sure to encourage readers to find their own happiness. Stories in this collection will inspire readers to pursue their dreams, find their passion and seek joy in their life. This book continues Chicken Soup for the Soul's focus on inspiration and hope, reminding readers that they can find their own happiness.

978-1-935096-77-1

Find Your Happiness

Chicken Soup for the Soul

Changing the world one story at a time®

www.chickensoup.com